Gender, Ethnicity and Political Ideologies

D0949150

Why do women support ideologies that depend on their own subordination? Does their positive identification with such ideologies question the whole feminist project? Does the use of women as symbols of cultural identity legitimise a denial of their rights as human beings? These are the questions that have been tackled by this new study, which develops a feminist perspective on the political issues of the post-Cold War era such as nationalism, inter-ethnic conflict and democratisation.

Gender, Ethnicity and Political Ideologies presents a broad range of international case studies such as inter-ethnic conflict in former Yugoslavia, the emergence of a 'male democracy' in Chile, the lack of equal rights for women in Israel, the role of women in the French Far Right's ideology and the sense of empowerment that Islam gives to many young Muslim women in Britain. Also included is an analysis of nationalist ideologies that can divide women from each other and define their role in reproductive terms.

This is a challenging new study that asserts the importance of a feminist politics which enables women to understand and work with each other across the boundaries that so effectively divide them. It will be essential reading for those in search of a rigorous analysis of the role and significance of women in a rapidly changing political landscape.

Nickie Charles is a Reader in Sociology at the University of Wales Swansea. **Helen Hintjens** is a Lecturer in Development Studies, University of Wales Swansea.

Gender, Ethnicity and Political Ideologies

Edited by Nickie Charles and
Helen Hintjens

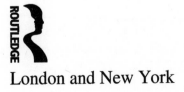

London and New York

First published 1998
by Routledge
11 New Fetter Lane, London EC4P 4EE

Simultaneously published in the USA and Canada
by Routledge
29 West 35th Street, New York, NY 10001

© 1998 Selection and editorial matter Nickie Charles and Helen
Hintjens; individual contributions © the contributors

Typeset in Times by
Ponting–Green Publishing Services, Chesham, Buckinghamshire

Printed and bound in Great Britain by
MPG Books Ltd, Bodmin, Cornwall

British Library Cataloguing in Publication Data
A catalogue record for this book is available from the
British Library

Library of Congress Cataloging in Publication Data
Gender, ethnicity and political ideologies / edited by Nickie Charles
and Helen Hintjens.
        p.   cm.
    Includes bibliographical references and index.
    1. Feminism–Political aspects.   2. Women in politics.
    3. Ethnic relations.
    I. Charles, Nickie.   II. Hintjens, Helen.
    HQ1236.G4616   1997
    305.42–dc21   97–14242
                CIP

ISBN 0–415–14820–0 (hbk)
ISBN 0–415–14821–9 (pbk)

Contents

Notes on contributors

Haleh Afshar teaches Politics and Women's Studies at the University of York and Islamic Law at the Faculté Internationale de Droit Comparé at Strasbourg. She was born and raised in Iran where she worked as a journalist and a civil servant before the revolution. She is joint convenor of the Development Studies Association's Women and Development Study Group and has edited several books produced by this group; the most recent include *Women in the Middle East* (Macmillan, 1994) and (co-edited with Mary Maynard) *The Dynamics of Race and Gender* (Taylor & Francis, 1994). She is also convenor of the Political Studies Association's women's group. She remains active in feminist Iranian politics and has written extensively on the subject.

Sheila Allen is currently Adviser to the University of Bradford on Equal Opportunities and is Research Professor of Sociology. She has written and published extensively on nationalism and ethnicity from a woman's perspective. She is currently writing an advanced text for Oxford University Press on Women's Contributions to Sociology.

Sarah Benton works as researcher, editor and writer. She is former political editor of the *New Statesman* and Lecturer in Politics at Birkbeck College, London University.

Valerie Bryson is Senior Lecturer in Politics at the University of Huddersfield and has taught and researched at a number of other British universities, most recently Manchester and Bradford. Her publications include *Feminist Political Theory: An Introduction* (Macmillan, 1992). She is working on a book on *Feminist Debates: Issues of Theory and Political Practice*.

Nickie Charles is Reader in Sociology in the Department of Sociology and Anthropology, University of Wales Swansea. She is author of *Gender Divisions and Social Change* (Harvester-Wheatsheaf, 1993), co-author (with Marion Kerr) of *Women, Food and Families* (Manchester University Press, 1988) and co-editor (with Felicia Hughes-Freeland) of *Practising*

Feminism (Routledge, 1996). She is currently researching a book on feminist social movements and their impact on state policies.

Helen Hintjens is Lecturer in the Centre for Development Studies, University of Wales Swansea. Her main interests are in the post-colonial relations of Britain and France, especially in the Caribbean and in immigration policies. She is author of *Alternatives to Independence: Explorations in Post-colonial Relations* (Dartmouth, 1995). Other interests include gender and nationalism, West African development paths and ecofeminist perspectives on development.

Eleonore Kofman is Professor of Human Geography at Nottingham Trent University. She has published articles on gender and political geography and national identity in France and is co-editor (with Gillian Youngs) of *Globalization: Theory and Practice* (Pinter, 1996). Her current research interests include the politics of international migration in Europe.

Mirjana Morokvasic has worked at the Centre National de la Recherche Scientifique, Paris, since 1979, and teaches at the University of Paris X (Nanterre). She is author of several books and articles in the field of sociology of migration, gender studies and inter-ethnic relations. She is the author of *Jugoslawische Frauen: Emigration und Danach* (1987) and co-author (with Hedwig Rudolph) of *Bridging States and Markets* (1993), *Wanderungsraum Europa: Die Menschen und Grenzen in Bewegung* (1994) and *Migrants: Nouvelles mobilités en Europe* (1996). She co-ordinated *Logics of Exclusion*, a special issue of *Peuples Méditerranéens* on the Yugoslav disintegration and conflict (1993). She is currently working on a book based on her 1993–4 fieldwork in Vojvodina, Yugoslavia. She is also a member of the international network of women in the conflict zones, based in York, Canada.

Georgina Waylen is Lecturer in Politics at the University of Sheffield. Her main research interests are gender and politics and development, primarily in Latin America and the Caribbean. She is the author of *Gender in Third World Politics* (Open University Press, 1996) and co-editor (with Vicky Randall) of *Gender, Politics and the State* (Routledge, 1997). She is currently writing a book on gender, democratic consolidation and economic reform in comparative perspective.

Nira Yuval-Davis is a Professor and post-graduate course leader in Gender and Ethnic Studies at the University of Greenwich, London. She has written extensively on theoretical and empirical aspects of nationalism, racism, fundamentalism and gender relations in Britain, Israel and settler societies. She is co-author (with Floya Anthias) of *Racialized Boundaries* (Routledge, 1992) and co-edited (with Floya Anthias) *Women-Nation-State* (Macmillan, 1989), (with Gita Sahgal) *Refusing Holy Orders: Women and Fundamentalism in Britain* (Virago, 1992), (with Daiva Stasiulis) *Unsettling Settler Societies: Articulations of Gender, Ethnicity, Race and Class* (Sage, 1995) and (with Helma Lutz and Ann Phoenix) *Crossfires: Nationalism, Racism and Gender in Europe* (Pluto, 1995). Her latest book is *Gender and Nation* (Sage, 1997).

Preface and acknowledgments

In February 1993 we jointly organised the annual conference of the women's sections of the British Sociological Association and the Political Studies Association at the London School of Economics. Its focus was 'Gender, Sexuality and Identity: Commonalities and Difference'. With the exception of Valerie Bryson's chapter and our introductory chapter, all the chapters in this volume originated as papers presented to that conference. At the time the mass rape of Bosnian women was in the headlines and the war in former Yugoslavia was a major focus of debate, particularly its vicious division of former friends and neighbours along ethnic lines and the effect of these divisions and related political ideologies on women. These concerns are reflected in the book which explores the interrelation of gender and ethnic identities and the way in which gender and ethnicity are used to create and maintain social and cultural boundaries.

We wish to thank everyone who came to the conference for making it such an enjoyable event, and particularly those women who felt that the conference was important enough to travel from various countries of the former Soviet bloc. Their input into the conference and the issues raised for women by the collapse of communism are reflected in our introductory chapter.

We also wish to thank our contributors for their forbearance and patience in what has been an unconscionably long time between the conception of this book and its appearance in print; the editors of the series, Haleh Afshar and Mary Maynard, who had faith in the project from the beginning; and our two editors at Routledge, Caroline Wintersgill and Vicky Smith, the one for being enthusiastic enough about the idea to issue us with a contract and the other for helping us see it through to fruition.

Finally, as we live and work in Wales, which enjoys its own form of nationalism, we end with a newly invented and very clearly gendered myth of origin of the Welsh nation. This poem by Nigel Jenkins provides a counterpoint to, and illustration of, some of the arguments which follow.

THE CREATION

When God clocked off from work one day,
Having put the finishing touches to Wales,
The Archangel Gabriel begged the Creator
To divest His opus of some of its veils.

'She's the finest,' said God, 'of all my creations,
A land of quite extraordinary charms,
From her alpine peaks and salmon-packed streams
To her golden coast with its prosperous farms.

'Her people I have blessed with laverbread and cockles,
Cwrw Felinfoel* and great mineral wealth,
They'll be wizards of rugby, singers and bards,
And they'll speak the language of heaven itself.'

'But haven't you, Boss,' the Archangel demurred,
'Haven't you somewhat overpaid 'em?'
'Not,' replied God with a devilish smirk,
'Not if you look at the neighbours I've made 'em.'

* The 'best beer in the world' according to the poem's author.

Nickie Charles and Helen Hintjens
Swansea, November 1996

1 Gender, ethnicity and cultural identity: womens 'places'

Nickie Charles and Helen Hintjens

> Modernity moves east, leaving post-modernity in its wake; religious revival, ethnic renaissance, roots and nationalism are resurgent as modernist identity becomes increasingly futile in the West.
>
> (Friedman 1991: 360, cited in Eriksen 1993: 151)

This book aims to develop a feminist perspective on the political developments referred to in the opening quotation, analysing them as gendered and as having specific effects on women. These developments are often contradictory, involving the emergence of right-wing nationalisms, inter-ethnic conflict and religious fundamentalism and, at the same time, processes of democratisation. In parts of the former USSR and Yugoslavia ethnic and national identities have formed the basis of political cleavages, resulting in bloody conflict and processes of 'ethnic cleansing' not seen in Europe since the end of the Second World War. On the other hand there have been moves towards democratisation and a free market economy in many former communist societies and in some these processes go hand in hand (Milic 1993). In the west the New Right has been in the ascendant and, in the name of freedom, has deregulated the market and attempted to reduce the role of the state. At the same time, the frontiers of western Europe are being locked and barred against outsiders (and even against the 'outsiders within'). In many parts of the world religious fundamentalism has become powerful (Sahgal and Yuval-Davis 1992: 2). In the USA Christian fundamentalist movements have been instrumental in trying to restrict women's reproductive rights and Islamic fundamentalism is a significant political force which, in countries like Iran and Pakistan, wields state power (Klatch 1994; Papanek 1994). In contrast, in Latin America there has been a move from authoritarian dictatorships towards democracy, a process which has something in common with those occurring in parts of the post-communist world. Many of these political ideologies include prescriptions for gender-appropriate behaviour and use women as potent symbols of cultural identity.

The focus of this book is on the gendered nature of these ideologies and their implications for women. This also involves an exploration of ethnicity: defining and controlling women is central to demarcating ethnic and national boundaries. An equally important concern is the relation between these ideologies and feminism and the implications for feminism of women's choosing to support ideologies and regimes which restrict their ability to control their own lives. In this introductory chapter we discuss the gendered nature of nationalist ideologies, the ambivalent relationship of women to national and ethnic collectivities, women's importance to the maintenance of these collectivities, and the problems they encounter with gendered and ethnically based notions of citizenship and democracy. Finally, we discuss the implications for feminist politics of divisions between women based on ethnicity, national identity and class.

NATIONALISM, GENDER AND ETHNICITY

Most theorists of the origins of nationalism and nation-states have ignored their relation to gender, focusing instead on ethnicity as the basis for national identity (Anderson 1983; Gellner 1983; Smith 1986). A partial exception to this is Mosse (1985) who analyses the relation between European, particularly German, nationalisms and sexuality. This linking of sexuality and nationalism was an important departure from previous analyses and provides a useful starting point for a consideration of gender, ethnicity and nationalism. Mosse argues that the nationalist ideologies which emerged in late eighteenth and early nineteenth-century Europe were associated with attempts on the part of national bourgeoisies to create national collectivities in their own image. This image was grounded in a specific gender division of labour, sexual orientation and ethnicity which involved notions of respectability and appropriate sexual behaviour, 'manliness' and a complementary role for women, and ideas of racial superiority (Mosse 1985). Thus men were represented as honourable, courageous and active in the public domain while women were guardians of morality and tradition in the private sphere; masculinity was 'the foundation of the nation and society' while women were 'the guardians of the traditional order' (Mosse 1985: 17). This gender division of labour was class-based and reflected bourgeois morality. The folk tales that were being transformed into fairy tales by the brothers Grimm in Germany at the time reflect these gender stereotypes. Snow White became the epitome of bourgeois respectablity and feminine virtue, being transformed from someone who would 'do the cooking' for the dwarfs when they were working in the mines to someone who was admonished to 'keep house for us, and cook, sew, make the beds, wash and knit, and keep everything tidy and clean. . . . In the evening, when we come home, dinner must be ready' (Zipes 1983: 53). Heterosexuality was defined as normal while male homosexuality and masturbation were dangerous and posed a threat to manliness and hence to the nation. Homosexuals were considered 'abnormal – strangers outside the tribe – and judged to be a threat to society' (Mosse 1985: 25) as were 'foreigners'. These strictures applied to male homosexuality; lesbians were not named until towards the end of the nineteenth century when they too came to represent a travesty of womanhood and respectability (Mosse 1985).

In the early nineteenth century nation-states self-consciously created symbols to represent the nation. As Eriksen (1993) points out, these symbols had to be powerful enough to guarantee not only the rational but also the emotional allegiance of the citizenry; hence the nation is represented as the bourgeois family writ large, the family to which citizens owe their primary emotional allegiance. Images of women as chaste, modest mothers and preservers of tradition were central to the ideology of nationalism. Women who deviated from this role were despised as transgressing the bounds of respectable womanhood.

The national collectivity is also represented in stories, stories which Sarah Benton (Chapter 2) refers to as myths of origin and myths of foundation. Myths of origin tend to be associated with essentialist ideas of 'race' or ethnicity and often include stories of men vanquishing women. Myths of foundation, in contrast, are about human, usually male, acts on which the nation-state is founded and involve stories about a fraternal group of men overthrowing paternal power. Myths of origin tend to be patriarchal whereas myths of foundation are fraternal and create men as citizens. Both types of myth 'tell a story of the proper order of society', embodying a gender and sexual order to which members of the nation or putative nation are expected to conform. They also render normal (and invisible) specific power relations: between women and men, dominant and subordinate classes, the young and the old.

In the twentieth century nationalism has been associated with movements for independence, liberation and revolution in different parts of the world. The gender and sexual order they envisage varies considerably, depending in large part on their class nature but, for many, the mobilisation of women in support of social change has been important. Indeed, most of them define a public, productive role for women as well as a private, reproductive one. Jayawardena differentiates between national independence movements led by an indigenous bourgeoisie and national liberation struggles or socialist revolutions led by the proletariat or the proletariat in alliance with sectors of the bourgeoisie (Jayawardena 1986). Both are committed to women's emancipation, but those which are associated with the working class differ from those associated only with the bourgeoisie in imagining a more active role for women of all classes. Thus, in the USSR and in eastern Europe, women were represented as mothers and as workers and were expected to fulfil both these roles. In Nicaragua the revolution was symbolised by a woman carrying a baby in one arm and a gun in the other. The modernising movement of Reza Shah in Iran in the early part of the century, on the other hand, restricted itself to challenging the seclusion of mainly middle-class women, a seclusion symbolised by the veil, and expanding women's access to education and the professions. In Turkey, reforms were more extensive, granting women political rights as well as encouraging their participation in education and employment, but leaving most rural and poor urban women untouched (Kandiyoti 1989; Najmabadi 1991; Toprak 1994). Women's contribution to nation building was not only through giving birth to future citizens but also through educating them in the values and attitudes appropriate to a modern nation-state. Nationalist movements which were orientated towards socialism, however, defined women as workers as well as mothers and transmitters of cultural values. These differences relate to the class or classes which are leading the movement and the national collectivity which they are imagining and representing symbolically.

In the last years of the twentieth century nationalism takes many different forms. It has become allied with religious fundamentalism, a political ideology associated with the petty-bourgeoisie, the landed classes and the religious establishment (Afshar 1989; Kandoyoti 1989; Moghadam 1994); in parts of former USSR and Yugoslavia it is associated with extreme ethnic intolerance and violent conflict; and in parts of western Europe and North America it is associated with movements for autonomy within the framework of a liberal-democratic state (Davies 1996). It has been argued that the nationalism associated with religious fundamentalism has arisen in response to the failures and dislocations resulting from attempts to modernise and westernise (Kandiyoti 1991; Moghadam 1994). What has become known as ethnic nationalism in former state socialist societies is a response to the collapse of all-encompassing state control and the search for new or revived collective identities. The gender order imagined by both these types of nationalism is generally rooted in an idealised past, in an agrarian society, and women's role as mothers and guardians of cultural identity, symbolising stability in the face of change, is paramount (Helie-Lucas 1994). Men are active in the public sphere, women are centred in the private domain where cultural continuity is guaranteed along with the identity of family, community and nation. Such movements reassert a national cultural identity which has been undermined by modernisation and/or westernisation (Fantasia and Hirsch 1995). They require women to be mothers first and foremost and to produce sons who can defend the nation and daughters who can carry on its traditions. Women's sexuality is to be put to use for the cultural community – nation or ethnic group – to which they belong.

Images of women as mothers, as well as representing the nation, can also unify disparate ethnic groups. In an interesting chapter on South Africa, Gaitskell and Unterhalter (1989) argue that symbolic representations of women as mothers have been used by both the Nationalist Party and the African National Congress (ANC) in different ways at different times. For the Nationalist Party, Afrikaner women as mothers have represented the purity of the Afrikaner nation while, for the ANC, motherhood has been used as a means of uniting women across different ethnic groups in attempting to forge a national identity which can override ethnic divisions. This symbolism does not directly challenge women's reproductive role and its importance for the gender order, but it challenges the ethnic basis of national identity and points to the importance of representations of women in the creation of a national identity. It also points to women's potential for uniting across national boundaries and women's problematic relation to nationalism. The identity of women as mothers can be constructed as shared across ethnic, national or class boundaries, thus providing a loyalty at odds with national identity (Eriksen 1993: 20; Gaitskell and Unterhalter 1989: 71; see also Valerie Bryson, Chapter 7 in this volume). This was evident during the conflict in former Yugoslavia when Serbian, Croatian, Slovenian and Bosnian mothers protested against the use of their sons as cannon fodder (Drakulic 1993; Milic 1993). They were subsequently divided from each other on the basis of national and ethnic identity, as Mirjana Morokvasic shows in Chapter 4 in this volume. Many women in former Yugoslavia have, however, voiced their preference to remain neutral and Morokvasic describes the efforts of groups of women to continue communicating across the ever-hardening borders and boundaries that seek to divide them. In continuing to communicate with each other and oppose the fighting, women are refusing to be cast in the role of passive and problematically complex territory for men to fight over. They are self-determining subjects, and may often pay a high price for being so. She asks why the media in particular seems complicit in the process of compartmentalisation, being apparently unwilling to convey stories of 'love, tolerance and solidarity across these borders'. Indeed, she and Sheila Allen (Chapter 3) both argue that to represent the war in former Yugoslavia as an inter-ethnic conflict 'borders [*sic*] on disinformation of a highly dangerous kind'.

Women's association with motherhood and the domestic sphere can also be used to resist authoritarian regimes, colonial domination or totalitarian states. Thus the mothers of the disappeared in countries such as Chile and Argentina during military rule protested against the disappearance of their children and grandchildren as Georgina Waylen discusses in Chapter 8.

Women as mothers in a time-honoured way were forced into a defence of their families and communities. They took their private role as mothers into the public realm of politics (Westwood and Radcliffe 1993). Similarly, veiled women participated as militants in the Algerian revolution, posing a challenge to patriarchal gender relations as well as to French colonial rule (Fantasia and Hirsch 1995). Women in both these situations, while not challenging symbolic gender boundaries, were actually transgressing the deeply gendered public–private divide. Georgina Waylen argues that in Chile, during the period of military dictatorship, the junta attempted to 'abolish the public sphere' and that this led to the 'politicisation of the private sphere'. Similarly, in eastern Europe the private sphere of the family assumed great importance during the state socialist period and women had a significant role within it; it was the site of resistance against an overbearing and controlling state (Einhorn 1993; Havelkova 1993).

NATIONALISM, IDENTITY AND RIGHTS

Nationalism defines who belongs and who does not belong to the national collectivity, and prescribes appropriate gender and sexual identities by which genuine members of the nation may be recognised. National identity is also associated with specific forms of sexuality and particular ethnicities. Right-wing nationalisms, such as Nazism or the Pinochet dictatorship in Chile, condemn homosexuality, glorify women as mothers and demonise 'foreigners'. In a sense, if nationalism is ethnically based and defines ethnicity as something that runs in the blood then it necessarily involves a tight control of women's sexuality in order to define and maintain the boundaries of the ethnic community. Liberal nation-states, on the other hand, appear not to be so exclusively based. Those who belong are granted citizenship rights. This raises important questions about the relation between nationalist ideologies, identity politics and a rights-based politics. National-isms which are based on essentialist notions of identity define those outside the collectivity as different. Within the collectivity there are also differences: differences between men and women and differences in sexual orientation and class positioning, some of which are allowable and some of which are not. Women's difference from men is essential (in more than one sense), and gives them a special place within the collectivity; their membership, however, is often dependent on prescribed behaviour symbolising an ethnic identity. This identity is shared with men of their collectivity and marks them off from 'other' women. However, other differences are not allowable and mark those who exhibit them as potential enemies within. This reliance on notions of shared identity within the collectivity and difference from those outside it is apparent in the ideology and politics of the Front National discussed by Eleonore Kofman (Chapter 5). 'Immigrants' are defined as essentially different from 'French' people and therefore, in the interests of preserving unique ethnic identities and cultures, deserve to be repatriated to their native land. As Balibar puts it:

> What racism, nationalism, and sexism seem to have in common is that they are all categories which . . . divide the universality of the human species into exclusive transhistorical groups which are supposed to be separated by *essential* differences, or to become self-conscious and act *as if* they were separated by essential differences.
>
> (Balibar 1994: 192)

The differences between 'ethnic-nationalisms' and those incorporating notions of citizenship are explored by Sarah Benton (Chapter 2) and Sheila Allen (Chapter 3). Benton argues that nationalist ideologies and myths of nation are predicated on a sexual order which excludes women from the polity. This raises an important question as to whether this exclusion is an inevitable feature of nationalism or whether there are significant differences between, on the one hand, nationalisms based on essentialist notions of gender and ethnic identity and, on the other, those based on the ability to speak a common language (which can be learned) and citizenship rights.

Benton implies that myths of origin rely on essential identities to define belonging, hence resulting in exclusionary ideologies of nationalism, whereas myths of foundation are potentially more inclusive of women and 'foreigners'. Sheila Allen's focus on identity and the way in which it has been theorised and used as a basis for exclusionary politics is relevant to this debate. In contradistinction to the idea that identity is essential and given at birth, or at least imbibed with your mother's milk, Allen argues that identity is situational. Her discussion of the fluidity of ethnicity in former Yugoslavia and the way that ethnic categories were imposed on the participants by outsiders and hardened by the experience of war demonstrates the way that an identity-based politics divides women from one another and disallows any 'mixing' of identies. This suggests that the significance of ethnic and national identities for women (and for men) varies and that in certain contexts they may not be important at all.

Feminist politics is not immune to the problems associated with identity politics. As Allen points out, an important assumption of feminist thought is that 'the subordination, oppression and exploitation of women are not respecters of national boundaries' (p. 58). But what assumptions about gender relations are involved here? Does feminism assume that women have interests in common which are opposed to the interests of exclusionary nationalisms? Implicit in Allen's chapter is the view that feminism as an ideology is opposed to nationalisms which are based on exclusionary definitions of identity and belonging, but at the same time there is a danger of essentialising identity/difference within feminism, as in arguing that it is in the interest of all women to oppose nationalism. A possible way out of this impasse is a rights- rather than identity-based politics. This is implied by Allen in her comment that basing inclusion on 'national identity, rather than . . . legitimate claims to citizenship rights within state structures, is to accept ideological constructions of nationhood which function to deny such rights' (p. 60). This contrast, between belonging defined in terms of a (mythical) national identity, on the one hand, and in terms of citizenship rights, on the other, also ties in with Sarah Benton's distinction between myths of origin and myths of foundation and her observation that the latter provide the greater potential for the inclusion of women on equal terms with men. For of course, right-wing nationalist ideologies most certainly include women but define their 'place' in very specific ways. An identity-based nationalist politics, such as has emerged in former Yugoslavia, is not only divisive and exclusionary in ethnic terms but also dangerous for women because maintaining a particular cultural identity involves the control of women's reproductive capacity and a curtailment of their autonomy. Both Allen and Benton distinguish between nationalisms based on essentialist notions of identity which are exclusionary of those who do not share that identity, and those that are based on citizenship rights which, both argue, are potentially more inclusive of women and of 'other' ethnic groups. Mirjana Morokvasic (Chapter 4) and Eleonore Kofman (Chapter 5) explore specific examples of exclusionary, ethnically and racially based identity politics in former Yugoslavia and in France, taking up several of the issues raised by Sheila Allen.

CONTROLLING SEXUALITY, MAINTAINING BOUNDARIES

Women's problematic relation to the nation and their greater or lesser exclusion from full citizenship led Virginia Woolf to state that 'As a woman I have no country' – an issue explored by Sheila Allen and Nira Yuval-Davis in their chapters. As we have already seen, asserting that women have shared experiences and interests as mothers can be used as a way of reducing the significance of ethnic or national identities. At the same time, defining women as reproducers of their collectivity may lead to the control of their reproductive potential and their sexuality in the interests of maintaining boundaries (Moghadam 1994; Papanek 1994; Yuval-Davis and Anthias 1989). The ambivalent and different relationship of women to their national or ethnic collectivities, and the significance of women's sexual and reproductive roles to this ambivalence, is made explicit by the existence of regulations which 'relate to them specifically as women, wives and mothers'

(Yuval-Davis 1995: 20). An illustration of such regulations is provided by Valerie Bryson's discussion (Chapter 7) of women's citizenship in Israel where, despite a rhetoric of gender equality and Jewish women's participation in the military, women's citizenship is circumscribed by religious law and democracy has not been extended to the domestic sphere. Thus, state laws govern 'the public worlds of politics and employment' while religious laws govern the private sphere and hence women's sexual and reproductive rights. Bryson notes that 'in matters concerning marriage and divorce, minority groups are governed by Muslim, Druze or Christian courts and Jews by the Rabbinical courts' (p. 140). Similarly, Muslim Personal Laws or Family Codes affect 'about 450 million women who live in Muslim countries and communities' (Helie-Lucas 1994: 394). These regulations, which govern marriage, divorce, child custody and inheritance, differ in different parts of the world, incorporating local traditions and, at the same time, claiming legitimacy from Islam. Helie-Lucas writes:

> Belonging to a specific Muslim community is equated with accepting all the religio-cultural aspects which make for this society. The Semitic tradition of veiling and/or secluding women in the Middle East and North Africa; female genital mutilation in Egypt, Sudan and other countries of West Africa; or the Hindu tradition of caste and dowry in India and Sri Lanka are all specific to the regions where they prevail. Nevertheless, Muslim peoples and certainly women are made to believe that their local traditions are part and parcel of being a Muslim and – in the final analysis – are Islamic.
>
> (Helie-Lucas 1994: 395)

In many countries the state delegates control of the family and women's sexuality to communal or religious authorities and/or to male heads of household (Helie-Lucas 1994; Kandiyoti 1991; Walby 1990) thereby gaining men's political support (Molyneux 1991; Stacey 1983). For instance, murders of Palestinian women, when they are carried out by Palestinian men to defend 'family honour', are tolerated by the Israeli authorities. In this they are complicit with Palestinian community leaders who support such actions, defining them 'as part of Arab folklore and tradition'. It is argued that this complicity facilitates Israeli control of Palestinian communities as well as reinforcing male control of women's sexual behaviour (Al-Fanar report 1995: 37).

Male control of women's sexuality and reproductive capacities is often an integral part of nationalism (Yuval-Davis and Anthias 1989). Indeed, myths of origin often include stories about control being brought to bear (by men) over women's sexuality, and women's fecundity being assigned a proper place – a heterosexual relationship within the domestic sphere

(Benton, Chapter 2). This place which is assigned to women means not only that women's sexual behaviour is circumscribed but also that 'other' men must not be allowed sexual access to them; such access not only impugns the honour of the family and community but also sullies the purity of the nation. Control of women's sexuality is particularly significant for right-wing nationalist ideologies which define belonging in terms of essentialist notions of 'race' or ethnicity. According to this type of ideology, the only way of maintaining the purity of the group is by ensuring that sexual access to women is possible only for men who 'belong'. Thus women are central to reproducing the collectivity but they are also its weakest spot – sexual access to them by an 'outsider' destroys their value to the nation. These issues are explored by Eleonore Kofman (Chapter 5) in her discussion of the gender and sexual dimensions of the ideology of the French Front National and by Mirjana Morokvasic in her Chapter 4 on the Yugoslav war.

The ideology of the Far and New Right in France, specifically the Front National (FN) of Le Pen, can be seen as an example of a specific myth of origin which has been 'invented and reinvented' (in Allen's words) to counter the degeneration and decadence of contemporary French society. Benton argues that myths about an essential ordering of society can be used as a benchmark against which to measure contemporary society. This is highlighted in the title of Kofman's chapter, 'When society was simple . . .'. Contemporary French society is compared to a golden past – when men were men and women were women – and is found wanting. While these right-wing nationalist ideologies justify social divisions in terms of biology, their attitude to sexual divisions is contradictory. On the one hand, European civilisation is seen as superior to 'immigrant' cultures because of the rights and freedoms enjoyed by women but, on the other hand, these rights and freedoms threaten the reproduction of the nation because they go hand in hand with a lowering of the birth rate. Indeed, one of the bases of the FN's criticisms of immigrant culture is the position of Muslim Arab women and the way they are treated by their men. Yet, for the Front National in France, as for the Islamic Salvation Front in Algeria, a woman's place is in the home. The Right's views on the family, sexuality and women's reproductive role are associated with active opposition to abortion (including raids on abortion clinics) and dire warnings about AIDS, immigration and homosexuality. Sexual metaphors are used to warn about the vulnerability of the French nation to invasion and thereby destruction – mainly through a mixing of French women with 'other' men.

The Far Right, of which the Front National is an example, is to be differentiated from the New Right in so far as the New Right celebrates differences of 'race' and gender and the inequalities associated with them. For them differences between the sexes denote complementarity rather than unequal power relations, as feminists would argue (see p. 100). Movement towards sexual equality is rejected because it undermines sexual difference, making men into 'women of masculine sex' and de-sexing women (rather in the vein of Lady Macbeth).

Kofman discusses women's support for the Far and New Right, arguing that right-wing women do not necessarily accept all the strictures on women's proper place laid down by the male leadership. An interesting difference between right-wing women and men relates to fears of sexual violence on the part of 'immigrant men'. This is a major concern in the ideology of the right, but right-wing women do not 'necessarily associate sexual harassment and rape with immigrants'. Although Kofman does not go into these issues in great detail, she presents a more nuanced and contradictory picture of the qualified support given by women to right-wing parties which shows that although right-wing women accept the prime importance of their role as mothers within the family, they do not necessarily accept that this role should be exclusive.

Sexual access to women of one collectivity by men of another represents the destruction of that collectivity, hence rape and impregnation of enemy women is often part of war and has been a mark of the so-called ethnic cleansing in former Yugoslavia (Brownmiller 1976; Einhorn 1993). Several of the authors in this volume consider the significance of rape to ethnic and national identity. Mirjana Morokvasic points out that in former Yugoslavia rapes are condemned only when they are committed by 'other men' and can be interpreted as crimes against the nation: to the extent that they are 'only' crimes against women they are ignored. Sarah Benton also argues that mass rape in war is a way of impugning the honour of a nation and undermining the power of enemy men. Indeed, rape symbolises the inability of men to protect their women and, as such, features in national myths of foundation. Benton observes that 'Rape in legend frequently symbolises the destruction of male authority, which has lost its essential quality of rule, the will and power to protect the weak'. Sheila Allen discusses rape in war, questioning whether women 'need' a national identity and arguing that exclusionary nationalisms are dangerous for women. These dangers, and the way they are manipulated for political ends at women's expense, are graphically and movingly illustrated in Morokvasic's chapter. As Allen comments, 'All women share a common interest in not being raped by the male "enemy" just as they do in not being raped by their "protectors"' (p. 59).

Violent sexual access to women can be used as a means of destroying boundaries and making them permeable. The repeated rape of women during the Yugoslav war was interpreted as an assault on national identity; it ensured that women gave birth to 'enemy' babies rather than babies of their own nation (Einhorn 1993: 106). In Morokvasic's words: 'The stories of raped women kept in custody until they could no longer abort spread simultaneously in Croatia and in Serbia and were quasi-identical: the "Others" raped "Our" women, they want to spoil "Our Nation"' (p. 80). Conversely, a means of maintaining boundaries is controlling women's sexuality so that it is directed towards the reproduction of the collectivity. In Israel, for instance, as Valerie Bryson discusses (Chapter 7), women's role as reproducers of the nation is given heightened significance by both Palestinians and Israelis in an attempt to outnumber the enemy. This is also the case in former Yugoslavia, as Morokvasic shows in Chapter 4. The importance of controlling women's sexuality to the creation and maintenance of boundaries can be illustrated by events in former Yugoslavia which bring out the significance of women's bodies as markers of ethnic boundaries. In the late 1980s in Kosovo, an autonomous province with a majority Albanian and minority Serbian and Montenegrin population, the alleged rape of Serbian women by Albanian men was manipulated by the Serbian authorities to separate the Serbian and Albanian communities and restrict the mobility of women. Thus the threat of rape was used as a way of strengthening ethnic boundaries, and increased control of women was crucial to this demarcation (Meznaric 1994).

Boundaries, and our idea of boundaries, are also hardened by bounded language, which often has an implied or explicitly gendered content. The euphemism 'ethnic cleansing' is one example of such divisive political language. The implication is that inter-ethnic mixing of people in families and community life involves the creation of human waste, and the pollution of the collective self, the *ethnie* or nation. As Benton puts it, 'Only pure fluids – blood and semen and rivers – transmit moral purity and racial belonging; if contaminated, they also transmit disease and decay' (p. 34). Such beliefs are apparent in the discourse of the Front National on the contamination of the French nation with AIDS, allegedly imported by immigrants. Multicultural families, villages, towns and state communities thus come to be seen as inferior to homogenous, supposedly pure ones and, in former Yugoslavia, they have been destroyed in a violent attempt to create 'pure' nations. Mixed offspring and mixed societies, instead of being regarded as the product of a creative, vital interaction, are seen as the product of an illicit and messy mixing of foreign substances with native substances in the body of the mother or mother country.

THE DOMESTIC SPHERE AND CULTURAL IDENTITY

The domestic sphere, and women within it, are regarded as significant for the transmission of cultural identity. This is accepted not only by political movements seeking to preserve cultural identities but also by modernising states. The attempts of such states to establish universal citizenship rights based on the idea of free and autonomous individuals often pits them against communities defending their right to maintain specific cultural traditions and ways of life. This conflict, and the compromises reached, are often played out in the sphere of women's rights and can be seen as a conflict between universal, individual rights and particularistic, group rights (Sahgal and Yuval-Davis 1992) – a contradiction between equality and sameness, on the one hand, and identity and difference, on the other. In the interests of establishing universal rights, modernising states may attempt to transform social relations which are perceived as standing in the way of 'progress'. Thus in the Soviet Union after the 1917 revolution laws were passed giving rights to women, such as the right to free-choice marriage and the right to abortion. Molyneux argues that socialist modernisation usually involves three types of reforms: removing the control of kin over marriage, redefining relations between the sexes and reforming laws affecting women as child bearers and rearers (Molyneux 1991: 241). This happened in the USSR after 1917 and in China post-1949 and was often met with a violent response on the part of men wishing to retain control over 'their' women. Indeed, many thousands of women lost their lives attempting to exercise their newly granted rights (Buckley 1989; Davin 1987). In these circumstances, challenging the social position of women was understood and intended as a challenge to the production and property relations underpinning traditional communities and patriarchal kinship relations (Molyneux 1991: 254). The destruction of these relations was a necessary part of modernisation and industrialisation.

Kandiyoti argues that because the domestic sphere, and women within it, represents the maintenance of tradition and cultural identity, it assumes a heightened significance in the face of a modernising state which undermines cultural diversity by the granting of individual, universal rights (Kandiyoti 1991). This also happens in the face of a state which appears to control every aspect of its citizens' lives, as in former eastern Europe and the USSR (Einhorn 1993), in states where the political sphere is abolished, as in Chile, or, indeed, in a state which embodies institutional racism, as in Britain and other liberal democracies.

> Citizens . . . turn to their primary solidarities both to protect themselves from potentially repressive states and to compensate for inefficient representation. This reinforces the stranglehold of communities over their women, whose roles as boundary markers become heightened.
>
> (Kandiyoti 1991: 14)

In this situation, control over women in the domestic sphere becomes one of the prime ways of preserving cultural traditions which are perceived as threatened.

The significance of the private sphere for the continued reproduction of particularistic cultural identities is assisted by the liberal state's distinction between public and private which makes it possible for different rules to apply in each sphere. In Britain, for instance, domestic violence is treated differently from an identical assault that takes place in public because of its 'private' nature. Leaders of minority ethnic communities are, therefore, able to argue that the jurisdiction of the state should not extend into the private sphere, thus ensuring the maintenance of their control over those cultural practices embodying the cultural identities of their communities. Some of these practices, however, may be detrimental to women's health or may result in their deaths and some are deemed illegal by the host society. This poses a problem for feminists who have taken on board the criticism of western feminism as ethnocentric and imposing western values on non-western cultures, and has led some to a position of cultural relativism and an inability or unwillingness to criticise any cultural practices for fear of being labelled ethnocentric or racist. These fears are played on by those who defend cultural practices which feminists define as oppressive to women. In France, for instance, women who mounted a legal challenge to parents practising clitoridectomy on their daughters were 'fiercely attacked both by fundamentalists of all sorts and by the liberal Left who support "the right to be different"' (Helie-Lucas 1994: 405). The women mounting the challenge were both French and migrants. Cultural relativism is associated with multiculturalism which, in Fred Halliday's words, 'while calling for tolerance and diversity between cultures and communities . . . too easily allows for the imposition of uniformity within them' (Halliday 1995: 17).

In Britain the theory of multiculturalism demands that different cultures be respected and their autonomy not interfered with. However, as Yuval-Davis points out, this approach to collectivities fails to recognise contradictions within them (as was made clear by the film *Bhaji on the Beach* and responses to it within the Asian community in Britain) and essentialises them as fundamentally different and other (Sahgal and Yuval-Davis 1992: 8). It also favours those with power within those collectivities. This tendency to collapse the members of a group or community into one amorphous whole also lies at the heart of many forms of right-wing nationalist and fundament-alist politics. At the same time, it is an impulse which can emanate 'from below', appearing to reflect a search for security through complete identi-fication with the greater body of 'the people', whether in terms of class, gender, nation, religion or culture (Fromm 1960: 122). A recognition of contradicitions within minority communities, as within any society, makes possible an understanding that their members may experience conflicting loyalties and fragmented identities. These contradictions open the door to alliances between women across collective boundaries. Nira Yuval-Davis takes up these issues in Chapter 9, discussing the way multiculturalism benefits fundamentalist leaders because of its view that the autonomy of minority cultures should be respected. An idealisation of communities, and the assumption of identity (sameness) within them, is shared by multiculturalism and fundamentalism. She criticises this assumption, arguing that a politics based on identity not only is exclusionary, but also fails to take account of differences within communities or within particular social categories such as 'woman'. Haleh Afshar in Chapter 6 also discusses contradictions within ethnic minority communities by focusing on the response to Islam by young Asian women in Bradford. She argues that their adoption of a Muslim identity in the 1980s was due to a 'sense of crisis' (p. 108), partly engendered by increasing racial conflict and partly by a denial of rights on the basis of a specific construction of British national identity. This provides an example of the negative effects of defining national identity in terms of essential attributes and using such a definition to exclude certain groups of people, particularly black people, from full citizenship rights. It also points to the importance of disentangling citizenship rights from national identity.

Afshar discusses the power of Islam in similar terms to those used by Benton and Kofman, that is, it describes a golden age existing in the past with which modern – particularly western – society is compared and found wanting. This myth of origin is powerful in leading young Muslim women to adopt a Muslim identity, not least because of the positive views of women that are to be found in the Qur'ān. She shows that young Muslim women negotiate an identity for themselves which, as far as they are concerned, is in keeping with Qur'anic teaching but which may be in opposition to the men of their own collectivity. Thus Muslim men may attempt to control and police women's behaviour in the public sphere as a means of protecting 'their' women and their community's honour. Young women and their mothers do not necessarily accept this sort of control and may successfully oppose the rule of their fathers and brothers while maintaining a positive, Muslim identity. This discussion shows that although women may adopt identities which appear to outsiders to involve their subordination and confinement to domesticity and reproduction, they negotiate the content and meaning of these political ideologies and religions and, in so doing, often come up against male authority. Their interpretation of a 'woman's place', however, seems to be far less restrictive than the ideas held by men.

Afshar's ethnographic material demonstrates the point made by Yuval-Davis that women have ambivalent relations to their collectivities. This emphasises the situatedness of identity discussed by Sheila Allen and the problems associated with an identity politics which assumes that identity is essential and fixed and shared by all members of a specific collectivity. As an alternative to feminist identity politics Yuval-Davis puts forward the idea of transversal or coalition politics, a politics which recognises that women are different, that they speak from different positionings and that these different positionings result in partial and different knowledges; and which, at the same time, recognises that different women can come together through a process of dialogue to construct a shared position on particular issues. This is a politics which, while recognising the possibility that conflicts between women may be irreconcilable, also recognises that these conflicts do not arise from some essentialised notion of identity which inevitably results in opposing interests and a politics of exclusion. Thus, while Sheila Allen asserts that women as women *do* share interests across national and ethnic boundaries (such as an interest in not being raped), Yuval-Davis argues that these interests have to be constructed on the basis of a mutually respectful dialogue.

DEMOCRACY, CITIZENSHIP, GENDER AND ETHNICITY

The granting of citizenship rights has historically been in response to struggles on the part of the working class, women and ethnic minorities and, in contemporary western democracies, these rights have been expanded to include women's reproductive rights (Einhorn 1993). However, even in liberal democratic states which apparently treat all citizens equally, citizenship rights vary and are dependent on class, ethnicity, sexual orientation and gender. In Britain, for example, white, middle-class, married, heterosexual women are viewed as suitable mothers and reproducers of the British nation and their breeding is encouraged while poor, single, working-class, black women's and lesbians' reproduction is regarded as being inappropriate and/or excessive. Black feminists have documented the way in which black women in Britain experience health care provision and the way that abortion, sterilisation and the injectable contraceptive Depo-provera may be forced on black women while the fertility of middle-class white women is encouraged (Bryan *et al.* 1985). Similarly sexuality can form a basis for unequal access to citizenship rights. Thus heterosexual marriage is recognised and legally sanctioned but only a few liberal states recognise homosexual marriage.

On the basis of this and other evidence, feminists have argued that citizenship is gendered and that a broader definition of citizenship is required that takes into account duties and responsibilties in the private sphere as well as in the public. This raises the issue of how a status such as citizenship which is based on equality (implying sameness) can incorporate difference (Marshall 1963). It is important to remember that contemporary western feminisms, while encompassing calls for equal rights and an expanded definition of citizenship, also stress the importance of difference. Indeed, many feminists insist that difference should be valued and respected, rather than denied in the interests of gender equality, and point to the gendered nature of a politics that is based on assumptions of sameness (Pateman 1988). This tension between calls for gender equality and the recognition of women's special needs and capacities has marked the history of western feminism and, arguably, nationalism (Bacchi 1990). It is because of this that western feminism is critical of the dualistic nature of Enlightenment thought which renders similarity and difference mutually exclusive and encloses women in the category of 'other' (Hekman 1990). Feminists thus argue for a wider conceptualisation of citizenship than has been evident in either liberal democracies or in most socialist societies; a conception that allows for difference and that is not constructed by the public–private divide (Charles 1993; Einhorn 1993; Eisenstein 1993).

Several of the contributors discuss citizenship and its gendered nature. Sarah Benton, in tune with her focus on origins, explores the importance of war to the emergence of citizenship, a citizenship shared among equals, arguing that the military origins of citizenship explain its masculine nature. Further, because citizenship has its origins in a brotherhood of men fighting and dying together, it excludes women and non-combatants. It is also predicated on men's separation from the private sphere: 'It is only the *separation* from household that allows men to become a fraternity' (p. 41). Citizenship is, therefore, gendered in its origins, but the further away from these origins a society moves, the more scope there is 'for women to come into their own'.

The question of the relation between war and citizenship is also raised by Valerie Bryson in her discussion of women in Israel (Chapter 7). In the Israeli situation women appear to have equality of citizenship which extends to a duty to serve in the armed forces. However, women's participation in the Israeli armed forces differs from that of men and excludes them from important routes into political power. In addition, neither Palestinian men nor women are required to serve in the armed forces. This evidence seems to support Benton's argument that war and participation in the military create a privileged fraternity to whom citizenship rights are granted, and that this fraternity is the embodiment of the nation.

Bryson's discussion graphically illustrates the inequalities and discrimination that arise when access to citizenship rights is defined in terms of national or ethnic identity. Even though Palestinians are citizens of Israel they do not enjoy the same rights as do Jewish people, and women's citizenship rights differ from those of men. This goes so far as providing free contraception to Palestinian women while providing Jewish women with a birth allowance and other forms of support for motherhood. These policies clearly demonstrate that the Jewish state is based on a gendered and ethnically exclusive form of nationalism. Indeed, Israeli feminists are concerned that the domination of the peace process by men, and the coming together of Jewish Orthodoxy and fundamentalist forms of Islam, may result in increased controls over women.

Against the idea that women's sexuality and reproduction are a legitimate arena for control by community or religious leaders or by the state, feminists have argued that citizenship rights need to include women's reproductive rights. These have been defined as including access to fertility control, child care provision, provision for parenting and sex education (Einhorn 1993: 91). In most post-communist societies women's reproductive rights, particularly the right to abortion, are under threat (Funk 1993: 11) and the resurgence of nationalist ideologies defining woman's place as the home coincides with high levels of unemployment. As Einhorn wrily comments, 'defining women as mothers with a "sacred duty" to reproduce the nation is occurring concurrently with and hence underwriting the economic need to shed labour' (Einhorn 1993: 106). It is a convenient way of getting women out of the work-force. In addition, the particularistic legislation protecting women as child bearers and rearers is being swept away in the name of democracy and the market. These processes are reinstating men's control over women's reproductive powers and represent a move from the public patriarchy of state socialism to a newly developing private patriarchy (Einhorn 1993; Eisenstein 1993). The church is centrally involved in debates on women's right to abortion (Fuszara 1993). These developments have led many to argue that the processes of democratisation that are taking place in eastern Europe and in Latin America are about male democracy (Einhorn 1993: 148; Eisenstein 1993; Jaquette 1994; see also Morokvasic, Chapter 4 in this volume). In both these contexts women were active in overthrowing repressive regimes, as in Algeria, but once this has taken place men tend to take over and dominate the more formal processes of political representation while women predominate at the informal, community level (Einhorn 1993; Jaquette 1994). Citizenship rights are defined in male terms; those pertaining to reproductive rights are problematised and come under attack or are regarded as the sphere of the religious authorities.

Georgina Waylen (Chapter 8) explores the transition to democracy that has taken place in Chile and the effect it has had on women's activism. She argues that while conventional politics was suspended under the Pinochet dictatorship, the community and the private sphere became politicised and women's political activism increased. With the return to what she terms 'competitive electoral politics', women's organisations and interests have been both incorporated and marginalised, and women's activism, at both formal and informal levels of politics, has decreased.

She analyses different forms of women's organisation, distinguishing between them on the basis of class and their relation to feminism. Both middle-class and popular feminist organisations, while not sharing a class identity or class-based interests, share an interest in reproductive rights, sexuality and domestic violence. Waylen documents the way in which class and gender interests, some of which were shared and some of which were antagonistic, were temporarily overcome in the alliance of women's organisations which came into being when the dictatorship began to be seriously challenged in the early 1980s, and which campaigned for 'Democracy in the country and in the home'. Subsequently, however, with the re-emergence of party politics, it was middle-class women and their demands which were integrated into formal politics rather than working-class women.

This integration had a gender dimension. Thus within the Christian Democrats, the largely male leadership opposed the women's demands for, among other things, reproductive rights and divorce, both of which are frowned on by the Catholic church, and opposition parties as a whole were reluctant to cede power to women within party organisations. Support was confined to 'general statements about women's equality' (p. 157). Incorporation into the formal political process led to the dominance of an equal-rights-based feminism associated with a concern to 'protect the family'. This ensured the reassertion of the public–private dichotomy and the establishment of a male democracy with no commitment to gender democracy in the home, and a gendered definition of citizenship based on involvement in the public domain. Democracy in Chile, therefore, embodies a specific class and gender order, but, at the same time, there is space for manoeuvre by women's organising within and outside the state.

This chapter suggests that transversal politics may be as difficult to achieve across class boundaries as it is across national and ethnic boundaries. This is particularly so if attention is not paid to the relations of exploitation which structure different classes within capitalist societies and which mean that members of the same ethnic and national collectivity are positioned in an antagonistic relationship with each other. Here class clearly enables some women to exercise power over other women, a power derived from their class positioning which also affects their ability to influence the processes of formal politics.

QUESTIONS FOR FEMINISM

Many of the political ideologies and movements discussed in this book define feminism or women's emancipation/gender equality as part of an alien state and/or ideology; hence maintaining or re-establishing a collective identity very often involves a rejection of gender equality (based on sameness) and feminism. In Iran, for instance, women's emancipation is associated with the west. Westernised women, who are usually upper-middle class, are seen as symbols of westoxification, an intoxication with all things western which is destroying Iranian cultural identity (Tavakoli-Targhi 1994). This makes it very difficult for women to assume a feminist identity or even to criticise 'Islamic' cultural practices. If they do they may be accused of betraying their culture (see Helie-Lucas 1994). Valerie Bryson suggests that the same may be true of Palestinian women in Israel (p. 134). The situation of Taslima Nasreen also exemplifies this problem. Her death has been demanded by Islamic fundamentalists in Bangladesh and she is now in exile in Sweden. Her crime was to 'challenge religiously sanctioned agendas that aim to subjugate women' (Cummins 1995: 53). In eastern Europe an assertion of cultural identity may equally involve a rejection of feminism, and women who are sympathetic to feminism may have to distance themselves from it for pragmatic reasons (Marody 1993; Siklova 1993). This may, however, result in critiques and modifications of western feminisms in order to develop a feminism that speaks to women's particular material and ideological circumstances (Najjar 1992; Schirmer 1993; Siklova 1993; see also Waylen, Chapter 8 in this volume).

Feminism as a political ideology and social movement claims to represent women's interests. It is patently obvious, however, that not all women assume a feminist identity and many are highly critical of feminism and feminists. In the context of the Third World, this rejection of feminism often arises from its association with western, middle-class women and with the negative consequences of modernisation (Barrios de Chungara 1978). Many of the political ideologies referred to in the opening quotation and discussed in this book are critical of modernity and attempt to assert cultural identities based on pre-(or post)modern traditions. Feminism is therefore vulnerable to attack because of its association with the modernist project. However, feminism has also developed a critique of modernism; it has been said that it straddles the modern–postmodern divide, relying on socially constructed identities for political mobilisation but recognising their fluidity and the existence of multiple, potentially conflicting, identities (Barrett 1992; Charles 1996). Thus western feminism recognises that women neither automatically share a gender identity nor do they necessarily have political interests in common. Their material circumstances and experiences differ significantly and a unity of interests between women from different cultures (and within the same society) cannot be deduced from their shared gender. Nevertheless, women's support for movements which curtail their autonomy and define their social role in purely reproductive terms has posed a problem for feminists, particularly as the validity of their experiences and the injustice of the circumstances against which they are organising have to be recognised. Such support clearly questions the claim of feminism to represent women's interests and even the possibility of there being such interests. Why do women support ideologies which depend on their own subordination? Does their positive identification with such ideologies question the whole feminist project? These questions are considered in the chapters that follow. Thus, Yuval-Davis notes the contradiction between the effect on women of fundamentalist politics, in terms of restricting their autonomy and control over their own lives, and their positively choosing to join fundamentalist or revivalist movements and gaining feelings of empowerment from so doing. She makes the very important point that the identities available to women are constructed within specific power relations which provide the framework of choice. Identities which seem to be disempowering in some circumstances may be empowering in others. Thus the young women interviewed by Haleh Afshar (Chapter 6) chose a Muslim identity, not because it subordinated them to the authority of their fathers and brothers – although it often did – but because it gave them dignity and pride in relation to members of other ethnic collectivities. Both involved relations of power, the one in the form of gender relations, the other in the form of relations between dominant and subordinate ethnic groups. And both forms of power were challenged by these young women's adoption and interpretation of a Muslim identity. Similarly, Eleonore Kofman and Georgina Waylen show that women do not necessarily accept all the strictures of the political ideologies they support when it comes to legislating a place for women, and are actively engaged in trying to change these ideologies. Sarah Benton suggests that women accept myths of origin which include stories of male control over female sexuality because such stories offer women a place *as women* and elevate their reproductive powers – as long as they are used in the service of the nation.

We wish to consider this issue by exploring the limitations of conceptualising gender equality (or gender democracy) in terms of legal and economic rights, a conceptualisation associated with liberalism and socialism as well as with western feminism. For socialism, women's participation in paid work together with legal rights is sufficient to ensure gender equality; for liberalism, women have the freedom to participate in paid employment if they so wish. Both ideologies assume a domestic sphere in which women are involved in reproductive and sexual activities. They enter the public domain only 'as workers demanding equal pay . . . or equal rights before the law' (Eisenstein 1993: 306). Both liberalism and socialism fail to recognise gender difference, assuming that gender equality involves relegating difference to the private sphere and/or making it irrelevant in the public sphere through providing child care, maternity leave and so on. Women are supposed to become surrogate men in order to achieve equality. Women are not present *as women* in the terms of either ideology, 'universal' rights are predicated on a masculine norm which *excludes* women in so far as they are different from men. Eisenstein argues that universal rights should include rights which are specific to women, such as reproductive rights, and rights that are specific to ethnic minorities, that is, rights that relate to difference. As currently formulated, equal rights do not encompass differences of gender or ethnicity (Eisenstein 1993: 310). In contrast, in nationalist ideologies and religious fundamentalism, women's specific role as mothers and reproducers of the nation is recognised and respected (in rhetoric if not in reality). Women's difference is valued rather than being devalued, there is no pressure on them to deny their womanhood and become the same as men, no pressure on them to assume a double or triple burden in the name of gender equality. In explaining women's allegiance to cultural practices which involve their subordination it is also important to take into account power. As Moghadam puts it, 'discrimination against women is not derived from culture, but from power' (Moghadam 1994: 22). Of course, this also means that we have to recognise the fact that women can oppress other women. Gender is not the only basis of power – class, seniority, ethnicity, 'race' and occupational position can and do give women power (Kandiyoti 1988). This power may help explain women's allegiance to ideologies which involve women's subordination; even though they may be disempowered *as women* they are empowered by their membership of other social categories.

Ironically feminism, unlike liberalism but like nationalism, recognises difference, including differences between women. However, unlike some forms of nationalism but like liberalism and socialism, it does not argue for difference to be the basis of exclusion, differences in identity should not provide the rationale for a politics of exclusion. This does not mean that identity politics have not emerged within feminism. The black feminist critique of white, western feminism revealed it to be a form of identity politics. In so doing it raised questions of how to overcome the essentialising of difference and identity, which is the basis of identity politics and makes it so exclusionary, and how to recognise commonalities as well as differences. These issues are explored by Sheila Allen and Nira Yuval-Davis in this volume. Allen stresses the situational nature of identity and the way in which supposedly essential aspects of identity are in fact socially constructed and therefore changeable. Yuval-Davis argues for identity politics to be superseded by a transversal politics which involves respect for difference, does not privilege one voice, and recognises the possiblity of constructing common political interests as women. Bryan Turner has similarly referred to the need to seek out dialogues of solidarity which stress similarities, while not engulfing differences (Turner 1989). This is no easy task, as women's involvement in inter-ethnic conflict, exclusive nationalisms and religious fundamentalism demonstrates. These movements are generally explicitly anti-universalist and anti-egalitarian, ignoring the real 'variabilities within categories and similarities across them' (p. 58).

It is important to provide an alternative to these movements, one which is based on universal human rights and, at the same time, takes into account and values difference. Feminism needs to accept its Enlightenment legacy and its basis in humanism (Lazreg 1990). This implies a set of moral values based on respect for the freedom and autonomy of individual human subjects. In many of the political ideologies discussed in this book, women's importance as symbols of cultural identity legitimises a denial of their rights as human beings. As Moghadam suggests, in order to counter this women have to be deconstructed as symbols of cultural identity and reconstructed as 'human beings' (Moghadam 1994: 22). This is a task that feminism is uniquely fitted to accomplish.

ACKNOWLEDGMENTS

We would like to thank Charlotte Davies, Valerie Bryson, Georgina Waylen and Vicky Smith for their helpful comments on earlier drafts of this chapter.

REFERENCES

Afshar, H. (1989) 'Women and reproduction in Iran', in N. Yuval-Davis and F. Anthias (eds) *Women-Nation-State*, London: Macmillan.

Al-Fanar report (1995) 'Developments in the struggle against the murder of women against the background of so-called family honour', *Women against Fundamentalism Journal* 6: 37–41.

Anderson, B. (1983) *Imagined Communities: Reflections on the Origin and Spread of Nationalism*, London: Verso.

Bacchi, C. L. (1990) *Same Difference: Feminism and Sexual Difference*, London: Allen & Unwin.

Balibar, E. (1994) *Masses, Classes, Ideas: Studies on Politics and Philosophy Before and After Marx*, London: Routledge.

Barrett, M. (1992) 'Words and things: materialism and method in contemporary feminist analysis', in M. Barrett and A. Phillips (eds) *Destabilising Theory: Contemporary Feminist Debates*, Cambridge: Polity.

Barrios de Chungara, D. (1978) *Let Me Speak*, New York: Monthly Review Press.

Brownmiller, S. (1976) *Against Our Will*, Harmondsworth: Penguin.

Bryan, B., Dadzie, S. and Scafe, S. (1985) *The Heart of the Race: Black Women's Lives in Britain*, London: Virago.

Buckley, M. (1989) *Women and Ideology in the Soviet Union*, Hemel Hempstead: Harvester Wheatsheaf.

Charles, N. (1993) *Gender Divisions and Social Change*, Hemel Hempstead: Harvester Wheatsheaf.

—— (1996) 'Feminist practices: identity, difference, power', in N. Charles and F. Hughes-Freeland (eds) *Practising Feminism: Identity, Difference, Power*, London: Routledge.

Cummins, A. (1995) 'Bhaji on the Beach', *Women against Fundamentalism Journal* 6: 52.

Davies, C. A. (1996) 'Nationalism: discourse and practice', in N. Charles and F. Hughes-Freeland (eds) *Practising Feminism: Identity, Difference, Power*, London: Routledge.

Davin, D. (1987) 'Engels and the making of Chinese family policy', in J. Sayers, M. Evans and N. Redclift (eds) *Engels Revisited*, London: Tavistock.

Drakulic, S. (1993) 'Women and the new democracy in the former Yugoslavia', in N. Funk and M. Mueller (eds) *Gender Politics and Postcommunism: Reflections from Eastern Europe and the Former Soviet Union*, London: Routledge.

Einhorn, B. (1993) *Cinderella Goes to Market: Citizenship, Gender and Women's Movements in East Central Europe*, London: Verso.

Eisenstein, Z. (1993) 'Eastern European male democracies: a problem of unequal equality', in N. Funk and M. Mueller (eds) *Gender Politics and Postcommunism: Reflections from Eastern Europe and the Former Soviet Union*, London: Routledge.

Eriksen, T. H. (1993) *Ethnicity and Nationalism: Anthropological Perspectives*, London: Pluto.

Etienne, B. (1989) *La France et l'Islam*, Paris: Hachette.

Fantasia, R. and Hirsch, E. (1995) 'Culture in rebellion: the appropriation and transformation of the veil in the Algerian revolution', in H. Johnston and B. Klandermans (eds) *Social Movements and Culture*, London: UCL Press.

Friedman, J. (1991) 'Narcissism, roots and postmodernity: the constitution of selfhood in the global crisis', in S. Lash and J. Friedman (eds) *Modernity and Identity*, Oxford: Blackwell.

Fromm, E. (1960) *The Fear of Freedom*, London: Routledge & Kegan Paul.

Funk, N. (1993) 'Feminism east and west', in N. Funk and M. Mueller (eds) *Gender Politics and Postcommunism: Reflections from Eastern Europe and the Former Soviet Union*, London: Routledge.

Fuszara, M. (1993) 'Abortion and the formation of the public sphere in Poland', in N. Funk and M. Mueller (eds) *Gender Politics and Postcommunism: Reflections from Eastern Europe and the Former Soviet Union*, London: Routledge.

Gaitskell, D. and Unterhalter, E. (1989) 'Mothers of the nation: a comparative analysis of nation, race and motherhood in Afrikaner nationalism and the African National Congress', in N. Yuval-Davis and F. Anthias (eds) *Woman-Nation-State*, London: Macmillan.

Gellner, E. (1983) *Nations and Nationalism*, Oxford: Blackwell.

Halliday, F. (1995) 'The literal vs the liberal', *Women against Fundamentalism Journal*, 6: 16–18.

Havelkova, H. (1993) 'A few prefeminist thoughts', in N. Funk and M. Mueller (eds) *Gender Politics and Postcommunism: Reflections from Eastern Europe and the Former Soviet Union*, London: Routledge.

Hekman, S. J. (1990) *Gender and Knowledge: Elements of a Postmodern Feminism*, Cambridge: Polity.

Helie-Lucas, M.-A. (1994) 'The preferential symbol for Islamic identity: women in Muslim Personal Laws', in V. M. Moghadam (ed.) *Identity Politics and Women: Cultural Reassertions and Feminisms in International Perspective*, Boulder, CO: Westview.

Jaquette, J. S. (ed.) (1994) *The Women's Movement in Latin America: Feminism and the Transition to Democracy*, Oxford: Westview.

Jayawardena, K. (1986) *Feminism and Nationalism in the Third World*, London: Zed.

Kandiyoti, D. (1988) 'Bargaining with patriarchy', *Gender and Society* 2(3): 274–90.

—— (1989) 'Women and the Turkish state: political actors or symbolic pawns?' in F. Anthias and N. Yuval-Davis (eds) *Woman-Nation-State*, London: Macmillan.

—— (1991) 'Introduction', in D. Kandiyoti (ed.) *Women, Islam and the State*, London: Macmillan.

Klatch, R. E. (1994) 'Women of the New Right in the United States: family, feminism, and politics', in V. M. Moghadam (eds) *Identity Politics and Women: Cultural Reassertions and Feminisms in International Perspective*, Boulder, CO: Westview.

Lazreg, M. (1990) 'Feminism and difference: the perils of writing as a woman on women in Algeria', in M. Hirsh and E. Fox Keller (eds) *Conflicts in Feminism*, London: Routledge.

Marody, M. (1993) 'Why I am not a feminist: some remarks on the problem of gender identity in the United States and Poland', *Social Research* 60(4): 853–64.

Marshall, T. H. (1963) 'Citizenship and social class', in T. H. Marshall, *Sociology at the Crossroads*, London: Heinemann.

Meznaric, S. (1994) 'Gender as an ethno-marker: rape, war, and identity politics in the former Yugoslavia', in V. Moghadam (ed.) *Identity Politics and Women: Cultural Reassertion and Feminisms in International Perspective*, Boulder, CO: Westview.

Milic, A. (1993) 'Women and nationalism in the former Yugoslavia', in N. Funk and M. Mueller (eds) *Gender Politics and Postcommunism: Reflections from Eastern Europe and the Former Soviet Union*, London: Routledge.

Moghadam, V. M. (1994) 'Introduction: women and identity politics in theoretical and comparative perspective', in V. M. Moghadam (ed.) *Identity Politics and Women: Cultural Reassertions and Feminisms in International Perspective*, Boulder CO: Westview.

Molyneux, M. (1991) 'The law, the state and socialist policies with regard to women: the case of the People's Democratic Republic of Yemen 1967–1990', in D. Kandiyoti (ed.) *Women, Islam and the State*, London: Macmillan.

Mosse, G. (1985) *Nationalism and Sexuality: Middle-Class Morality and Sexual Norms in Modern Europe*, Madison, WI: University of Wisconsin Press.

Najjar, O. A. (1992) 'Between nationalism and feminism: the Palestinian answer', in J. M. Bystydzienski (ed.) *Women Transforming Politics: Worldwide Strategies for Empowerment*, Bloomington, IN: Indiana University Press.

Najmabadi, A. (1991) 'Hazards of modernity and morality: women, state and ideology in contemporary Iran', in D. Kandiyoti (ed.) *Women, Islam and the State*, London: Macmillan.

Papanek, H. (1994) 'The ideal woman and the ideal society: control and autonomy in the construction of identity', in V. M. Moghadam (ed.) *Identity Politics and Women: Cultural Reassertions and Feminisms in International Perspective*, Boulder, CO: Westview.

Pateman, C. (1988) *The Sexual Contract*, Cambridge: Polity.

Sahgal, G. and Yuval-Davis, N. (1992) 'Introduction: fundamentalism, multiculturalism and women in Britain', in G. Sahgal and N. Yuval-Davis (eds) *Refusing Holy Orders: Women and Fundamentalism in Britain*, London: Virago.

Schirmer, J. (1993) 'The seeking of truth and the gendering of consciousness', in S. A. Radcliffe and S. Westwood (eds) *'Viva': Women and Popular Protest in Latin America*, London: Routledge.

Siklova, J. (1993) 'Are women in Central and Eastern Europe Conservative?', in N. Funk and M. Mueller (eds) *Gender Politics and Post-Communism: Reflections from Eastern Europe and the Former Soviet Union*, London: Routledge.

Smith, A. D. (1986) *The Ethnic Origins of Nations*, Oxford: Blackwell.

Stacey, J. (1983) *Patriarchy and Socialist Revolution in China*, Berkeley, CA: University of California Press.

Tavakoli-Targhi, M. (1994) 'Women of the West imagined: the Farangi Other and the emergence of the woman question in Iran', in V. M. Moghadam (ed.) *Identity Politics and Women: Cultural Reassertions and Feminisms in International Perspective*, Boulder, CO: Westview.

Toprak, B. (1994) 'Women and fundamentalism: the case of Turkey', in V. M. Moghadam (ed.) *Identity Politics and Women: Cultural Reassertions and Feminisms in International Perspective*, Boulder, CO: Westview.

Turner, B. (1989) 'From Orientalism to global sociology', *Sociology* 23(4): 629–38.

Walby, S. (1990) *Theorising Patriarchy*, Oxford: Blackwell.

Westwood, S. and Radcliffe, S. A. (1993) 'Gender, racism and the politics of identities in Latin America' in S. A. Radcliffe and S. Westwood (eds) *'Viva': Women and Popular Protest in Latin America*, London: Routledge.

Yuval-Davis, N. (1995) 'The Cairo conferences, women and transveral politics', *Women against Fundamentalism Journal* 6: 19–21.

Yuval-Davis, N. and Anthias, F. (eds) (1989) *Woman-Nation-State*, London: Macmillan.

Zipes, J. (1983) *Fairy Tales and the Art of Subversion*, London: Heinemann Educational.

2 Founding fathers and earth mothers

Women's place at the 'birth' of nations

Sarah Benton

THE WAR-MADE CITIZEN

When people assert that they are 'a nation', they have to find their origin. They tell stories of how and when they began as this collective entity. As it is a story of a unitary being, differences within that nation – of class or sex or race – have to be expunged, even though the conflict between different groups may be the motor of the story. If we want to know what those conflicts were, we have to rely on hints and allusions or infer something unspeakable from the silences.

A story of the origin of the nation is always of its moment. But it always reveals the character of the nation, explains a conflict, proposes its destiny, justifies a current action. The stories are varied and particular, which makes it remarkable how many assume men have possessed the women as a preliminary to their claiming control over their own story. The cultures in which most of the ancient stories originate grew from the 'epicentre' of the Mediterranean Levant, whose 'traditional' society is characterised by 'a persistent debasement of the female condition'.[1]

The stories that are sung aloud, telling us of founding fathers and enduring national traits, are often of successful wars against an outside enemy. They tell us of republics made by war, and those who took part are the first citizens of the republic. Whether or not women play heroic walk-on parts in this epic of heroism, the actual civic settlement at the end of war – such as the bestowal of land or state benefices – is almost invariably made in the interests of the male defenders of the nation. War, and the armies that make war, are as marked by their distinct times and places as any other human activity. What is strikingly constant is the fact of a link between citizenship and the division between women and men that war, and the preparations for war, enforce. It is this link with war and military preparedness that social contract stories and socialist histories, as the national myth, so often ignore.

MYTHS OF ORIGIN AND FOUNDATION

There is a difference between racial or ethnic myths of origin and myths of the foundation of the nation *as a state*. The differences have profound implications for the political status of women – although all nations will have versions of both types of story and versions which merge the two. (The nation itself, in Homi Bhabha's phrase, 'is an agency of *ambivalent narration*': Bhabha 1990: 3.) A teetering ambivalence is apparent in pre-nationalist discourse. For instance, Aristotle in *The Politics* proposes a mix of natural urges and conscious acts of man to account for the state. The 'aim and the end' of the state, he says, 'is perfection'. Perfection equals self-sufficiency and it is the natural urge of men to strive for self-sufficiency, which they have done through constantly enlarging the self to incorporate households, villages, the state. To understand this process, we have to 'look at the natural growth of things from the beginning', and this 'beginning' is the pairing of male and female for reproduction, with the addition of a slave to make a household 'according to nature for the satisfaction of daily needs'. Households associate to form villages; villages associate to form cities. The fact that men then consciously make their republic is a consequence of their *natural* capacity as political beings (a capacity which women don't have) to desire good and justice and to be able to discriminate between good and evil (Aristotle 1981: i, ii).

Many myths of origin belong in a folklore which claims for the nation an origin as old as time. 'Have you not seen Pharaoh in his might, claiming descent from the sun and moon, giving shade to the civilisation of our ancestors, the high edifices, the great relics?' wrote the Egyptian poet Ahmad Shawqi in an incitement to nationalism in the 1920s (cited in Hourani 1991: 342). In this original time, the people of the nation could be imagined as belonging to one family, of the same blood, with a common ancestor. Such imaginary times pre-date travel, miscegenation – and politics. Where a nation's history is elided with a story of royal descent, real people acting in real time to control their own destiny have to excoriate the royal myth, denouncing it as mere superstition, as in Russia in 1917. For origins in the mists of time obscure the question of the legitimacy of a royalist claim. States which still rely today on a myth of origin lost in the mists of time might be states where the leadership lacks popular political authority – such as monarchies which are best served when their claim to legitimacy is obscured in the mists; or the states of contemporary central and eastern Europe where the leadership cannot lay claim to an authentic political founding in the 1990–1 'revolutions'. Here there are no rules about who is a fit leader, and there is a gender anarchy. Women do not know their place. Should they be sexually available on the free market, or the kept housewives of enticing American TV serials?

Such myths of origin are different from myths of foundation, which are accounts of human acts and the beginning of politics. These range from modern history and journalism to the epics recited by Greek bards which 'recalled the foundation of their city and the establishment of ancient cults' (Grant 1970: 16). Founders were often brothers, symbolising the fraternity of the republic – one of whom often killed the other, symbolising the fratricidal strife which will destroy the city unless harmony can be instituted. Myths of origin, such as of Japan's descent from a Sun Goddess, may give a female a primary role.[2] Myths of state foundation almost certainly do not. All republics have myths of foundation, replete with founding fathers, founding acts and founding documents. (Nation-states which still sport a monarchy also carry half-buried republican myths of foundation, that is, stories of men creating a *res publica*. See, for instance, Benton 1996.)

National myths tell a story of the proper order of society – leaders and led, chiefs and peasants, men and women, a story of who should properly exercise power and be venerated. The details of that order must be glossed over – for how can the consent of the peasants or serfs, women and the excluded to their own subordination be said to have been secured? Or – more to the point in societies outside the liberal democratic mainstream – how can the lowly be expected to display gratitude for their protection to those who have violated them? In Britain and the USA in particular, the governing myth is that of the social contract, which rests on the premise that the consent of all individuals has been secured to their own subordination to the state. (For a critical discussion of this, see Pateman 1985.) Polities which developed outside this tradition, such as Japan's, may premise the duty to obey on an idea of displaying gratitude to parents or other protectors, including husbands. The expectation of gratitude can impose a greater burden on the powerless as well as serving to protect the powerful from their fear of envy. This is of particular importance for women whose position has been regulated by complex rules of debt and gratitude long before a notion of a republic of consenting adults has been created.

Myths expunged of unacceptable violence become the legends of a few brave men. Women and the conquered races are deleted from the national story. These purged tales are often revitalised in order to attack the existing order as corrupt, as having deviated, with fatal consequences from its true origin and purpose. (See Kofman, Chapter 5 in this volume, for a specific example of this.) Margaret Thatcher was wont to upbraid the British for having abandoned their heroic, adventurous character as manifest in such founders of the modern British nation as Sir Francis Drake. Leadership, in her discourse, should go to such entrepreneurs. Lenin's niece laments in 1996 that communism began going wrong as party leaders betrayed the true spirit of the founding Bolsheviks. Leadership belonged to a self-denying brotherhood.

THE PROSTITUTE AND SEXUAL ORDER

The implication so far is that myths are both indispensable to the life of a nation and that they necessarily exclude women who are defined as part of some lower order. How true is this implication, and if there is truth in it, why should women be so relegated?

Myths of origin have to grapple with the irresistible fact of female fecundity. She swells to great size, produces a new human being from her body, suckles it. From her body comes an unstinted flow of life-giving liquid. Yet she does not rule the world. Men have no such power of procreation, and are enslaved to the other-directed urgings of the penis. In pre-political legend, the female can be revered for her fecundity. Tiridates I, the first king of the Parthian Dynasty in Armenia, AD 66, paid homage to the goddess Anahit

who is the glory and *life-giver* of our nation, whom all kings honour, especially the King of the Greeks, who is the mother of all *sobriety* and a *benefactress* (through many favours, but especially through the granting of children) of all mankind, through whom Armenia lives and maintains her life.

(cited Ananikian 1925: 28, emphases in original)

Burrowing in these myths reveals fragments of stories of the control over sexual disorder (the goddess of sobriety) and the awesome sexual generosity and power of women. That women were seen as the original creators of order is suggested, says Ortega y Gasset, by etymology; the word 'order' derives from the word for 'to weave' (Ortega y Gasset 1973).[3] Less speculative are the associations with women's sexual power. In the Babylonian epic of the hero-founder Gilgamesh, Gilgamesh's male companion Enkidu is transformed from being a wild, solitary man-animal hunter into a fit heroic companion through the sexual giving of the harlot Shamhat. Acting on divine instruction:

Shamhat loosened her undergarments, opened her legs and he took in her attractions.
She did not pull away. She took wind of him,
Spread open her garments, and he lay upon her.
She did for him, the primitive man, as women do.
His love-making he lavished upon her.
For six days and seven nights Enkidu was aroused and poured himself into Shamhat.

(From Gilgamesh in Dalley 1989)

Larentia, the legendary foster-mother of Romulus and Remus, founders of Rome who were first suckled by a wolf, was also known as 'lupa', a word meaning both she-wolf and prostitute. In legend Larentia was known as prostitute saint or prostitute goddess before her reputation was changed to that of the foster-mother of the founder of Rome (Grant 1971: 106). This suggests that before the rule of respectability, there either was – or people in their respectable fastness imagined there was – a culture when women and sexuality were not consigned to the household, when free sexuality, fecundity, the life-sustaining milk and sex-enabling wetness of the female were accepted and venerated. Legends of societies before civilisation tell of a sexual life that takes place outwith the individual household – whether this is through the temple prostitutes (available to all men), the British system which Caesar reported in his *Commentaries* of groups of ten to twelve men sharing their wives, or the common practice of seizing women in neighbourhood skirmishes (Grant 1970). Herodotus gleefully records, from his position of assumed respectability, the 'wholly shameful' custom of Babylon and Cyprus in which *every* woman, regardless of status, had to go once in her life to the temple of Aphrodite and 'there give herself to a strange man'. 'The woman has no privilege of choice – she must go with the first man who throws her the money' (Herodotus 1954: 4). After she has lain with him, she goes home, where no amount of money can ever again seduce her to lie with a stranger, that is, the custom regulated the woman's sexual behaviour, but not as the man's private resource, rather as a common resource regulated by the city and its cult.

Women who give freely or publicly of their sexual powers become, in legend, shameful harlots. Otherwise sex is an account of the rape of women, meaning the seizure of women by men for the purposes of sex *and* procreation.[4] This, too, is common in epics. Even the Bible includes it as a preliminary to human culture: 'the sons of God saw the daughters of men that they were faire; and they took them wives of all which they chose' (Genesis 6). Although this act precedes God's recognition that henceforth men will be in command of their own affairs, it also directly precedes the coming of the Flood, through which all but Noah's family, and the animals in male and female pairs, are exterminated. It is as though Genesis tells a story of two beginnings; one in which there is sexual disorder culminating in the mass seizure or rape of women; and a second which gets off on the right foot, with the father-headed family and animal one-to-one pairings already in place. Women – as the source of life-giving wetness in the desert lands which originated these epics – are trumped by God/Nature with a death-bringing flood.

It is testament to the resonance in our political subconscious of this idea of sexual licence and women in common that for years Bolshevik revolution *meant* 'nationalisation of women'. That is, to a respectable hierarchical society the breakdown of a class hierarchy and political order means the breakdown of the sexual order; sexual order itself is predicated on the siting of female sexuality inside the private household. Sexual order becomes a synonym for civilisation. In the most dramatic breakdown of Britain's political order, the seventeenth-century civil war, 'people listened with delicious horror to reports of Ranter meetings, where, it was said, adherents drank freely, smoked, swore, took off their clothes and practised "community of wives"' (Gentles 1992: 89).

PASSING ON GOD'S RACIAL PURPOSE

After this perilous sexual licence, order (together with the consolidation of the magistracy as a form of elder brother dominance) was re-established in Britain by the 1690s. The divergence between myths of origin and myths of foundation becomes entrenched (though it is never absolute), as on the one hand, there are revolutions and upheavals which destroy the inheritance of authority and common belonging and, on the other, new nationalisms which buttress themselves with ideologies of pure racial origin and destiny. These absorb select morsels of 'scientific' theories of race which make them very attractive to the educated bourgeoisie. Versions of the origin of nations, in which the nation stems fully clothed from god's loins, are developed within a mounting hysteria about competition with other rival nations. The full clothing is national character, language, customs and the national constitution which, as Dickens' Mr Podsnap says of Britain: 'Was Bestowed Upon Us by Providence.'

A myth of divine origin usually goes alongside a myth of having a divine mission, of being a chosen people inhabiting a chosen land. The most clearcut example of this is nineteenth-century Afrikaner ideology, constructed out of a *mélange* of racial superiority, the sense of being under siege, the Calvinist heritage and theories of the elect. Nico Diederichs, future President of South Africa, said in 1936 that God willed that there should be nations, and 'had separated people into language groups, encouraged them to crystallise into nations and intends nations to exist until the end of time' or as D. F. Malan, who became leader of the National Party, said in 1937: 'We have a right to our nationhood because it was given to us by the Architect of the Universe' (Bloomberg 1990: 13, 26). Such myths, among other things, conveniently re-ascribe birth from the female to the male, in this case a definitely male God.[5]

National destiny was described by the German nineteenth-century nationalist, Friedrich Schleiermacher: 'For it is God who directly assigns to each nationality its definite task on earth and inspires it with a definite spirit in order to glorify himself through each one in a peculiar manner' (*Addresses on Religion*, cited Kedourie 1961: 58). At its simplest then, national destiny was for a nation – defined as an ethnically homogeneous people – to manifest itself as God's distinct creation, to bear witness to God's intention by being there. If it was God's will for them to be a distinct nation, then obviously it was God's will that Afrikaner women, who are largely absent from the story, should produce only pure Afrikaner babies. The story makes no sense unless the rigorous repression of sexual disorder is assumed.

Ironically, such ideologies are not necessarily repulsive for women. They offer women a distinct role *as* women. Not as citizens, but as the female part of the organic, homogeneous nation. The fact that pregnancy and childbirth are part of God's mission sanctifies their femaleness in a discourse which otherwise tends to associate femaleness with dark and terrifying sexual chaos. The same siege mentality, the same notion that the female contains the pure essence of the nation, the same paranoia which marks all power-holders who expect gratitude from the 'protected' lower order but harbour murderous desires towards them, also assumes that alien men want nothing so much as to possess and desecrate these holy vessels of men's honour. Their femaleness must be possessed by the nation, by men who are the nation's ordained mundane representatives (viz., husbands), never by alien men, never, never by the women themselves. (See Kofman, Chapter 5 in this volume, for a discussion of this in the context of the New and Far Right in France.)

In this racial nationalist discourse, women endow their national babies with more than life and succour; they also give them the mother tongue. As the nationalist German writer Fichte says, in *Address to the German Nation*, a conquered people who have given up their language are 'an echo resounding from the rock, an echo of a voice already silent; they are, considered as a people, outside the original people and to the latter they are strangers and foreigners' (cited Kedourie 1961: 67).

Language, the mother tongue, is drunk in with mother's milk in the motherland. As Germans and Russians wrestled in the nineteenth century with their lack of nation-states and their national ineffectuality, many voices were raised arguing that the nation must be refounded on its mother tongue. This, thought the linguistic nationalists, would distinguish the true German (or Russian) from aliens, because someone who has not drunk in their mother's milk will never speak the authentic language. Some slip of the tongue will always betray them.[6] Thus national motherhood was the one true source of national belonging.

THE SACRED ESSENCE

If women procreate the nation, ensure its survival in pure form, then they are worthy of reverence and should be incorporated as full-fledged members of the nation. (Aristotle says the village is created by 'sons and grandsons' to satisfy *more* than daily needs, but refers to these community offshoots as 'homogalactic', that is, suckling the same milk: Aristotle 1981: 1252b15.) This role as procreators of the nation is the essence of the claim to belonging made by right-wing, 'womanist' women, some of whom became prominent anti-suffragists in the nineteenth century. But the argument was desultorily used by suffragettes as well, some of whom adopted the prevailing eugenicist theories for their cause. The role of women, in this discourse, is not just to have babies and bring them up properly (i.e. inculcate proper nationalist values); it also falls on them to police the sexual disorder of both women and men. The language of moral purity (meaning sexual continence) hovered very close to the language of equal rights for women.

The national essence which must be transmitted is a bodily essence. It may be milk or blood or semen, sacred fluids all. This creates one of the chief contradictions which myth must resolve: how do men pass on the sacred fluids to each other without transgressing the boundary between acceptable and unacceptable sexual acts? The strain of upholding myths of national distinctness and destiny at a time – from about the 1870s to the 1920s – when there was an escalating movement in Britain and the USA to recruit all young men into paramilitary movements, from the Boy Scouts to Army reserves – was most evident in the edge of hysteria about homosexuality, moral cleanliness and racial degeneration which afflicted those times. Only pure fluids – blood and semen and rivers – transmit moral purity and racial belonging; if contaminated, they also transmit disease and decay. (See also Kofman's discussion in Chapter 5 of the dangers to the French nation posed by AIDS.) Mental, moral and physical diseases were inherent in non-white races. Syphilis was passed on by impure women; it was also, argued a body of medical literature, transmitted in Jews through the ritual sucking of the penis at circumcision by the *mohel*, the circumciser who either picked up or passed on syphilitic ulcers (Gilman 1993: 66). In Britain, experience of the empire appeared to confirm the link between race, disease and moral decay. This was particularly so in West Africa, the one posting to which no wife should ever be taken. The idea that both disease and national essence are transmitted by essential fluids is found in the common association between diseases and 'national' identity – i.e. the idea that different racial groups are more vulnerable to different diseases, and are thus identified by disease – or rather by invulnerability to diseases which the other carries. The vulnerability of the white man and – especially – the white woman to 'African diseases' was taken as testament not so much to the infectiousness of tropical diseases as the corruption of moral purpose which afflicted those who 'went native'. Women were more vulnerable to possession by the other because they inherently lacked self-possession.

The exchange of precious fluids among men was not staunched. The most sacred exchange was that of the blood oath, taken by the elites of brothers who would be the kernel of the new nation. Blood oaths were the *de rigeur* initiation for paramilitary brotherhoods from the IRA to the Palestinian Boy Scouts of the 1930s. Sometimes they just bled simultaneously from their wounds. No wonder Henry V became such a favourite text:

> We few, we happy few, we band of brothers
> For he today that sheds his blood with me
> Shall be my brother.

This is the politically correct form of transmission. But to sustain the nation, fluids must be passed from man to woman and from woman to child from their common font in the founder of the nation. Where national origin is claimed in God himself, then descent is from him via Adam via Eve (as the seventeenth-century patriarchalists asserted.) Outside the Christian tradition, another supernatural origin must be found. Most founders (again a moment when myths of origin and of foundation overlap) are orphans of divine or royal parentage. They are conveyed to their place in mundane human society by the sacred fluids of nature, usually a river. If women appear in these myths as actual or surrogate mothers, their bodies are merely the vessels for containing and safely conveying the sacred fluids of semen or milk or blood.

The Victorian culture in which these myths of origin and essences flourished was a culture both repelled and transfixed by sexuality, both irresistibly drawn to spending (money, semen) and aghast at wasting (capital, energy through masturbation). There was a terror of incontinence.[7] The idea of transmission by blood was for them both a metaphor and a scientific reality. The best known propagator of theories of racial superiority, Count Gobineau (1967), never doubted that 'racial essence' was passed on through blood.

Many of these apparently self-confident nationalist ideologies were invented at a time when the rise of other nations and modernity itself threatened to destroy the racial and sexual order. In imagery, it was essential to portray the good woman as immobile, a container, a form of safe deposit in which men could vest their secrets and their bodily needs, while she stood calmly guarding his most precious possessions in a world where everything, from loose women to national boundaries, moved with the unclutchable speed of the new telegraph system.[8] 'Like all symbols, the female embodiment of the nation stood for eternal forces', wrote George Mosse of the movement for re-founding Germany as a unified nation.

They looked backward in their ancient armor and mediaeval dress. Woman as a preindustrial symbol suggested innocence and chastity, a kind of moral rigor directed against modernity – the pastoral and eternal set against the big city as the nursery of vice.

(Mosse 1985: 98)

RAPE IN THE OVERTHROW OF PATERNAL POWER

It is the contention of both Gordon Scochet and of Carole Pateman that theories of the social contract, as the *original* act of civilisation, in fact must assume that a family order already exists in society (Pateman 1988; Scochet 1975). It is Pateman's argument that the ordering of society into individual households headed by men, who thus arrange for their own access to their own women, is a necessary precursor of the social contract – a sexual contract, in fact – which marks a transition from patriarchy to fraternal rule. This is not the place to pursue that argument – other than to observe that myths of origin are patriarchal myths which tell of the unbroken line from paternal font to the present; myths of foundation are social contract myths and are stories of fraternal rule. With a new beginning, new men create their own households, which means women must be wrested from the authority and care of their fathers. Like the American Declaration of Independence, marriage is both an assertion of independence and a declaration of war against the parents.[9] (Hence the symbolism in a wedding of the father consenting to hand his daughter to her husband. Without his formal consent, or bride-price or dowry contracts, the removal of his daughter would be a rape, or a seizure.) An order welded by systems of obligation, protection and gratitude precedes an order of consenting individual adults. It also persists after any founding of a republic as a sub-system within it, governing relationships between male citizens and their wives, adults with children, masters with slaves in the nineteenth-century USA, western European states with their colonies.

Stories of rape, such as the rape of the Sabine women which accompanies the foundation of the City of Rome, can be read as accounts of the seizure of women from paternal authority. Rape in legend frequently symbolises the destruction of male authority, which has lost its essential quality of rule, the will and power to protect the weak. Thus, just as Rome begins with a mass rape, so the rule of kings in Rome is ended and the republic inaugurated when Tarquin, the king's son, proves the misgovernance of kings when he rapes Lucrece. The actual circumstances of the overthrow of the house of Tarquin and the institution of consular rule are speculative. However, the mythology of the rape and the failed attempt of the wicked king's house to reclaim Rome have been handed down to the English through Shakespeare's

Rape of Lucrece and Macaulay's *Lays of Ancient Rome*. In Shakespeare's 'Argument' introducing *Rape of Lucrece*, father Lucius Tarquinius has already acted tyrannically by declaring war without 'staying for the people's suffrages'. Lucrece kills herself after being raped by Sextus Tarquinius, and revulsion at the rape and her martyrdom so move the people that 'with consent and a general acclamation the Tarquins were all exiled, and the state government changed from kings to consuls.' However, as a set of mythological tales, this was also read as a *return* to a form of strong patriarchal rule (the new consul Brutus reputedly has his own sons executed for treachery) and a rejection of the licentious and wayward behaviour of young men without a strong father. Macaulay eulogises the Roman state before fratricidal strife despoiled it:

> Then none was for a party;
> Then all were for the state;
> Then the great man helped the poor,
> And the poor man loved the great:
> Then lands were fairly portioned;
> Then spoils were fairly sold;
> The Romans were like brothers
> In the brave days of old.
> (XXXII, 'Horatio' in Macaulay 1842)

The symbolism of the rape of an innocent woman is used again by Macaulay in *Virginia*, an event which this time precipitates the downfall of the rule of the Decemvirs, and which explicitly refers back to the overthrow of the Tarquins.

> Now, by your children's cradles, now by your father's graves,
> Be men today, Quirites, or be for ever slaves!
> For this did Servius give us law? For this did Lucrece bleed?
> For this was the great vengeance wrought on Tarquin's evil seed?

Macaulay's verses, instructing readers on the civic virtues of Rome, were hugely popular, with new editions published almost every year from the middle of the nineteenth century and a number of them in India for use in the Empire. The anti-monarchical undertones in his evocation of republican virtue are muted in comparison with his plangent evocation of pure woman as the inviolable solace for man if civic life is to continue: 'Then leave the poor Plebeian his single tie to life – The sweet, sweet love of daughter, of sister and of wife', he apostrophises the rapacious tyrant in *Virginia*. Macaulay implies that the man who abuses political power is the man who abuses women and children – the purpose of political power is to protect the innocence of women, or to protect the sanctity of a man's home, his private domain. That rape is popularly understood as the symbolic failure of those holding (or claiming) political power is evident in much media reportage. This is also a meaning in many fictional treatments; for instance in the hugely (and unexpectedly) successful Pulitzer Prize winning novel, *To Kill a Mocking Bird* by Harper Lee (1989), the misgovernance of white political rule in the South is implied by their false accusation of a black man of rape. Macaulay's is clearly just the most popular of many attempts in the later nineteenth century to re-establish civic virtue on the basis of manliness, as a system of male protection of female virtue inside the sanctity of his own home.

Certainly, however the men of a nation might actually treat 'their' women, any failure by a political power to treat 'their' women in the rhetorical realm as both the bearers of the nation's honour and as frail beings in need of protection is the final political sin. After the whites of South Africa achieve Dominion Status in 1910 – in a welter of new rhetoric about creating a republic – the Afrikaners erect a commemorative monument to their suffering during the Boer War. The 1913 Women's Monument at Bloem-fontein, write Gaitskell and Unterhalter, is of stoically suffering women and dying children, mute testimony to the unspeakable brutality of the other side (Gaitskell and Unterhalter 1989: 61). The mass rapes of Chinese women by Japanese soldiers in the 'Rape of Nanking' in 1937, by West Pakistan soldiers of East Pakistan women in 1971, of Croatian and Muslim women by Serb soldiers in 1992–4, are but the most notorious examples of rape as an actual assault on women, on a nation's honour and on men's capacity to protect their women, as well as of a public response that the rapes prove the unfitness of the rapists' nation to exercise political power responsibly (see also Allen, Chapter 3, and Morokvasic, Chapter 4 in this volume). The 1948 Tokyo War Crime Tribunal pointedly established that rapes by the Japanese army throughout China and Manila were carried out with the approval of commanding officers (Friedmann 1985, vol. 2). And women in Tjepu, Java, 'were not killed, but were all raped several times in the presence of the commanding officer', said the military tribunal, as part of a general indictment of the Japanese for not respecting the Hague Convention of 1907 and thereby proving themselves uncivilised. False claimants to political authority fail to protect the weak. They do not establish order.

War is won by the just, and the just settlement of war sanctifies men as the protectors of their own hearths and homes.

WAR IN THE CREATION OF CITIZENS

Myths of foundation assume that the people exist already, in some sort of order. They would not otherwise have the collective resources to create the city or the republic. The occasions of these foundations, or rather of and in the myths of foundation, is war. This is in sharp conflict with theorists who see war, not as evidence of men's ability to organise collectively for a purpose, but of the absolute opposite. The 'war-mad man', condemned in the Iliad as 'having no family, no law, no home', is, says Aristotle severely, 'a non-cooperator like an isolated piece in a game of draughts' (Aristotle 1981: 1253a1). A huge body of political theory about citizenship and the state has developed outwith the experience of war; precisely as though war is an aberration, or a 'subhuman' or pre-political activity which does not need to be assimilated into the main corpus of political ideas.

The war-making function of the state, if not its very purpose, was commonly accepted in Europe before the spread of social contract theories and the belief that the state, or republic, had been brought into existence in order to keep the peace. Hobbes marks the transition with his famous dictum that 'the condition of Man . . . is a condition of Warre of every one against every one' (Hobbes 1914: 67). The transition is from medieval society, with its idea that it is the right, sometimes duty, of kings to conduct war to the mercantile societies of the seventeenth and eighteenth centuries, in which the civil individual is a powerful agent and in which peaceful commerce and domestic harmony are the nation's destiny.

Belief in an endemic connection between war and the foundation of states was revived in a dispute in the last third of the nineteenth century between largely German and English anthropologists. The dispute is too complex to go into here but revolved around questions of whether states were formed spontaneously all over the world as a product of the same social and psychological forces in all societies, whether they were spread by conquest from a primary, conquering state or whether they were diffused by contact between people 'along the lines of least resistance and of greatest attraction' (MacLeod 1931: 70).[10] The theories of the foundation of a state all assume a prior society which was either a golden age of apolitical harmony or of quarrelsome and murderous disharmony. The peaceful state that is then founded is either the body which institutionalises a social compact (in MacLeod's term) or a product of a social compact to end disharmony. Whichever war-state theory is put forward, the originating conflict is presumed to be between men. In none of the theories is it argued that the state is founded *in order to* institutionalise a political system in which women are consigned to an individual household, each headed by a man. Yet the existence of this household sphere is assumed to be part of the peaceful order institutionalised by the social contract. Only the assumption that women constitute part of each individual man's inalienable private domain makes sense of Rousseau's paradoxical prior demand for the social contract: 'the total alienation of each associate, together with all his rights, to the whole community'. For he surely does not mean that a man's wife and hearth be alienated to the whole community, nor that women constitute equal members of the body politic (Rousseau 1966).[11]

The social contract – a myth of foundation – creates citizens. It creates men as citizens. It creates a separate domestic sphere of households in which the daily business of sustaining and reproducing life goes on. The man who heads the household is the man who is the citizen in the public sphere. What's the link?

THE CIVIC-MILITARY HIGHER ORDER

One link is the experience of war. Nothing so fits man for citizenship as service to the nation through military duty. Of course, this is not a qualification for citizenship in a feudal order, where belonging is governed by rules about status, obligation, protection and gratitude. But once there is pressure for political belonging from men in their own right, proof of belonging and fitness have to be demonstrated in some other way, and no experience throws up such consistent, such irresistible demands for suffrage as popular military service. The nation belongs to those who make it and protect it, and who most obviously makes it but the military? Many of the debates about citizenship in eighteenth- and nineteenth-century Europe and America were conducted through debates about who should, who must, be eligible for military service. That women might serve in militias (let alone standing armies) was unthinkable, and nothing so consolidated the gulf between men and women in the evolution of political ideas as the link between civic belonging and military service (see Bryson, Chapter 7 in this volume). In Britain this was established not in feudal times, when the *fyrd* was summonsed only sporadically, but from the second half of the eighteenth century, after the Militia Act of 1757.

However much the language of citizenship appears to be an argument for the treatment of all as equal individuals (even if women are not counted as individuals) the argument must also be understood as the *creation* of a citizenry which is separate from, and superior to, the non-citizen. That is, even radical arguments for citizenship from the eighteenth century are simultaneously about creating a sphere of political equality and creating a sphere of political superiority. What fits a man for citizenship, and marks him as superior, is his ability to command a household – bearing in mind that until the twentieth century only householders had the franchise and a household, by definition, included women, children and servants, all of whom were subject to the command of the head of household. The citizenry were not 'the people'; they were rather the non-commissioned officers of the nation.

War churns up these distinctions, war thrusts men into a communal male life, cutting them off from their households. It is only the *separation* from household that allows men to become a fraternity. In the words of Ralph Barton Perry, the American who headed the movement at the start of this century for universal military training to redeem the American nation through redeeming its manhood:

> Military training brings a man into contact with his fellows solely upon the basis of fellow citizenship. For the time at least, the differences of wealth, education, locality, taste, occupation, and social rank which divide Americans as effectively as though they lived on different continents or in different centuries, are lost sight of. Men are brought face to face with the elemental fact of nationality.
>
> (Cohen 1985: 260)[12]

In fact, in all military service, men do not have households as they move round the country, foraging, pillaging and generally earning a reputation as the scum of the earth. The fear that separation from household made men into brutes ran through many of the arguments from the eighteenth century for militias, rather than standing armies. Militia service gave a man an education *par excellence* in the fraternal bonds of citizenship while retaining his root in the family. Woodrow Wilson, President of the USA during the First World War, said: 'We must depend in every time of national peril, in the future as in the past, not upon a standing army, nor yet a reserve army, but upon a citizenry trained and accustomed to arms' (cited in Cohen, 1985: 3). The dangers of men loosed from home had been learned from the past. In England's Civil War, service in Cromwell's army inspired some men – common soldiers – to 'usurp the pulpit' claiming an equality with preachers that appalled even the non-hierarchical churches (Gentles 1992: 101). But the experience of military service, particularly during a war, also convinced the men that they were a superior fraternity, transformed by the experience of hardship, privation and above all by killing for a higher cause into the elect of the nation. The brotherhood which is the kernel of the republic, in whose image of manly virtues the republic is fashioned, is also the elect. War, then, creates the overwhelming need to reinforce or restore distinctions in the peace settlement which follows it. For unless the citizens are petty monarchs of the household domain, what ennobles the republic as a distinct and higher order? It is intrinsic to social contract theory that somehow a new collective will is created, in which men can put aside selfish, private pursuits and think for the good of all – as men do in war, but *only* in war. What social contract myth glosses over is how this transformation comes about; it excises the war which precedes the constitutional settlements of actuality and the imagination.

The 1689 British Declaration of Rights, for instance, after the 'Glorious Revolution' of 1688, was in no sense a bill of rights for the individual. It confirmed that sovereignty lay with the 'king in parliament' and did not assign sovereignty to the people (Speck 1988: 140). However, the judgement that the Revolution was merely 'the restoration of power to the traditional ruling class' and 'demonstrated the ultimate solidarity of the propertied class' perhaps underestimates the significance of the enshrinement of the political status of rural gentry and city freeholder (Hill 1961: 275–6).

PROTESTANT PILLARS AND MAGISTRATES' RULE

These men became the magistracy of England and Wales and in the next two centuries were the chief political authorities in local life. Most importantly, the authority to call out the militia, and adjudicate on who was eligible for service, and thus the authority to preserve the status quo against violent disturbances, lay with them (see Babington 1990). Significantly, one of the key points of the 1689 Declaration was the denial of the king's power to maintain a standing army and the assertion that 'subjects which are Protestants might have arms for their defence', a clause understood to be a defence of the role of militias as well as the supremacy of the Protestant brotherhood. In actuality, then, in England and Wales in the late seventeenth century we see the public realm being defined as a hierarchy, with a monarch, a parliament and a small fraternity comprised of men of property, heads of household, with the right to bear arms. The Protestant religion which they are pledged to defend has confirmed the right of men in their own households directly to interpret and uphold God's law without mediation by a Pope.

These settlements both restore an order after the chaos of war and institutionalise the political status of the brotherhood which won the war. The process of institutionalisation is the *sine qua non* of peace-time political order. For a paradox is at the heart of the idea of fraternal rule, and this paradox is that fraternity can *only* be maintained outside the household. The selfless, communal experience of brotherhood, which is the model of civic virtue, is unsustainable. It is febrile and hysterical. The Spanish historian, Jose Ortega y Gasset, posited that the grouping of men around a military leader is an 'hysterical contagion', creating the 'neurotic origin of the state' (Ortega y Gasset 1973: 129). (Freud also pointed to the hysteria that binds military men, and scatters them in a panic when their leader disappears: Freud 1985: section V.) The unsustainable hysteria of the fraternity in whose honour the republic is founded has to be set off against a stable, binding, separating order, that is, the individual household in which the brother is re-grounded as stalwart Head of Family. Of course, acts of settlement after disorder are specific to their time and place. It is, however, notable how commonly women are excised from the political apparatus and mythology after the upheaval – even when, as also commonly happens, the settlement explicitly recognises women as citizens. When the upheaval, whether war or revolution, has demanded the mass mobilisation of men as soldiers, then the settlements also, indeed primarily, recognise men as citizens, as the makers of the nation. The excision of women from politics is consequent on this primary recognition of men. It counters the hysteria of the brotherhood. The further in time a society moves from war, from military mobilisation, from the moment of fraternity, the greater the opportunity for women to come into their own.

NOTES

1 The fact that this was a common characteristic of widely varied societies so startled the great anthropologist (and Resistance fighter) Germaine Tillion that it shaped her studies in North Africa and impelled her most reprinted book, *The Republic of Cousins*, from which this is quoted (Tillion 1983: 12).

2 Goddess myths usually associate goddesses with the fruitfulness of the earth and the glory of new life (see Baring and Cashford 1993). One reason for the disappearance of goddess myths from myths of national origin has been the estrangement of people from the earth with industrialisation and agribusiness.

3 As a Spanish writer, he cites the Spanish word *urdir*, meaning to lay the warp – and hence to plot. The Latin *ordiri*, meaning to begin a web, has the connected meaning of to begin.

4 The English word rape comes from the Latin *rapere*, to seize, carry off, snatch. The alternative word, violate, from the Latin *violare* (to injure or dishonour), allows the same ambiguity as to who is in the injured party in a rape. The belief that it is the patriarchal family which is dishonoured was institutionalised in twentieth-century conventions on war crimes and human rights. The idea that rape is a hurt to the individual woman is relatively recent (see Khushalani 1982).

5 The affinities between the conservative, racist republicanism of the Afrikaner polity, the Dutch Reformed Church and the Orange Order of Northern Ireland are as notable as their obverse in the 'libertinism' of the Amsterdam which gave them birth.

6 In Mikhail Bulgakov's novel *The White Guard*, first published in 1926, the pretensions of one character to political leadership of the Ukraine are scorned when he fails to pronounce a test series of Ukrainian words correctly.

7 Men's fear of fear in public places, recorded in many accounts of schoolboy punishment and of going into battle, is often expressed as a terror of public urinary incontinence.

8 Lewis Mumford, the historian of cities, judges the creation of receptacles to be the great innovation of the neolithic period. The shift from phallic forms to round containers expressed, he thought, woman's nature and her social dominance at this time (Mumford 1987: 24).

9   'The primary intention' of the Declaration of Independence was 'to separate one people from another people', writes J. G. A. Pocock. 'All the indictments of George III's personal role and actions, which introduce the claim that his authority over the colonies is dissolved by reason of his misgovernance, serve to introduce the Declaration's chief verbal performance, which is a declaration of war' (Pocock 1988: 58).

10 MacLeod's (1931) book summarises the dispute, which included the work of William Rivers, reintroduced to English readers in Pat Barker's First World War trilogy (Barker 1991, 1993, 1995).

11 I agree with Judith MacCannell's argument (MacCannell 1991) that Rousseau can, at this moment, be read for his attempt to restructure our concept of self, which is specifically *not* founded on the repression of mothers, but 'on repressing the father – for the benefit of the son'. This is in tune with the eighteenth-century radical political thought which was preoccupied with the freedom of new civic, fraternal societies to discount the weight of their patriarchal ancestors. This took for granted that women lacked a political self.

12 The capacity of fraternal life to rid the nation of class distinction was admired by reformers and struck terror into British army officers, whose rigorous enforcement of the niceties of rank survived two world wars and innumerable small colonial wars.

REFERENCES

Ananikian, M. H. (1925) *Armenian Mythology*, vol. 7, *Mythology of all Races series*, Boston, MA: Archaeological Institute of America, Marshall Jones.

Aristotle (1981) *The Politics*, trans. T. A. Sinclair, Harmondsworth: Penguin.

Babington, A. (1990) *Military Intervention in Britain*, London: Routledge.

Baring, A. and Cashford, J. (1993) *The Myth of the Goddess: Evolution of an Image*, Harmondsworth: Penguin.

Barker, P. (1991) *Regeneration*, London: Viking.

—— (1993) *The Eye in the Door*, London: Viking.

—— (1995) *The Ghost Road*, London: Viking.

Benton, S. (1996) 'The 1945 Republic', *History Workshop Journal* Spring 1997 43: 249–57.

Bhabha, H. (ed.) (1990) *Nation and Narration*, London: Routledge.

Bloomberg, C. (1990) *Christian–Nationalism and the Rise of the Afrikaner Broederbond in South Africa*, London: Macmillan.

Bulgakov, M. (1971 [1926]) *The White Guard*, London: Collins.

Cohen, E. A. (1985) *Citizens and Soldiers: The Dilemmas of Military Service*, Ithaca, NY: Cornell University Press.

Dalley, S. (1989) *Myths from Mesopotamia*, trans. S. Dalley, Oxford: Oxford University Press.

Freud, S. (1985 [1921]) *Group Psychology and the Analysis of the Ego*, vol. 12, London: Pelican Freud Library.

Friedmann, L. (1985) *The Law of War: A Documentary History*, 2 vols, New York: Random House.

Gaitskell, D. and Unterhalter, E. (1989) 'Mothers of the nation: a comparative analysis of nation, race and motherhood in Afrikaner nationalism and the African National Congress', in N. Yuval-Davis and F. Anthias (eds) *Woman-Nation-State*, London: Macmillan.

Gentles, I. (1992) *The New Model Army*, Oxford: Blackwell.

Gilman, S. (1993) *Freud, Race and Gender*, Princeton, NJ: Princeton University Press.

Gobineau, Count (1967 [1915]) *On the Inequality of Human Races*, trans. A. Collins, New York: Howard Fertig.

Grant, M. (1970) *The Ancient Historians*, London: Weidenfeld & Nicolson.

—— (1971) *Roman Myths*, London: Weidenfeld & Nicolson.

Herodotus (1954) *The Histories*, trans. A. de Selincourt, Harmondsworth: Penguin.

Hill, C. (1961) *The Century of Revolution* London: Nelson.

Hobbes, T. (1914 first published [1651]) *Leviathan*, London: Dent.

Hourani, A. (1991) *A History of the Arab Peoples*, London: Faber & Faber.

Kedourie, E. (1961) *Nationalism*, London: Hutchinson University Library.

Khushalani, Y. (1982) *Dignity and Honour of Women as Basic and Fundamental Human RIghts*, The Hague: Martinus Nijhoff.

Lee, H. (1989) *To Kill a Mocking Bird*, London: Mandarin.

Macaulay, T. B. (1842) *Lays of Ancient Rome*, London: Longman, Brown, Green & Longmans.

MacLeod, W. C. (1931) *The Origin of History and Politics*, New York: John Wiley.

MacCannell, J. F. (1991) *The Regime of the Brother*, London: Routledge.

Mosse, G. (1985) *Nationalism and Sexuality*, New York: Howard Fertig.

Mumford, L. (1987) *The City in History* London: Peregrine.

Ortega y Gasset, J. (1973) *An Interpretation of Universal History*, trans. M. Adams, New York: Norton.

Pateman, C. (1985 [1979]) *The Problem of Political Obligation*, 2nd edn, Cambridge: Polity.

—— (1988) *The Sexual Contract*, Cambridge: Polity.

Pocock, J. G. A. (1988) 'States, republics and empires: the American founding in early modern perspectives', in T. Ball and J. G. A. Pocock (eds) *Conceptual Change and the Constitution*, Lawrence, KS: University Press of Kansas.

Rousseau, J.-J. (1966 [1762]) *The Social Contract*, London: Dent.

Scochet, G. (1975) *Patriarchalism in Political Thought*, Oxford: Blackwell.

Speck, W. A. (1988) *Reluctant Revolutionaries: Englishmen and the Revolution of 1688*, Oxford: Oxford University Press.

Tillion, G. (1983) *The Republic of Cousins: Women's Oppression in Mediterranean Society*, London: Al Saqi Books.

Yuval-Davis, N. and Anthias, F. (eds) (1989) *Woman-Nation-State*, London: Macmillan

3 Identity: feminist perspectives on 'race', ethnicity and nationality

Sheila Allen

The aim of this chapter is to suggest some possible ways in which feminist perspectives on identity can be developed to take account of gender and the complexities of racial, ethnic and national divisions. It considers the kinds of approaches that have been adopted by social scientists, the way feminists have approached the issue of identity and identity politics and the current use of the term 'identity' in popular discourse.[1] It makes no claim to be exhaustive in terms of the literature. This is not out of some sense of false modesty, nor is it simply that the literature which could be drawn on is voluminous. It reflects rather the current situation in which identity has become a recurring referent in popular media discourse. We are confronted daily with events which are interpreted, at least in part, as matters of identity. Is identity used when there is no understanding or no readily available explanation of events or of the actions of others? Is this more likely to be the case in times of rapid social change accompanied by widespread disruption? (This question is also addressed by Haleh Afshar, Chapter 6 in this volume.)

Identity also appears with increasing regularity in academic discussions. For example, at a conference on women's role in building the 'new' Europe, with participants from across Europe and the former Soviet Union (held in Athens in the autumn of 1991), it was constantly stated that everyone needs a national identity (Allen 1991). This unqualified statement was extremely puzzling to me. Three women, one from Cyprus, one born in Tashkent, now living and working in Moscow, and I were the only ones to ask what this meant and to raise doubts about its relevance, especially for women. Either our queries were met with blank incomprehension, or the meaning and relevance were taken to be so self-evident as to need no explanation. The emergence or re-emergence in Europe of nationalisms, and of exclusive ethnicities reinforcing racialised structures and practices, pose a considerable challenge to many understandings and explanations developed by social scientists, including feminist scholars. Given the widespread use of the term 'identity', the ways in which it has been conceptualised and its use as a tool of analysis deserve close attention. The questions raised by its current usage are much more than intellectual puzzles. They are intimately related to issues of human action, moral purpose and the range of choices available. The social conditions and the individual circumstances in which choices are embedded are relevant to the interpretations made about identity/identities.[2] I first consider theories of what I shall call 'the identity problematic' and the ways in which it has been conceptualised and investigated. I then discuss perspectives from feminist approaches which modify, and in some cases significantly reshape, the ways in which this problematic is discussed. Finally I take up some issues in the current popular discourse which are of particular relevance to women.

IDENTITY IN THE SOCIAL SCIENCES

The use of the term identity has not been widespread in social science until comparatively recently. However, questions about the relation between the individual and society, which involve issues of identity and are referred to as the identity problematic, have been at the core of much European social thought over at least the past four centuries.

There are two major ways of conceptualising this relationship within the social sciences. One is where each human being is seen as an individual entity separate from others, not living in isolation, but in association with them. The problem to be investigated then starts with the individual who exists prior to and outside the social, and the explanation is couched in terms of the links between the individual and society. The second way depicts individuals as part of the social relations in which they engage, both in the sense of direct personal interaction and indirectly as part of wider structures, of which they are not necessarily aware. The task then becomes one of explaining how the mechanisms of social interaction and social structure operate, both to create human beings as social persons and how in turn these social persons influence the structures of which they are a part. In addition to these broader conceptualisations but integral to them is a range of questions about the individual's/social person's understanding or perception of her/himself. It is around these that the narrower concept of identity has been focused. There is a further assumption to be noted, which is not always made explicit, but is incorporated into theoretical models and into common-sense thought, that of the mind and body dualism. It is not my intention to pursue the ramifications of this assumption in any systematic way in this chapter, though I recognise their importance to a feminist unravelling of mainstream depictions of women.

In the sociological literature reference to identity is relatively scarce. This is due in part to the discipline tending to eschew over long periods anything which might be interpreted as psychological or individualistic reductionism. If we look to the identity problematic, however, we find that this is theorised, albeit at different analytical levels and within very different paradigms, in the work of many nineteenth- and twentieth-century social theorists (for an overview see Burkitt 1991; for the philosophical underpinnings see Benton 1977).

Despite the differences of approach and emphasis within them, classical social theorists, such as Marx, Weber, Durkheim and Parsons, were all concerned with explaining the construction of self as part of societal order and change. Their ideas have been developed by others and the problems addressed remain central concerns within sociology (see e.g. Z. Bauman 1978; Elias 1982). Burkitt, after reviewing a wide range of social theorists, argues against any division between society and the individual and concludes that

> there are many levels of dynamic agency within the personality. . . .
> These different levels are always interwoven with and determined
> by social relations and activities of production, communication and
> power. . . . Only if we begin from the study of social relations and
> activities can we truly understand how individuals are social selves.
>
> (Burkitt 1991: 215)

The social self, or identity, is therefore theorised within sociology as being socially constructed and embedded in specific social relations.

Since the early 1980s the issue of identity has been addressed, particularly with regard to gender and 'race', within the context of debates on modernism and postmodernism. It is claimed that the dominance in western social science of theoretical approaches which saw in industrialisation a pattern of social change which subordinated all social statuses to the market and production relations created a mode of theorising inappropriate to the late twentieth century. Without going into any further detail at this point we have to note that most theorising of change and development, whether of a Marxist or liberal variety, presumed that statuses such as gender, ethnicity, 'race' and sexuality were subordinate to those produced by economic rationalisation and ever more centralised systems of power.[3] In most accounts of the development of western industrial economies, neither capitalists nor labourers were depicted as having any gender, ethnicity, 'race', religion or nationality. It was not that these social attributes did not exist, but according to the models of development adopted they belonged to 'traditional' societies and, through the processes of industrialisation, were marginalised and so became less and less relevant to understanding societal relations.

Much about this model of development has a clear purchase on the creation of modern societies and I would not wish to suggest that we cast it aside. Rather, the task is to hypothesise and investigate how and when the processes and structures of modernisation/industrialisation construct and incorporate statuses such as those related to gender, ethnicity, 'race', religion and nationality. Although sociologists were antipathetic to seeing ethnicity as anything more than a relic of 'traditional' societies and did not incorporate it into core theorising, it was not by any means totally neglected. When ethnic groups or categories were recognised as relevant they were explained by exogenous factors and as instrumentally functional. Moreover, they were also conceived as situationally specific, applicable to and used in relations outside the market. Thus, while structuring personal, religious, cultural or kinship boundaries and actions, they were absent in market relations. In some situations they could be externally imposed by dominant others, defining some or all relations between dominant and subordinated categories; a set of ethnic labels emerging or disappearing according to other political or socio-economic forces. Identity structuring was absent from much sociological work on race and ethnic relations; for example, Goulbourne (1991); Rex (1986) and Schermerhorn (1970) do not discuss it and the emphasis is on group processes and boundary maintenance in what were variously labelled plural or heterogeneous societies.

There was, in addition, a scepticism about ethnic identities claiming long histories or authenticities derived from primordial ties (see Allen 1995; Allen and Macey 1994a; Smith 1986). A scepticism by no means altogether misplaced. Whether considering traditions (cultural beliefs, rituals, ceremonies, ways of doing things) or collective memories of shared pasts, as nations, tribes, peoples or clans, a degree of scepticism is appropriate. Many such claims turn out to be recent, modern inventions or reinventions; the products of conflicts of material interests or struggles over 'authentic' identities linked to claims to civil, political and social rights (Hobsbawm 1984; see also Benton, Chapter 2 in this volume). McCrone (1992) in his discussion of late-twentieth-century Scotland and the phenomenon of nationalism refers to the selective remembering involved in nationhood. 'Events can be linked across centuries so that the "Scottish people" can stretch across centuries. "Remember Bannockburn" may seem a daft stricture in the late twentieth century when no-one can imagine what it was like to be there' (McCrone 1992: 198). But the stress is on continuity and McCrone argues that 'social scientists and historians have little power to prevent this selective remembering, and confronting myths with "facts", has little impact because myths survive almost in spite of facts' (McCrone 1992: 199). For the sociologist the task is to explain under what conditions the mythical past is brought into play and how it is constructed and reconstructed in terms of the present. (See Kofman, Chapter 5 in this volume, for a discussion of this.)

One of the most pressing current examples to which such analyses are to be applied is that of the former federal state of Yugoslavia. The ethnic map, here as elsewhere, deals with majorities/minorities but can be used as an exclusionary tool in the hands of majoritarian politicians. The reality in many of the Yugoslav republics is somewhat different. Bosnia, for instance, at the time of its recognition as an independent nation in 1992, had a population of Yugoslavs, with a mixture of ethnicities and religions. Bosnians were those born or living in Bosnia; they were Serb and Croat and, if they had a religious affiliation, the Croats were Catholics and the Serbs were either Orthodox Christians or Muslims. The reality was, as many now know, by no means this simple; thus the Bosnian Muslims like the Serbs are 'ethnically' Slavs. The boundaries drawn in the public discourse use a mixture of religious, ethnic and national markers and so compound the confusion. There are also people of other religions who are rarely mentioned. In addition patterns of intermarriage were common, so that many had not only partners from 'other categories', but also parents from 'different' religions or ethnicities. All of these were neighbours and kin, especially but not only, in urban contexts, sharing their daily lives, over several generations. The description and explanation of who is killing whom and why is interpreted in terms of ethnicity/religion and nationalism. Selective remembering is part of this process not only by the powerful parties directly involved, but also by most reporters and commentators. Ethnicity linked to nationalism and religion is claimed to have overridden all other identities in the conflict. Other descriptions, explanations and interpretations, in which these are used as symbols to mobilise support in struggles for political and economic dominance, are by and large ignored. (See Morokvasic, Chapter 4 in this volume for another explanation.)

In an unusually reflexive article on the reporting of the fighting in former Yugoslavia the situation was described not only as highly dangerous for journalists, but as facing them with a moral quagmire 'in a brutal multisided conflict' (Keating 1993). One journalist admitted the difficulties of reporting the complexities in which at times 'you had to approach people carefully [*sic*] and say "Excuse me are you Croats? Oh sorry you're Muslims . . . you're shooting at . . . um . . . Serbs? Oh, the Croats!"' Despite this, she went on to argue that viewers at home 'like to identify with one side. Where are the good guys? Who are the bad guys? . . . and if it is not clear, then people lose either sympathy or interest' (Adie 1993). Constructing clarity where none exists, albeit in order to hold an audience, may be seen as necessary by some reporters, and as such it tells us something about how exclusive categorisations are imposed and transmitted. But it tells us nothing about the identities of those involved and borders on disinformation of a highly dangerous kind. What is clear is that identity is not simply an individual matter, but a social product located in time and space. It is not a fixed static entity, but has to be seen as a dynamic process.

It is in order to make sense of the present that a historical perspective, including the role of mythical pasts, and a comparative approach building on the most rigorous theories and methods developed by social scientists are essential. Before taking these points further, I shall explore work which deals with identity in terms of individual perception or understanding of self.

The discussion of identity *formation* is predominantly to be found in the field of psychology, especially in developmental psychology, psychoanalysis and social psychology (Harre 1979, 1983; Kelly 1955; Laing 1965). A range of studies have used a narrow concept of self and attempted to construct measures which will tell us from what 'self-concept' is derived, how it is constituted and in some cases whether it accords with or deviates from 'reality'. These studies rely heavily on mechanistic (non-reflexive) theories of socialisation. Moreover, the view that identity is formed during childhood or in adolescence and only marginally modified later, if at all, is still accepted relatively uncritically. Evidence that these assumptions are, to say the least, problematic is not hard to find. Bauman, for instance, discussing the stages at which Jewishness played a role in his life says 'there are three stages in which Jewishness played some role in my life. On the whole, for most of my life and the greater part of it, Jewishness played a very small role, if at all' (Z. Bauman 1992: 226–7). These stages were the eruption of anti-Semitism in Poland in 1968, the publication of Janina Bauman's book on her experiences in the Warsaw ghetto (1986) and later when he 'discovered that peculiar condition in which Jews were cast during the period of rapid modernisation and assimilation in the second half of the nineteenth century' (see also Z. Bauman 1991). My awareness of my Irishness developed largely in my 30s and 40s and its significance has changed many of the ways I see the world and feel about my identity. Henry (1983) details the processes by which she, long settled in North America, chooses as an adult to look into her national/ethnic roots. Many inhabitants of former Yugoslavia have recently found their ethnic, national or religious affiliations eclipsing all the others. After 1991 these have been made to carry very different meanings and consequences for those involved and for those reporting on them in the media. While it is impossible to know whether the imposed exclusive categorisation becomes a matter of self-identity, those trapped in such situations are faced with few options but to conform to them.

Occasionally voices are heard which relate different stories. Two, both from BBC Radio Four's PM programme, can be taken as examples. The woman in Sarajevo described by the reporter as a Muslim, crying, 'What do I care about the mosque? It is my neighbours who are with me living in cellars, we are all together Serbs and Muslims, that I care about' (1992). Or the young student from Sarajevo University living in Edinburgh, who was introduced by the interviewer as a Muslim, but she kept laughing and giggling and saying, 'We didn't actually think in those terms, you know, religion wasn't important.' She explained that her friends were drawn from all religious/ethnic groups and it was the same for her parents living in Tuzla. Religion had not been an important defining characteristic, but sharing in the many religious holidays did mean you could enjoy cake provided by your or your friend's grandmothers (1993). Identity, and the way identities are imposed on people, especially in potentially conflictual situations, is something that has to be investigated.

Existing research, which explores empirically how individuals define themselves, especially in conflict situations, is problematic both in terms of the methods employed and the conclusions reached. For instance, Weinreich's (1986) research into racial and ethnic identity is unable to take into account social change and assumes a distinction between personal and social identity which he sees as being related but does not theorise this relationship (Allen 1994). With regard to the methods used to investigate identity formation it is, I would argue, inappropriate to use questionnaires or even one-off interviews. An illustration of the problems that can arise from this is to be found in studies carried out in Northern Ireland using questionnaires. These produced findings which suggest that few define themselves in religious terms (Hutnik 1992). Ethnographic accounts give a rather different picture, that of a public avoidance of issues such as religious affiliations which may provoke anger or embarrassment in others. Such avoidance is confirmed by my own experience in Northern Ireland and the rest of Ireland where my religious affiliation is assumed (always wrongly) and ignored. I am never questioned about it. Outside Ireland among the Irish diaspora (both Protestant and Catholic) it is raised usually, but not always, with hostility. Heaney's poem entitled 'Whatever you say, say nothing' indicates the complexities of interpretation in situations of long-running conflict. Maybe the fact that religious definitions were used by few is an indication, not of the irrelevance of religion, but of its centrality to the lives of the respondents. Understanding what is not said, *reading the silences*, is a crucial aspect of any investigation of identity (and also nationalism, see Benton, Chapter 2 in this volume), but one not available through questionnaires or tests. The complexities of social life are part of the processes of data collection and these cannot be encapsulated in twenty statements either by the respondent or the researcher. It is because of such limitations that these methods appear to be inappropriate and distorting, especially where conflict exists and mixed and multiple identities carry personal and social costs. Milner's comment remains at least partially applicable:

Identity is a concept which has been much used and abused in psychological theory. The term 'identity' has been a repository for a variety of imprecise ideas about what people are and how they see themselves. It has been all things to all theorists

(Milner 1975: 45)

The perspectives of interactionism and symbolic interactionism have in a variety of ways been concerned with combining 'the subjective aspects of group life with an appreciation of its objective features' (Lal 1986: 285). Drawing as it does on the intellectual histories of sociology, as well as social psychology, it cannot be said to represent one coherent or consistent set of perspectives (see Fisher and Strauss 1978 for a fuller discussion). Nevertheless, both the theories of Mead (1934) and the work of Blumer (1969) on method are useful. In essence, Mead argued that the self was to be conceptualised as having two components, the I and the me, and it was through the dialogue between them that a sense of self develops. Again we are dealing with a process, not a static entity and the potentiality for multiple selves over time or location is not to be seen as in contradiction to an integrated self. This potentiality is not limitless (or random). It is precisely the structuring of the limits which sociologists investigate. Additionally, there is no necessity for the self I think and feel I am, to be either that which others assume me to be, or the same as the groups with which I behaviourally identify. The discrepancies between my concepts of myself and those that others hold of me may be of great significance to me, but how far I can act on them in any situation is not only up to me, but also a matter of structural and cultural location.

Blumer stressed the need for methods to bridge the structural approaches to social research and the accounts given by individuals, of their sense of self and their world. In particular, following not only Mead but also Park, he worked on the level of group interaction and advocated forms of participant observation, which facilitated the researcher in 'developing a familiarity with what is actually going on in the sphere of life under study' (Blumer 1969: 39).

The variety of methods used in investigating a wide range of problems, including 'race' relations, urban communities, industrial relations and collective behaviour carried out by innumerable sociologists demonstrate the strengths of both sociology and social psychology and offers a great deal more insight into the social bases of identity than the narrow ones pursued in much psychology. Symbolic interactionism does not, however, go far enough conceptually.

Interactionism shares some of the features of the ethnographical approaches used by, among others, anthropologists who have also been concerned with issues of identity. Some of their studies have been justly criticised for lack of attention to asymmetrical power structures in which their subjects are located (see Mason 1986). But not all studies have neglected these aspects. Those of Mirpuris in Bradford and Pakistanis in South London, for instance, demonstrate the strength of an urban anthropology which pays close attention to the concerns with and meanings derived from 'homelands', the translation of these in minority situations and the imposition of majority perceptions (Saifullah Khan 1974, 1976, 1977, 1979). The work of some anthropologists is of particular relevance in exploring conceptualisations of identity and these will be considered in the final part of this section.

Epstein (1978) made the concept of identity central to his discussion of ethnicity and ethnic groups in North America and Africa. He argues that when this is done 'new perspectives on old dilemmas' are possible. He points out, what should be obvious to social scientists, that ethnic identity is meaningful only where those of different ethnic origins are brought together in a common social context and is only one among many possible identities. While ethnicity is conceptualised as a social mechanism classifying groups or categories, frequently involving relations of dominance, hierarchy and social stratification, he sees the generating of ethnic identity as a psychosocial process. Epstein stresses early childhood experiences and influences in ethnic identification and the security, trust and affirmation of oneself that association with fellow ethnics confers in polyethnic situations. However, as this is only one of many possible identities he allows that whether it is taken up is partly a matter of choice, but a choice always within social and unconscious elements of constraint. There are points of similarity here with the arguments of Mead noted earlier.

Epstein's three brief but carefully crafted essays are interesting and insightful and deserve much closer attention than they have received in debates on 'race' and ethnicity in Britain. Barth (1969) has been accorded more prominence than Epstein, but he is concerned with relations between ethnic groups, particularly boundary maintenance and permeability; according to Fox, Barth uses an ethnocentric market model which 'strips cultural identities of their constituting effect on individuals' (Fox 1990: 6). Cohen (1969, 1974) was also critical of Barth's approach and in his work on Nigeria developed a two-dimensional model in which the symbolic and the political are autonomous, but dialectically interrelated in such a way that ethnic solidarity and awareness mesh together in social action. Cohen (1981) carries these ideas forward in his study of Creole identity as an elite in Sierre Leone.

One of the major strengths of anthropology and sociology in investigating the structuring and perception of action has been the stress on fieldwork methods and ethnographic studies.

IDENTITY AND FEMINISM

The 'politics of identity', both within feminist social science and in women's movements during the 1980s, have to be rethought. In the first the concept of difference has been stressed (see Barrett 1987; Maynard 1994) and in the second differences, most notably of class, 'race', ethnicity and sexuality, used as grounds for exclusion. In the late 1980s and even more in the 1990s differences of religion and nationality have been given a higher profile. (See also Yuval-Davis, Chapter 9 in this volume, for a discussion of identity politics).

I am not arguing that differences between women do not exist. The recognition of them is an important corrective to earlier Eurocentric, particularly white North American, approaches (Allen *et al.* 1991).The need to be sensitive to and appreciative of the different experiences of women across and within states is now, if not taken for granted, well argued in much of the literature. This clearly indicates that neat boundaries and arbitrary lines cannot encapsulate the specificities of subordination. Concentrating on difference served to highlight how, in mainstream social science, gender has remained unincorporated in analyses of social formations. Interpreting gender as though the relations of inequality between men and women are one-dimensional has not been helpful. Some women do have greater power and resources than some men, but not as far as men in their own social groups, however defined, are concerned. In attempting to discuss feminist perspectives on gender and to incorporate 'race', ethnicity and nationality we need to bear in mind the degree to which, both in social science and in practice, women have been defined as the 'other' (De Beauvoir 1974). This perception has been so taken for granted that women are defined in relation to men, particularly as mothers, wives, sisters and daughters, while men are taken to be representative of a non-gendered subjectivity, of non-gendered human beings. (See also Benton's discussion of citizenship, Chapter 2 in this volume.)

A reflexive awareness about oneself and others is anchored in day-to-day activities in which we produce and reproduce 'appropriate' behaviours. It is unnecessary for us to think actively about much of this in order to carry on 'as normal'. If asked, we could describe in some way, who we are, what we are doing and why. Such descriptions are not just in our minds, but combine our thoughts and feelings, our presuppositions of the enquirer's expectations and our relative statuses. In developing an understanding of the processes involved in the creation and reproduction of ourselves, from a feminist perspective, questions about the presumptions underlying and the common-sense knowledge associated with 'normal' human activities have constantly to be raised. Otherwise the distortions embedded in dominant modes of social thought and everyday language that male equals human are reinforced.

In the creation and reproduction of the self, gender is a fundamental dimension in all societies. Psychology, psychoanalysis, philosophy and sociology have not ignored this altogether, but have fairly systematically neglected or distorted it (Sherif 1987). As Harding (1987: 187) warns, 'if grounds for accepting knowledge claims are in perfect fit with the claim advanced, we should worry about what kinds of knowledge are being suppressed, subjugated, sent underground'. This cautions us to question the taken-for-granted presuppositions of man-made science and the man-made world. For example, for some white, middle-class, educated women in North America and northern Europe, Friedan's (1963) attempt to explicate 'the problem that has no name' changed their ways of seeing/knowing/ understanding themselves; it did not change their 'objective' situation. It facilitated the connections between the personal and public spheres en-capsulated later in the statement 'the personal is the political'. Further questions were raised. These were not only about white middle-class women's identity formation, but also about women in different classes, cultures and about women of colour.

The range of diverse conditions in which women are located is vast, but these differences are neither random nor absolute. The current 'trafficking' in women and young girls, within and across borders, organised and controlled by men, brings into sharp focus exploitation for monetary reward and sexual gratification. Spivak (1992) gives a particularly vivid portrayal of the experiences of a daughter of a bonded labourer in decolonised India. Through these she analyses the global meanings of 'The persistent agendas of nationalisms and sexuality, encrypted [on the gendered body] in the indifference of super-exploitation' (Spivak 1992: 113).

Friedan and others argued that only when alternatives are available can women first see that there is an unnamed problem and second move towards what she terms 'self-actualisation'. Underlying this train of thought is a culturally and historically specific conception of available alternatives, of choice and of self-actualisation, that of voluntaristic individualism. If these specificities are not recognised and addressed, serious distortions enter feminist theorising. Three points, in particular, need to be borne in mind, all of which relate to the self/society debates discussed above. First, available alternatives exist in all societies, as comparative and historical work has shown. It is not only in modern societies that women have alternatives. The questions to be investigated are those which have been central in mainstream social science, reshaped to include women, such as under what conditions are alternative ways of acting perceived. Second, when perceived, what are the cultural and material barriers to be overcome, what resources are available, what are the costs and gains involved in any particular course of action and how do these vary for different groups of women? The third relates to Friedan's conception of self-actualisation. Self-actualisation is not simply or necessarily an individual project as she indicates; her view is that of white, liberal North America, and is therefore culturally specific and partial. Conceptualisations of the self as socially constructed are to be understood and realised through collective/group/community activities. The contribution of feminist thought lies in the recognition that all these activities are gendered and so are social selves. In feminist practice, therefore, any moves towards self-actualisation include others.

The debates on difference within feminism have been around two issues. One about which women to include/exclude and the other about whether women have more in common with men and children in their own group than with women defined as different. A range of political and intellectual positions has been taken on both these issues. For instance, it has been argued that other divisions, most notably those of class, colour, ethnicity, religion and nationality, cut across those of gender so that only women sharing one or more of these have a common identity and a common basis for action. (These issues are explored further by Afshar, Waylen and Yuval-Davis, Chapters 6, 8 and 9 in this volume.) In modernist theories, as noted above, class relations take precedence so that men and women of the same class are assumed to have common interests as against those of another class. Within this general approach some of those concerned with race and ethnicity argued that *within* classes, fractions developed along racial and ethnic lines, but neglected to theorise their articulation with gender. In postmodernist discussions multiple differences are posited as central to the understanding of the realities of social divisions, inequalities and dis-empowering exclusions (Seidman 1992). However, where patriarchy and the capitalist market not only remain, but also are in the ascendancy, the adoption by feminists of postmodernist and deconstructionist perspectives and vocabularies is arguably premature. Virginia Woolf's statement 'As a woman I have no country' provides a starting point for thinking about what feminist analyses have to offer in the present context.

IDENTITY AND THE SUPPRESSION OF DIFFERENCE

In the heterogeneous societies of the contemporary world the postmodernist critiques of universalism carry an attractive plausibility into which the concept of identity neatly fits. However, identity denies and suppresses differences *within* socially created categories and emphasises differences *between* them (cf. Yuval-Davis, Chapter 9 in this volume). Identity X has meaning only in relation to a not-X identity and logically assumes a categorical equivalence of all X's and a categorical difference from all not-X's. Such logic does not describe any social reality. If we accept that individuals derive their identity from their history, from parents, grandparents and significant others, and from their biography in which the particular combination of relationships and experiences is unique to each individual, then the simple dichotomy of sameness and difference quickly evaporates. We are left to deal with variabilities within categories and similarities across them. In postmodernist discourse some identities are listed but not explained, described but not ordered. To overcome these shortcomings requires an exposition of multiple identities latent or otherwise and a theorising of the social relationships in which they are embedded and through which they may be activated.

One of the critiques of dominant social thought consistently put forward by feminists is that it defines women as other. This is exactly what discussions of identity produce, unless the complexities of social divisions and their ordering are addressed directly, without employing the common dichotomous approach of self/other, mind/body, subject/object and nature/culture. Recognising and theorising the interconnections across boundaries is both an intellectual and practical task of considerable difficulty. Especially as in European societies, as well as in social thought, dichotomous categorising abounds impeding the development of fruitful dialogue and a plurality of non-threatening identities.

If we examine the current conflicts and war discourses among politicians and in the media we can see the stark outcomes when identity 'turns the merely different into the absolutely other' (Young 1990). In feminist thought the subordination, oppression and exploitation of women are not respecters of national boundaries. On the contrary, women are used in defining boundaries, and asserting the dominance of some men over other men through the protection of 'their' women (Guy 1992). Societies always portray their women as more virtuous than women of other groups and therefore in need of protection according to Obbo (1989). The notions of protector and protected are central constructs of war (Stiehm 1982). To protect 'their' women they engage in violent conflict and rape the women of 'their' enemies. The frequent use of rape in the discourse of men warring over national boundaries is not a recent phenomenon (see Benton, Chapter 2 in this volume). Nor is the use of gendered language to describe a nation unusual. Nations are raped by others or, as in colonial situations, said to be waiting to be raped by others. For feminist scholars the recognition of male discourses and praxis in this regard is essential. The attempt to gain international recognition of rape as a war crime grew out of the reporting of rapes in the former Yugoslavia and elsewhere. While agreeing with this attempt to internationalise the criminality of rape and a whole battery of other crimes against women and young girls, it is important to recognise the functions of the male discourse on rape, including war rape (see Kofman, Chapter 5 in this volume). Rape in war serves two functions. One as a *rite de passage* where soldiers prove their loyalty to the nation by raping the women of the enemy and the other as a means of attacking the enemy through his women.[4] All women share a common interest in not being raped by the male 'enemy' just as they do in not being raped by their 'protectors'. If we recognise that in national, ethnic or race conflicts, rape functions to divide and disunite women, then we, along with Virginia Woolf, begin to question the meaning of such statements as 'Everyone needs a national identity'.[5]

ISSUES OF EXCLUSION AND MARGINALITY

An understanding of the many differences which mark heterogeneous societies leads to an acknowledgment that any simple dichotomous categorising carries with it mechanisms of exclusion and marginality. In my concluding section I shall take two examples of these from Britain that have not so far been dealt with by feminists, but to which in my view their analyses are of particular relevance.

There is general agreement that historically the ideologies of nationalism and racism have been intertwined in British imperialism and that in the post-war period we have witnessed a growth in British, or more particularly English nationalism, as an exclusionary force to deny racialised minorities a British/English identity with full rights of citizenship (Gilroy 1987; Miles, 1987a, 1987b; Solomos 1989). The British nation is a myth, relying heavily on Anglo-Saxon origins and ignoring the different racial, linguistic, cultural and national composition of those living in the British Isles over many centuries, but the British state is a reality (see Benton, Chapter 2 in this volume). In its imperial mode this state defined all those living in the UK or one of its colonies as British *subjects* with varying rights according to gender and 'race'/ethnicity. The post-imperial phase, first through immigration control legislation and then through legal categories of nationality, has produced a progressive reduction of rights for those not holding full British citizenship, with gender and patriality playing crucial and continuous roles in the construction of Britishness by the British state. The *de facto* exclusion of the black British from such constructions raises important political and sociological questions (see Allen 1989a, 1989b; Allen and Macey 1994a; Goulbourne 1991). This is a specific example of much wider phenomena, including the plight of refugees, asylum seekers and migrant workers in western and central Europe and the situation of many groups of ex-citizens of the former Soviet Union. To construct the problem as one of national identity, rather than one of legitimate claims to citizenship rights within state structures, is to accept ideological constructions of nationhood which function to deny such rights (Morokvasic 1991, 1992; see also Afshar, Chapter 6 in this volume).

Identity, when construed as uni-dimensional rather than as composed of shared attributes and part of social relations, leads to a marginalisation of those who do not fit the categories of 'X' and 'not-X'. The example in Britain which most readily comes to mind is the division of people into black and white. This is highlighted in the politics and policies surrounding transracial adoption and fostering.[6] The arguments for 'same race' adoption are couched in a variety of terms, but identity has always been prominent among them. Differences of, for instance, class, of natural and adoptive parents or siblings of 'mixed' origins, or of birth mothers of the 'wrong' category all become subsumed under a genetically based dichotomous orthodoxy. This acknowledges little of the multiple characteristics of selves in a society divided horizontally and vertically, where power differentials are central, and so the issue remains clouded. Practitioners leave it unexplored, policy makers adopt politically expedient solutions and academic researchers, including feminists, do not confront it. At present it is only in the writings of people like Jackie Kay (1991) that the harshnesses and the strengths of the circumstances surrounding, and the feelings involved in 'transracial' adoption in Britain are given a reality and a veracity. In a racially ordered society there are very serious questions to be addressed, but these require not simple dichotomies or claims and counter claims of racism, but painstaking, hard work of rethinking in non-exclusive ways the experienced vulnerabilities, particularly of women and children, in a patriarchal and class-divided society.

The concept of identity not only marginalises those categories taken as not fitting a norm which confers sameness, but also excludes all those individuals and families of 'mixed' descent or affiliation. Research into those for whom this 'mixed' condition is a normal way of being and living is scarce. What research exists tends to pathologise them, seeing them as abnormal individuals with identity problems, as threatening to ordered social relations in crossing dominantly construed boundaries, and thus strongly reinforces populist stereotypes (see Alibhai-Brown and Montague 1992; Spickard 1989; Stahl 1992). In Europe many people have mixed affiliations and origins. Social scientists need to explore the conditions under which these are productive and creative and those which promote them as destructive and alien.

Unless we ground our discussion and research in as rigorous analyses as we possibly can and risk offending those with particularistic interests or beliefs, which we are almost inevitably bound to do, we shall be unable to contribute to the understanding of present problems and the specific ways in which they affect women across Europe. Insights and theoretical propositions derived from the many attempts by feminist scholars to develop an epistemology and research methodologies which treat women as central actors not as 'other', are especially relevant to devising research which will take 'mixed' conditions as normal. I see no difficulty in accepting that some people, including myself, think of themselves simultaneously as an outsider and insider, a stranger and an in-group member in ethnic, national and class terms. How we are perceived is a different matter. The study of processes by which identity has come to be the equivalent of sameness and to command such a dominant position in social thought and practice with all the consequences of exclusion and marginality constitutes an urgent research agenda to which feminist analyses have much to offer.

ACKNOWLEDGMENTS

This chapter draws on Allen (1994) with the kind permission of Taylor & Francis Ltd. My thanks are due to many friends and colleagues for discussions on some of the issues raised, in particular Mirjana Morokvasic and Gill Olumide.

NOTES

1 In my own work I have rarely, if ever, used the term 'identity'. Its current widespread use in relation to 'race', ethnicity and nationality indicates that its analytical status needs close attention.
2 The term 'choice' is problematic. There is no consensus on its meaning. In some voluntaristic models it is conceptualised *as though* individuals make choices in a social vacuum, abstracted from the constraints of the socio-economic, gendered and racialised structures in which they live. This is clearly not adequate.
3 'Race' and ethnicity have been conceptualised in a variety of ways (for a discussion of these, see Anthias 1992). In this chapter they are used as social constructs embedded in social relations, not as unchanging attributes of individuals, voluntaristically chosen. Both can be major social markers between categories, imposed by dominant others and may provide bases of solidaristic relations. The processes by which these potentials can be turned into social realities can be explained only within broader theories of social relations. The increasing use of the term identity in relation to both is highly problematic and, as I argue in this chapter, has to be seen as a particular variant of the general question of the mutually interactive relations of self and society.
4 One comment made to me by a Yugoslav sociologist at the 1993 conference

was that frequently the first question to be put by journalists, as they arrived in war zones, was 'Is there anyone here who has been raped and speaks English?'

5 It has been customary in western Europe to use the term 'nation-state' which implies the state is coterminous with the nation. This is by no means so in most cases (see Allen and Macey 1994a for further discussion). The state can be multinational and a nation can exist without being a state (see McCrone 1992).

6 These emerged only some twenty years after religion ceased to be the excluding criterion used by almost all agencies (see Allen and Macey 1994b)

REFERENCES

Adie, K. (1993) Contribution to R. Keating, 'When reporters go over the top', *Guardian* 18 January.

Alibhai-Brown, Y. and Montague, A, (1992) *The Colour of Love*, London: Virago.

Allen, S. (1989a) 'Social aspects of citizenship', public lecture Queens University, Belfast, May.

—— (1989b) 'Women and citizenship: the British experience', paper presented to International Seminar, 'The Participation of Women in Politics and Decision Making Processes', Istanbul, December.

—— (1991) 'Diversity and commonality: building a dialogue', paper presented to International Conference, 'Building a Europe without Frontiers: the Role of Women', Athens, November.

—— (1994) 'Race, ethnicity and nationality: some questions of identity', in H. Afshar and M. Maynard (eds) *The Dynamics of Race and Gender*, London: Taylor & Francis.

—— (1995) 'Nationalism: ethnicity and gender', paper presented to the European Sociology Conference, Budapest, 30 August–2 September.

Allen, S. and Macey, M. (1994a) 'Some issues of race, ethnicity and nationalism in the "New" Europe: re-thinking sociological paradigms', in P. Brown and R. Crompton (eds) *A New Europe: Restructuring and Social Exclusion*, London: UCL Press.

—— (1994b) 'Sociological perspectives on adoption: the implications of the transracial discourse in Britain', paper presented to the World Congress of Sociology, University of Bielefeld, Germany.

Allen, S., Anthias, F. and Yuval-Davis, N. (1991) 'Diversity and commonality: theory and politics', *Revue Internationale de Sociologie* 2: 23–7.

Anthias, F. (1992) *Ethnicity, Class, Gender and Migration*, Aldershot: Avebury.

Barrett, M. (1987) 'The concept of difference', *Feminist Review* 26: 29–41.

Barth, F. (1969) *Ethnic Groups and Boundaries*, London: Allen & Unwin.

Bauman, J. (1986) *Winter in the Morning*, London: Virago.

Bauman, Z. (1978) *Hermeneutics and Social Science*, London: Hutchinson.

—— (1991) *Modernity and the Holocaust*, Cambridge: Polity.

—— (1992) *Intimations of Postmodernity*, London: Routledge.

Benton, T. (1977) *Philosophical Foundations of the Three Sociologies*, London: Routledge & Kegan Paul.

Blumer, H. (1969) *Symbolic Interactionism: Perspective and Method*, Englewood Cliffs, NJ: Prentice Hall.

Burkitt, I. (1991) *Social Selves: Theories of the Social Formation of Personality*, London: Sage.

Cohen, A. (1969) *Custom and Politics in Urban Africa*, Berkeley, CA: University of California Press.

—— (1974) *Two Dimensional Man*, Berkeley, CA: University of California Press.

—— (1981) *The Politics of Elite Culture*, Berkeley, CA: University of California Press.

De Beauvoir, S. (1974) *The Second Sex*, Harmondsworth: Penguin

Elias, N. (1982) *State Formation and Civilisation: The Civilising Process*, vol. 2, Oxford: Blackwell.

Epstein, A. L. (1978) *Ethos and Identity: Three Studies in Ethnicity*, London: Tavistock.

Fisher, B. M. and Strauss, A. L. (1978) 'Interactionism', in T. Bottomore and R. Nisbet (eds) *A History of Sociological Analysis*, London: Heinemann.

Fox, R. G. (ed.) (1990) *Nationalist Ideologies and the Production of National Culture*, Washington, DC: American Anthropological Association.

Friedan, B. (1963) *The Feminine Mystique*, London: Gollancz.

Gilroy, P. (1987) *There Ain't No Black in the Union Jack*, London: Hutchinson Education.

Goulbourne, H. (1991) *Ethnicity and Nationalism in Post-Imperial Britain*, Cambridge: Cambridge University Press.

Guy, D. J. (1992) '"White slavery", citizenship and nationality in Argentina', in A. Parker, M. Rosso, D. Sommer and P. Yaeger (eds) *Nationalisms and Sexualities*, London: Routledge.

Harding, S. (ed.) (1987) *Feminism and Methodology*, Milton Keynes: Open University Press.

Harre, R. (1979) *Social Being: A Theory for Social Psychology*, Oxford: Blackwell.

—— (1983) *Personal Being: A Theory for Individual Psychology*, Oxford: Blackwell.

Henry, F. (1983) *Victims and Neighbours: A Small Town in Nazi Germany Remembered*, Bergin and Garvey.

Hobsbawm, E. (1984) 'Mass-producing traditions: Europe 1870–1914', in E. Hobsbawm and T. Ranger (eds) *The Invention of Tradition*, Cambridge: Cambridge University Press.

Hutnik, N. (1992) *Ethnic Minority Identity: A Social Psychological Perspective*, Oxford: Clarendon.

Kay, J. (1991) *The Adoption Papers*, Newcastle: Bloodaxe.

Keating, R. (1993) 'When reporters go over the top', *Guardian* 18 January.

Kelly, G. A. (1955) *The Psychology of Personal Constructs*, New York: Norton.

Laing, R. D. (1965) *The Divided Self*, Harmondsworth: Penguin.

Lal, B. B. (1986) 'The "Chicago School" of American Sociology, symbolic interactionism, and race relations theory', in J. Rex and D. Mason (ed.) *Theories of Race and Ethnic Relations*, Cambridge: Cambridge University Press.

McCrone, D. (1992) *Understanding Scotland: The Sociology of a Stateless Nation*, London: Routledge.

Mason, D. (1986) 'Introduction: controversies and continuities in race and ethnic relations theory', in D. Mason (ed.) *Theories of Race and Ethnic Relations*, Cambridge: Cambridge University Press.

Maynard, M. (1994) '"Race", gender and the concept of difference in feminist thought', in H. Afshar and M. Maynard (eds) *The Dynamics of 'Race' and Gender*, London: Taylor & Francis.

Mead, G. H. (1934) *Mind, Self and Society: From the Standpoint of a Social Behaviourist*, Chicago: Chicago University Press.

Miles, R. (1987a) 'Recent Marxist theories of nationalism and the issue of racism', *British Journal of Sociology* 38 (1): 24–43.

—— (1987b) 'Racism and nationalism in Britain', in C. H. Husband (ed.) *'Race': The Continuity of a Concept*, London: Hutchinson.

Milner, D. (1975) *Children and Race*, Harmondsworth: Penguin.

Morokvasic, M. (1991) 'Fortress Europe and migrant women', *Feminist Review* 39: 69–84.

—— (1992) 'Chez nous, la Guerre', in M. Morokvasic (ed.) *Yougoslavie: Logiques de l'exclusion*, special issue of *Peuples Méditerranéens* 61: 3–5, 279–93.

Obbo, C. (1989) 'Sexuality and economic domination in Uganda', in F. Anthias and N. Yuval-Davis (eds) *Women-Nation-State*, London: Macmillan.

Rex, J. (1986) *Race and Ethnicity*, Milton Keynes: Open University Press.

Saifullah Khan, V. J. (1974) 'Pakistani villagers in a British city: the world of the Mirpuri villager in Bradford in his village of origin', unpublished Ph.D. thesis, University of Bradford.

—— (1976) 'Perceptions of a Population: Pakistanis in Britain', *New Community* 5: 222–9

—— (1977) 'The Pakistanis: Mirpuri villagers at home and in Bradford', in J. L. Watson (ed.) *Between Two Cultures*, Oxford: Blackwell.

—— (1979) 'Work and network: south Asian women in south London', in S. Wallman (ed.) *Ethnicity at Work*, London: Macmillan.

Schermerhorn, R. A. (1970) *Comparative Ethnic Relations*, New York: Random House.

Seidman, S. (1992) 'Postmodern social theory as narrative with a moral intent', in S. Seidman and D. G. Wagner (eds) *Postmodernism and Social Theory*, Oxford: Blackwell.

Sherif, C. W. (1987) 'Bias in psychology', in S. Harding (ed.) *Feminism and Methodology*, Milton Keynes: Open University Press.

Smith, A. D. (1986) *The Ethnic Origins of Nations*, Oxford: Blackwell.

Solomos, J. (1989) *Race and Racism in Contemporary Britain*, London: Macmillan.

Spickard, P. R. (1989) *Mixed Blood: Intermarriage and Ethnic Identity in Twentieth Century America*, Madison, WI: University of Wisconsin Press.

Spivak, G. C. (1992) 'Woman in difference: Mahasweta Devi's "Douloti the Bountiful"', in A. Parker *et al.* (eds) *Nationalisms and Sexualities*, London: Routledge.

Stahl, A. (1992) 'The offspring of interethnic marriage: relations of children with paternal and maternal grandparents', *Ethnic and Racial Studies* 15 (2): 266–83.

Stiehm, J. H. (1982) 'The protected, the protector, the defender', *Women's Studies International Forum* 5 (3/4): 367–76.

Weinreich, P. (1986) 'The operationalisation of identity theory in race and ethnic relations' in J. Rex and D. Mason (eds) *Theories of Race and Ethnic Relations*, Cambridge: Cambridge University Press.

—— (1989) 'Variations in ethnic identity: identity structure analysis', in K. Liebkind (ed.) *New Identities in Europe*, Aldershot: Gower.

Young, I. M. (1990) *Justice and the Politics of Difference*, Princeton, NJ: Princeton University Press.

4 The logics of exclusion

Nationalism, sexism and the Yugoslav war

Mirjana Morokvasic

And when the next war started,
The women said: **NO!**
And locked up their brothers, sons and husbands in their homes
(Erich Kästner)

Scarcely a human being in the course of history has fallen to a woman's
rifle
(Virginia Woolf)

Most of us in Yugoslavia's post-Second World War generation grew up
with war stories. These stories were told by women and women were their
main protagonists.[1] My early childhood was marked by these stories,
perhaps because their tellers and the people they were about were women I
loved or simply knew, or, if the stories were about those who were no longer
alive, I knew their children, relatives or friends. The way these women acted
was familiar to me: they helped and protected others, they were in a
relatively weak position but sometimes their solidarity, courage, 'sang-
froid', pragmatism or knowledge of languages protected them in the most
dangerous situations. A few of them did not survive the war or were left
invalids. I remember now the one who helplessly watched her house being
set on fire and burnt down by the withdrawing occupier troops, another one
escaping the celebratory violence of male liberators, and the teacher of mine
who survived the dreadful concentration camp of Jasenovac. I also listened
to stories about women who were executed and others who took food to
starving prisoners, looked after the children of other women who were at
the front, hid the partisans, and so on. It was as if self-evidently, naturally,
women did what they thought had to be done. These female experiences
remained in the sphere of the local and personal, there was no attempt (on
the part of those who told the stories) to generalise about women resistance
fighters as heroes of the revolution.

The vast majority of *heroes* were men, I learnt later at school, as were the *unknown soldier* and the important dignitaries of the party. According to the poems we learnt by heart and recited on important dates and commemorative occasions, women were their *mothers* or *sisters*. At that time I do not think that I was aware of the strangeness of this gendered perception of history. After all, I was born in a country in which *'brotherhood and unity'* was one of the most important slogans. It was only some years later that I noticed that *sisters* were mentioned only in reference to *brothers*, and that women I knew about, who, in my opinion, also deserved a place in the history books, were simply not there. Although in my native language 'homeland' is of feminine gender, men were the ones who spoke and acted in its name as is the case for other nations (Lutz *et al.* 1995); but ultimately they also acted against it – as I try to show in this chapter.

For years I was deeply convinced that war would never happen again in that region. The suffering had been so tremendous, the horrors perpetrated so immense, that it was unimaginable that something similar could ever happen again. 'There is no revolution, no ideal in the world, that is worth spilling blood for again', asserted an old partisan friend of mine. And yet, at the age of 18, full of hopes and ideals, she had joined the resistance. I believed her: from now on we would be immune to war, thought I.

I was wrong. Yugoslavia became a theatre of atrocities unseen in Europe since the Second World War: millions of refugees, destruction, torture, rape, robbery. Of all the east Europeans, Yugoslavs or ex-Yugoslavs are experiencing the most difficult and the most tragic 'transition to democracy'.

We were all taken by surprise and perhaps 'that is one of the reasons why we could not do much to prevent the war' (Djuric 1995). Indeed, in various analyses of the Yugoslav situation there were several warnings of a possible political impasse after Tito's death (Martinet 1971). In the late 1980s, especially, studies focused on the dangers of transition and the improbability of the Yugoslav state surviving (Glenny 1990; Krulic 1991; Pavlowitch 1988; Rupnik 1988, to mention just a few). These warnings came when the Yugoslav drama was already in preparation, but the country itself was not yet the focus of media attention and there was little international awareness of the situation. Other warnings came when it was already too late and they were not taken seriously. Take, for instance, the example of Georgy Konrad's speech in October 1991:

There are in the Eastern part of the Continent many more nations than states, and – should each nation manage to create a state of its own as a realisation of its historical dreams – a number of new states could be created. Homogeneous nation states would nevertheless not be created by such a multiplication of states, not to mention all the frontier conflicts that this would engender, because minorities would still exist. Since there would be no room for them in such states, they would be restless and there would be no peace in this region of the world if the creation of nation states in the post-communist era became a dominant political doctrine. A solution must be a multinational multicultural state which as a federation would be capable of respecting multiple and complicated allegiances of individuals.[2]

What we are witnessing at the end of the twentieth century is the return of nations and its ugliest face can be seen in former Yugoslavia. Here 'new democracies' have been constructing political systems based on exclusion and discrimination against 'Others', culminating in violence and aggression against them. 'Others' are members of ethnic groups who are identified as outsiders and those who refuse to identify themselves in national terms (traitors!), as well as those with different political opinions, those who are weaker, etc. In these male-dominated and male-represented 'new democracies' (in reality the extreme nationalist regimes) women are the largest social group to be discriminated against and excluded from decision-making processes and from representative bodies.

How has it all been possible? Media coverage of the drama has been unprecedented. Since the beginning of the conflict in the early 1990s numerous studies have tried to shed some light on what has happened and why. While a few have succeeded in making sense of the extremely complex situation, shedding light on the multifaceted dynamics which led to war (Woodward 1995, among others), many have muddied the waters, contributing to the confusion created by the simplistic interpretations promoted by the media and attributing the conflict to 'ethnic hatred', 'historical incompatibilities', 'one-sided aggression', the dream of 'Great Serbia', and so on. This chapter is a modest contribution towards answering this question. But, given the complexity of the situation, it can shed light only on some aspects. It is limited to a discussion of internal factors and is in line with a trend in the literature which explains what has happened to Yugoslavs as an outcome of the internal contradictions of the system, that is, as a follow-up of the previous system and not as a break with it.

Contrary to the widespread assumption that this is an inter-ethnic conflict, based on 'historical and traditional antagonisms', it can be shown that the war was ideologically prepared, provoked and carried out by the male power elites (some only changed their shirts). These elites are the product of a rushed and badly managed process of socialist urbanisation. They are incompetent, patriarchal rulers who have grasped hold of nationalism in order to remain in power. Only, in contrast to their communist predecessors who were acting 'in the name of History and towards a better future for everybody' (at least they were universal in their rhetoric), the present ones

are acting in the name of the interests of their nation, its salvation and purity
– which, they believe, can be achieved only by a total dissociation from the
Other, by destroying every reminder of a common past (i.e. 'impurity') and
by physical elimination in order to achieve 'ethnically pure' nation-states.

Hence the 'urbicidal' aspect of the war, destruction of the cities as places
of mixing and of centuries-old civilisation, places of openness and of
tolerance, destruction of bridges as witnesses of historical exchange and
physical bonds between groups presently at war and which the warring elites
try to present as historicaly, traditionally enemies. Hence also the treatment
of women by the nationalists, as by definition more open towards the Other
(Ivekovic 1993) and therefore more vulnerable, as guardians of purity but
also more likely to endanger the project of ethnic purity: women are to be
either excessively protected or violated – depending on whether they are
perceived as 'Ours' or 'Theirs' (Lutz *et al.* 1995; Yuval-Davis and Anthias
1989; see also Benton, Chapter 2 in this volume).

The status that nationalists assign to women of their own group
represents a formidable regression in comparison to their previous status
of formal equality in socialism. As for women of the 'other' group they are,
as in all wars, seen as victory trophies, objects of gratification for the
warrior. Many women, especially those who have themselves been victims
of violence, are instrumentalised and may adopt the nationalist cause of
their own group. A relatively small number of others resist and struggle for
a universal good, peace.

The argument of this chapter is that both in the case of the disintegration
of the country and as far as the position of women is concerned, there has
been a continuity and not a break with the socialist past. I am arguing that
both nationalism and patriarchal sexist ideology have been a constant in the
history of Yugoslavia, and that socialism, in spite of its official discourses
concerning the national question and the position of women, did not bring
about a notable and lasting change. Under the polished surface of education,
law, women's equality, the right to work, to participate politically or have
free access to abortion, there was a rigid system which maintained itself
within the communist framework. The position of women has deteriorated
even more since the so-called transition to 'new democracies'. And finally,
one can argue that the disastrous effects of the war on women are an
extension of the way in which socialism had 'solved' the national and the
women's question: they reach a paroxysm in sexual violence against women
in the name of the nation.

Nationalism and sexism are deeply interwoven, one nourishing the other
and relying on the other. One could say that Yugoslav women have always
experienced contradictions. In the socialist system it was between, on the
one hand, the official discourse of women's equality and, on the other,

women's own reality in which patriarchal values prevailed. In the present nationalist 'new democracies' there is a contradiction between the symbolic importance of 'woman' for the nation, the official discourse which puts women on a 'pedestal', and their marginalisation, exclusion from the political scene and increased violence against them.

FROM SOCIALIST TO ETHNIC 'DEMOCRACY': NATIONALISM AS A TOOL IN THE HANDS OF THE POWER ELITES

The war was not a consequence of historical hatred but was necessary in order to create conditions under which the people, transformed into members of different 'entities' or ethnic collectives, will themselves say: 'We cannot live together any longer'. The nationalist propaganda which preceded and prepared the way for war found fertile ground, prepared by the way the socialist system had treated and solved the 'nationality question'. Socialism needed the 'pre-socialist history of ethnic hatred to glorify its victorious present, in order to create and sustain the socialist history of brotherhood and unity' (Zarkov 1995: 109).

A number of analysts locate the beginnings of this process of dislocation, which accelerated in the late 1980s in the 1960s and, particularly, the 1970s when there were visible signs of rising nationalism: it had however been a significant force throughout the socialist period, both as discourse and as political practice. The political use of nationalism by the ruling power elites of the former Yugoslav republics induced a process of economic and political disintegration (Goati 1996). Scierup (1991) was among the first to analyse the general 'ethnification' of political processes in former Yugoslavia as a characteristic product of the socialist state system rather than as a perpetuation of past ethnic conflicts. The country was a victim of two contradictory trends: a trend towards economic integration, a unified Yugoslav market necessary for successful integration into the international economy, on the one hand, and a trend towards political and economic fragmentation (decentralisation in the local language), on the other. The latter centripetal forces were gradually destroying the bonds that kept Yugoslavia together, while keeping the national communist power elites intact. In this permanent competition between decomposition and re-composition, it was the former that won.

The system of self-management which was the model for internal policy served as a source of fragmentation. It did not undermine the state bureaucracy by giving more decision-making power to the workers (as in its rhetoric), but on the contrary, amplified the power of local oligarchies where political megalomania was coupled with a narrowness of economic vision (Scierup 1991). This tendency towards particularisation in the economy and the transfer of the economic functions of the federal state to the constitutive republics began after 1968 and received its legitimisation in the Constitution of 1974. From then on, the state apparatuses of the republics, with their ethno-national ties and loyalties, became the vehicle for centralising political power which was no longer at the federal level. The Communist Party had independent national organisations in each republic and in the autonomous regions. And because the national communist power elites were no longer, in their terminology, defending the class interests of the working people but the national interests of all of 'US' (i.e. everybody of the same nation), their power was more absolute in character (it was easier to identify with the 'mother Nation' than with the working class).

The national economies of the republics tended to be more and more dependent on foreign capital, know-how and technology, but were increasingly isolated from each other. 'The most dynamic process throughout the seventies and the eighties was that of closing up.' In the mid-1970s only about 3 per cent of all enterprises extended beyond the borders of a single republic and, in the mid-1980s, the figure had dropped to 2 per cent. Inter-republic trade did not exceed 25 per cent of the total while 99 per cent of investments came from within the republics (Djuric 1995: 125).

In the Constitution of 1974 the republics were declared to be responsible for their own economic developement and for the economic development of the federal state, so that the latter was stripped not only of responsibility but also of any opportunity to influence the economic development of its constitutive republics. The prerogatives of the federal state were thus paralysed. In practice this meant the establishment of nation-states at the level of republics long before there could be any question of their secession. The ruling sub-elites (at the republican level) disregarded the interests of the state as a whole. The Yugoslav Federation was left without its most important functions and gradually became a complex and ungovernable state whose efficiency diminished (Madzar 1994).

Despite its rhetoric of 'brotherhood and unity', Yugoslavia was virtually a state without Yugoslavs (Mrdjen 1996). Exclusive forms of belonging to one of the constitutive nations were either openly encouraged or at least considered as normal and natural. This can be seen in the way the Population Census categories were manipulated: all the options within the 'nationality category' were exclusive of one another, that is, one could not be at the same time Yugoslav and Serb, Yugoslav and Croat, etc., but had to choose one or the other. This means that a supranational category 'Yugoslav', representing citizenship, was put on the same level as categories of nationality and, by definition, in opposition to them. Consequently the category Yugoslav was never chosen by more than 5 per cent of the population. Another example is the transformation of a religious identification as 'muslim' into a nationality category 'Muslim' in 1971. This had a double effect: it reduced the number of Yugoslavs (those muslims previously choosing the category Yugoslav now turned to the category Muslim); it also established a close link between religious and national identity – if a muslim could not be anything else but a Muslim (not a Croat or a Serb or a Macedonian), then, as Zarkov perceptively points out, by implication a Serb could not be anything but orthodox, and a Croat could only be catholic (1995: 107). In the present post-communist, post-Yugoslav states these exclusive forms of belonging to one's nation have been developed to an extreme. For example, though unconstitutional, questions relating to religion, blood and ancestry are often decisive in the attribution of citizenship.

The importance of 'blood' and 'soil' has not changed since communism, nor have the ways in which they are constructed. In the case of so-called mixed marriages for instance,

> what has changed are the values ascribed to these mixtures. In socialism they were praised as victorious results of 'brotherhood and unity', while in nationalism they are condemned as 'treason' to the purity of specific nations. In both cases however, it is 'purity' that is normalised and constructed as natural.
>
> (Zarkov 1995: 110)

Ironically, a completely opposite manipulation of nationalism and national identity has in Yugoslav history served the same purpose: after the Second World War the communists, because they were the only force which could erase national antagonisms and, with their 'brotherhood and unity' ideology, unite the population of Yugoslavia across national lines, gained power. Gradually, however, they started building on these very antagonisms in order to remain in power. Although there were earlier outbursts of nationalist rhetoric, the first real break with 'brotherhood and unity' came from Milosevic and the manner in which he exploited the situation of the Serbian minority in Kosovo (this is also discussed by Charles and Hintjens, Chapter 1 in this volume).[3]

In the late 1980s the novelty was that everywhere the nationalist power elites sought the support of the masses: their strategy succeeded in transforming their own antagonisms into inter-ethnic hostilities which ultimately led to war. One has to remember that the military conflict was preceded by a media war (Pejic 1993): for several years the population had been exposed to the systematic broadcasting of news and reports which were a direct invitation to hate and to kill the Other. This media propaganda was needed to destroy the important legacy of forty-five years of peaceful coexistence. There was one television station in each republic of former

Yugoslavia. Each was founded by the Communist Party which wanted to establish complete control over the media. Consequently the media, especially television, began to broadcast programmes on 'our' interests, they then stopped representing 'other's' interests; and ultimately they established a closed news market and of course a closed society (Pejic 1993).

The war was, however, still not an inevitable outcome of this process. Rather – if we consider the internal factors alone – it was ultimately the result of a series of unilateral and hostile initiatives on the part of political elites. Goati (1996) enumerates a number of these decisions which were taken in Serbia, Croatia and Slovenia in a period of less than two years.[4] The conflict among the republican elites polarised, first on the issue of the political system (decentralised-pluralistic versus centralised-monistic) and second, on the issue of the future of the Yugoslav state (federation versus confederation). With the help of the media, the advocates of these opposing tendencies systematically emphasised the threat posed by the Other and the external enemy served as an instrument for internal homogenisation. Hostile feelings developed into hostile actions. Thus the fracture of republican elites had been transformed into an inter-ethnic conflict with the focus on issues of 'identity' and of 'national survival'.

These elites in conflict agreed on one important matter: they were against having the first free elections on the level of the federation. Thus the population was not given a chance to demonstrate its opinion about a further state project in truly democratic free elections on the federal level, before it got completely intoxicated by the merciless nationalistic propaganda; no formation of a transnational Yugoslav party was allowed and in the first free elections, which took place in 1990 in each republic separately, the nationalist parties had a sweeping victory. The terrain was also favourable to nationalists because of the disastrous economic situation, existential insecurity and the drastic fall in the level of living of the population.

Later, as the war started, the only way the population could show its disagreement with the politics of violent disintegration of the country was through massive demonstrations for peace, in particular in Bosnia-Herzegovina, and through massive desertions from the federal and other armies. Hundreds of thousands, mostly young and highly educated people, 'voted with their feet': they left the country before large-scale conflict took over (Morokvasic 1996). None of the new states has so far declared an amnesty for these young people which would guarantee them a safe return.

During this at first gradual and then rapid ethnification of society, of the emergence of policies of exclusion of the Other and closure, there has been a simultaneous process of silencing women and their disappearance from the public scene, as the next section will show.

WOMEN AS LOSERS: FROM INSTITUTIONALISED EQUALITY TO 'MOTHERS OF THE NATION'

The brothers' project for sisters' emancipation

There is something paradoxical about the status of women in post-communist societies, including the post-Yugoslav 'new democracies': while they promise improvement for the population in general, the status of women deteriorates as far as employment rights and the possibilities of employment are concerned. The argument of this section is that the position of women in socialist Yugoslavia was not as good as it seemed and that it has deteriorated even further in the new ethnic democracies.

The socialist system did indeed proclaim equality between men and women, it opened up possibilities for political participation, gave women the right to employment, to abortion and so on, but at the same time it left gender relations practically intact, maintaining and reproducing the patriarchal system. The foundation of the socialist egalitarian project was women's massive participation in the war of national liberation from 1941 to 1945; 100,000 were active as partisans and almost as many were either killed or wounded. The Antifascist Front of Women (AFZ) brought together some 2 million women. They acted primarily as a support for male-dominated resistance groups (Sklevicky 1984); the AFZ was created by the Communist Party, the party co-ordinated and steered all its activities until it decided to abolish it as early as 1950. (It was the first of the 1941–5 institutions to be abolished.) Nevertheless the massive participation of women in the war and in the AFZ left an important legacy: it became a source of spontaneous emancipation of women from the traditional patriarchal system of subordination in the family. Women experienced their country's liberation as their own (Milic 1993). The socialist rhetoric in which the 'emancipation of women' had an important place, at least suggested possibilities – though these possibilities were beyond the reach of the majority of women. The result was formal, institutionalised gender equality: civil, political and social rights were experienced by women not as something granted to them but as achieved and deserved. However in spite of the changes that had occurred in life outside the family (i.e. for 'women at work') there were hardly any changes within the family itself. Women remained subordinated and discriminated against and in practice were stuck with the well-known double burden (Morokvasic 1984). Their reaction was a gradual withdrawal from public life and a return to the family and home. This, along with the disappearence of women from the political sphere of influence, provided fertile ground for nationalist ideologies to develop: women became symbols of nationalist politics and at the same time ever more numerous victims of war and everyday violence (Djuric 1995: 122).

The socialist project for women's emancipation, one has to recall, was implemented in an extremely heterogeneous country where the status of women mirrored the stage of development and also varied enormously depending on whether women came from urban or rural backgrounds. Socialism not only concentrated on women who were active in the labour force (i.e. a minority) but also did not question or require the transformation of gender relations. So women, in spite of having *de jure* equality, could not achieve *de facto* equality because of traditional gender relations both in the family and in society at large. Roughly two-thirds of the female population of Yugoslavia lived in circumstances which were removed from the socialist ideal of 'woman at work': they were not active in the labour force,[5] but were 'dependants'; and the more underdeveloped the region the higher the rate of female dependency: over 90 per cent in Kosovo, 69 per cent in Bosnia-Herzegovina, and between 58 and 50 per cent in the more developed regions of the country (Djuric 1995: 128).

Formal equality was proclaimed in education as well. There was indeed an advance in the educational achievement of women during the socialist period: the illiteracy rate went down and the level of education improved. Despite this, however, men and women were affected differentially so, as far as the literacy rate is concerned, the gap between them increased. Likewise, improvements in educational level did not eradicate discrimination against women in employment and their concentration in the typically female sectors, neither did it help them get better-paid and more interesting jobs (Kavcic 1990). Besides, although women represented only one-third of the work-force, they were more than half of the unemployed. Moreover, it was the less-educated and less-skilled women who tended to find jobs more easily and it was gender rather than ethnicity that was the major determinant of woman's position in the labour market throughout the republics of former Yugoslavia (Blagojevic 1991). To sum up: not only was the socialist project of women's emancipation likely to affect only a minority of women (those who were not 'dependants' and who were in the more developed parts of the country), but even the otherwise notable improvements in the sphere of schooling and education neither eradicated discrimination nor facilitated women's access to the labour market.

Exclusion from the political scene in the 'new democracies'

In the 'new democracies women find themselves more and more excluded, even from those spheres which they previously occupied in the socialist state' (Djuric 1995: 132). On the one hand, the worsening has occurred because of the overall economic disaster and, on the other, assumptions about the proper role of women (never seriously questioned under socialism) have contributed to this exclusion, finding legitimisation in nationalist ideology. The political representation of women in the Federal Parliament before disintegration was 55 per cent compared with 2 per cent in the assemblies of the republics. Their representation in the new post-Yugoslav states is about the same.[6]

One can therefore say that the election results were distorted in the first multiparty elections which were experienced by women as chaotic. The programmes presented did not include those issues that would attract them. Most party leaders presented an extremely aggressive, masculine image. It is typically an aggressive and violent masculinity that was launched as the universal masculinity. Those men who opposed war and violence 'were not men'. This significantly reduced women's participation and contributed to their orientation towards the parties they knew; this benefited those who already had power and needed only elections to legitimise it.

Women in nationalist discourse

Women often embody the nation, they are bearers of its honour and love. In nationalist discourse woman is either the mother of the nation or the sex object. She is either a protector and regenerator of the collective or a possession of that collective. These symbolic images have been used by the media, in particular in the preparatory stages of the war, thus getting the nation ready to face the enemy. As a matter of fact the 'enemy' had to be constructed: having been a part of 'US', as our neighbour, cousin, friend, it had to be turned into 'THEM'. One of the most famous media images was that of a young woman with a gun over her shoulder, marching through the fields with one child in her arms and two others by her side. Another one was the image of a nun also with a gun in her hands, which accompanied the story of nuns attacked and raped in the Serb monasteries in Kosovo. These images conveyed a clear message: these women were ready to defend their 'own identity' by means of violence. Only, their 'own identity' was not the individual self, but a superior collective: family, nation, church (even Christianity against Islam). This even implies sacrificing the individual self for the higher cause of the collective. Raped women were also directly exploited as a symbolic image of the threat that mixing represents for a nation (Meznaric 1994). As we shall see in the next section, in nationalist discourse rapes are condemned only in so far as they are committed by men of the other group. Thus images of women under threat or violated serve to homogenise the nation and to define its boundaries in relation to others. This reaches a paroxysm in war.

Even when women are not directly present in the images of a nation, nationalist discourse is implicitely addressed to them. In the nationalist construction of the image of the Serbian nation for instance, the Others are 'Albanians who have too many children'. Whether explicitly or implicitly, this concerns non-Albanian (Serbian or Macedonian) women too: they are those 'who do not have enough children' – so the Serbian (or Macedonian) nation is 'threatened with extinction'. All the post-Yugoslav post-communist nationalists expected women to accomplish their 'duty' towards the nation and bear more children. Their constitutions protect women as 'mothers' and address them as guardians of ethnic purity – allegedly the basis for the existence and maintenance of the group. That is why their sexuality has to be controlled. Well-known demographers started calculating the number of years it would take for the Serbian nation to disappear if the birth rates did not increase, poets were producing verses in praise of the fertility of women of their nation, legislators came up with draft bills which threatened the reproductive rights acquired by women (namely the right to abortion). These draft bills were discriminatory and exclusionary: for example taxing childless couples and depriving those with three and more children of social assistance. In Croatia the streetcars carried posters: 'each unborn baby is an unborn Croat', whereas after a political meeting brother Croats were urged to 'go home and make a new Croat' (see also Bryson, Chapter 7 in this volume).[7] This was all echoed and amplified by the media. It is only thanks to the vigorous reaction of independent feminists that the adoption of these retrograde bills was prevented (Djuric 1995; Milic 1993). Nevertheless, in spite of the absence of anti-abortion laws, it is much more difficult for women to obtain abortions in new democratic Croatia than it was in the previous socialist Croatia.[8]

WOMEN IN WAR, WOMEN AGAINST WAR

A war always becomes a war against women and the Yugoslav war is 'an extreme male war', as Helke Sander (1992) said. Women can fully claim that this is not their war – they were already virtually absent from the political scene when the nationalists took over and have since been even more marginalised by them. 'The nation has taken over without having asked us women', says the Belgrade feminist Zarana Papic (1993).

With the militarisation of the conflict, women clearly emerged in their vast majority as victims, either indirectly as victims of everyday violence, economic disaster and political chaos in the states at war, or as direct victims of the warring parties, killed, raped, forced into prostitution, as refugees and displaced persons. A minority of women is active either in supporting the war – fighters and nationalist supporters, or in opposing it – peace activists and 'mothers against the war'.

Everyday violence and humiliation

In war the majority of the population is transformed into victims and most of them are women.[9] Violence against women has increased everywhere. They also face male violence where the bombs and grenades seem remote. The 'SOS line for women and children victims of violence' from Belgrade registered more calls from battered women than ever before; the use of guns and other weapons among the civilian population in general and in cases of violence against women has dramatically increased.[10]

But most women have to cope with ordinary life, trying to turn it into the 'normal' given the circumstances. Wheareas in a queue in Sarajevo one risks one's life, elsewhere there is daily humiliation coupled with the risk of facing uncontrolled violence. Here is a quote from a letter from Sarajevo in 1993:

> You would not recognise the city, half destroyed with grenades, trees in parks cut down for heating, we are living, or rather, surviving, hungry. We live on humanitarian aid which we get every 21 days: a little oil which we use for light instead of electricity which we have not had since October, we do not have water, we have to walk two to three kilometres to get it. We do not know if we will come back wounded or will be shot dead on the way. We also get a little flour, a little sugar, sometimes milk powder and once in a while a tin of corned beef. Someone with Deutschmarks can even buy something: a kilo of beans costs 25 DM a kilo, one kg onions is 15 DM, one candle is 2 DM. I have not seen vegetables and fruit for months. My pension in BH bonds is enough to get a kilo of bread or a roll of toilet paper.... If one does not get privately a parcel from Croatia or Serbia, one can die. But all this is not so horrible when a life is at stake: please do something for my son. If he at least could leave this hell.

The woman who wrote this letter is now a displaced person somewhere in Europe, so is her son.

About the same time my 81-year-old mother wrote from Belgrade, the capital of the country which, according to its official propaganda, had nothing to do with the war, but which in fact had most responsibility for it.

> If one does not get up at four o'clock in the morning and queue for bread, one does not get any. It is the same with milk, I have not had fresh milk for the past six months. The same with meat, I do not remember when I

had it last . . . one day I saw a piece of meat at the butchers and I thought I could buy a bit for your aunt and me. The piece was already sold. My pension is enough to buy several kilos of potatoes at the market or several packages of soup. Should something happen to me, I would not even be taken to the hospital, they do not have medicine, not even for the younger ones.

Like millions of other citizens of former Yugoslavia she has been robbed by the state banks of her hard currency savings.[11] That is the unbearable thought for many who can still hardly grasp what has happened to them, let alone those who have been displaced by force, lost their children or friends in war: 'It is with our money that they are financing their war!'[12]

Refugees and displaced persons

This war has displaced several million people; many have lost members of their families or have been forcefully separated from them for many years or for ever (Morokvasic 1992). Most of those who left the country did so before 1993, before the governments of the states of destination introduced measures – in particular visa requirements – to stop further arrivals. They are in general a young, urban population, with a high educational and professional profile. Women represent less than half of the refugees currently dispersed abroad, mostly in different countries in Europe (the majority in Germany), but also in North America, Australia and New Zealand.[13] Some of these people will remain, particularly in those countries which offer them more than a 'temporary protection' status. The majority will have to return to their countries of origin where the recent, theoretically peaceful conditions should allow it. Repatriations from Germany, where temporary protection status was abolished in 1996, are already under way and most 'voluntary returns' are scheduled for 1997.

Among the internally displaced persons women and children represent over 80 per cent. They have usually lost everything and are separated from close members of their family. Even if they have not been victims of physical violence they have experienced situations of fear, witnessed executions and carry the psychological scars. There is little prospect of return to their home regions: the September 1996 elections in Bosnia-Herzegovina were a testing ground and have shown that only a small number of voters dared return to vote in their former place of residence (14,000 out of over 100,000 expected).

The displacement of the population is not only a consequence of the conflict and tensions, but also a strategy of the warring parties and their ultimate aim in this war over territories and boundaries. From the very beginning individual suffering of all kinds has been used and manipulated for the purpose of constructing new national histories. Journalists in the service of the new power elites, politicians, film makers, novel writers, and also some social scientists, used refugee narratives/testimonies to form the image of their own nation as victim or used them in the service of a nation they considered to be the victim (or against the aggressor). In such productions the individual disappears and is replaced by the collective. There are a few texts which reflect critically on this strategy (Bausinger 1996; Greverus 1996; Korac 1996; McNeill and Coulson 1994; Nikolic-Ristanovic *et al.* 1995, to mention only those relating to the Yugoslav drama).

Women victims of sexual violence

Rapes have always been part of the male war strategy. It would have been a miracle had the present conflict in the Balkans gone without this ghastly practice. It is a generalised war crime which has so far remained unpunished. In spite of the complete dossier and testimonies prepared after the Second World War for the Nuremberg Tribunal, war criminals were not condemned for rape (Sander 1992; *Freitag* 23 November 1993). Korean women have spoken up about the rapes committed by Japanese soldiers only half a century later.[14]

Dominating, humiliating, conquering and destroying the Other is being done via women. The hatred and the violence are crystallised in rape, it becomes the instrument of war, the weapon of the conqueror over the conquered. Women are the gift of the warrior and his trophy, the proof of his victory over enemy males (i.e. the enemy group represented by males). That is why rapes in war usually have the following features: women are raped in public, or in front of their husbands, brothers, fathers; soldiers rape collectively, they have to have witnesses; it is also an initiation rite for those who are considered weak (i.e. not 'male' enough in war terminology) and finally, women are often killed at the end. 'I was the twentieth, all I remember was that she was dirty, full of sperm and that I killed her'.[15]

It took almost a year of war before the stories about raped women filtered into the media. Independent Zagreb feminists were the first to launch an appeal in spring 1992, but they were not taken seriously because they did not have a 'clear national approach'. It was only when the nationalists of the warring parties grasped the propaganda value of women's suffering that rape stories spread all over the media, both local and international. 'Raped Bosnian women, possibly pregnant and speaking English, were in great demand', a Zagreb feminist noted.[16] For a certain time Croat nationalists exhibited Muslim women as the prime victims of Serbian aggression, but stopped doing so when the hostilities between Croats and Muslims in Bosnia intensified because it became politically counter-productive. The stories of raped women kept in custody until they could no longer abort spread simultaneously in Croatia and in Serbia and were quasi-identical: the 'Others' raped 'Our' women, they want to spoil 'Our Nation'.

Almost all international observers pointed to the rape of women as a means of intimidation of the whole group, that is, it was implicitly or explicitly politically motivated (Amnesty International 1993; Helsinki Watch 1993; Jones 1994). Their information not only points to the systematic use of rape by Serbian forces, but also stresses that rape is used by all sides. In the international media, however, journalists, obviously overwhelmed by the complexity of the conflict, grasped the once-in-a-lifetime chance of an ideal news story and tried to simplify it as a conflict of the baddies against the goodies.[17] Their instrumentalisation of rapes, and the division of rape victims according to their nationality into goodies and baddies, clearly had other purposes and outcomes than denouncing rape as a crime against women and as a gendered political strategy in war: on the one hand, it demonised the Other, the barbarian rapist, the 'perfect aggressor' (the Others, the rapists, are always Serbs and the victims invariably Muslim and to a lesser extent Croat women), on the other, it aimed to destroy the transnational solidarity of women, who are less inclined than men to identify with the Nation only and its conquests.[18]

Thus in the media accounts, the rapes of Muslim women in Bosnia are 'unprecedented' because of the political purpose behind this practice, 'a systematic attempt to cleanse territories in order to establish Greater Serbia'.[19] Journalists or *ad hoc* women activists constructed their victims to fit this general political strategy of the Serbs (since the Serbs are only aggressors, the Serb victims are hardly ever mentioned).[20] They let the victims in their narratives set the priorities and point to the real issues:

> They [the raped women] did not want in any way to let rape overshadow the *real problem* which is the extermination and execution of thousands and thousands of men and women.
>
> (added emphasis)[21]

When quoted and requoted in respectable journals, by allegedly respectable social scientists, or when published in book form (Jones 1994; Nahum-Grappe 1996; Stiglmayer 1993, etc.) this information, collected in a questionable way and launched by the media, gains respectability and a legitimacy for the construction of 'historical truth'.

It is as if the rape of women as the usual war practice of men was not worthy of attention unless it was presented as a crime against a nation. Rape could be condemned only from a nationalist perspective. This is most clearly formulated by the US feminist and law professor Catherine Mackinnon

(1994) for whom rape is an attack on human rights only when it is associated with genocide. She, among others, gave a certain legitimacy to the figure of 50,000 to 60,000 raped women, which, although an underestimation (Nahoum-Grappe 1996), was widely circulated and is used even today; this is despite these figures having little basis in independent fact-finding (Neier 1993). Since it was apparently the first time in history that world-wide attention was focused on sexual violence against women in war while it was happening (and not decades after), the present case was important as a '*cas de jurisprudence*'.[22]

In this kind of argument women as individuals cease to exist. The value of their suffering is measured by the value of the suffering of their nation - they are good victims only as long as their nation can be demonstrated to be a good victim. The fact that women unwillingly speak of their atrocious experiences, preferring to stay silent about them or at least, if they speak, to preserve anonymity (Nikolic-Ristanovic *et al.* 1995) should at least make social scientists curious about those women who do talk and about the nature of their testimonies in front of the TV cameras. There is no evidence of such an awareness on the part of any of the great promoters of the uniqueness of the rapes in the Balkan war (Nahoum-Grappe 1996; Mackinnon 1994; Stiglmayer 1993). Ironically, rape becomes a political concern only when it ceases to be a crime against women and becomes exclusively a crime against the group to which a woman is assumed to belong (Zarkov 1995: 114). It is useful to refer to Ina-Maria Greverus's perceptive analysis of the use of testimonies and of professionalising the victims:

> Their [refugees'] stories, especially if they are stories of suffering, are being made into history. Native writers and ethnologists, national politicians and international critics and NGOs of every creed and kind are constructing the 'objective' written history of events out of the individual fates of 'lost lives'. . . . Out of their lost lives they are being raised into the witness stand, to testify for – or against – national history. But as witness, a person is only visible and audible in the witness stand, his individual testimony is being collected into a general one, his identity, his being is dissolved into collective identities. After the testimony he is invisible again or becomes captive of his own statement, turns into a monument of ideological fixations of the political and intellectual elites with ideological claim to leadership.
>
> (Greverus 1996: 281)

Because gender relations cross-cut other social and political relations and gender identities are constitutive elements of other identities, a war rape cannot be considered simply as a crime of men against women, but also not only as a crime against the state, nation, community. As a specific form of sexual violence against women it is also a specific gendered political strategy (Zarkov 1995: 115). Turning rape exclusively into a crime against an ethnic community obscures the fact that women are raped because they are both the 'female Other' and the 'ethnic Other'. In a war situation, however, they are primarily assaulted as women, their ethnic otherness can be constructed or deconstructed. This means that women of the enemy are the prime targets, but if the women of the enemy are not available, any other will do. So one soldier said that he would get DM 100 for each bus-load of women he could bring to his fellow soldiers. 'When women they wanted were not available, I brought others.' Whether or how his order-givers later checked women's nationality he did not know - for him it was important to get a load of women in order to get his money. This belongs too to the spectrum of the political use of rape in war (the aim being intimidation of the civil population) but tends to be forgotten by those who are scandalised by war rapes only when they are linked to genocide or when they are committed by an absolute aggressor on a perfect victim.

This issue of rape was focused on by the media for a relatively short period of time in 1992–3. It stopped being an issue while the war was still raging and women were no less and probably more raped. The question is whether rape will suffer the same fate before the International Tribunal in The Hague as it did in the Nuremberg Trials. It seems impossible to prosecute the perpetrators: the International War Tribunal in The Hague needs proof of an explicit order on the part of a military commander that his forces should rape. Otherwise, rape is considered an arbitrary act and the sole respons-ibility of a single soldier. It is in those terms that some asylum claimants from Bosnia were rejected in 1993: 'Rape and fear of war are not sufficient reasons for asylum, rape being a normal criminal act and not a politically motivated one.'[23] A man rapes a woman – and that is no longer in the jurisdiction of the International Tribunal. In practice these raped women may be considered as victims either of 'a banal criminal act' or of 'a normal war act'. When the war really ends, will women again be expected to hide their tragedy, 'their shame', while as usual monuments will be erected to male heroes and unknown soldiers?

Women adopting the nationalist cause and women fighters

Few women are actually involved in the creation of nationalist policies or practicies, but when they are, they do so mostly but not exclusively, in a way which is congruent with their place within a system of patriarchal domination, as mothers of heroes or protectors of their offspring (Djuric 1995). Some women's organisations were not only 'in line' with the nationalist political correctness of the moment but also actively engaged in nationalist policies and propaganda.[24]

Women fighters embracing the cause of the nation are even smaller in number. With war propaganda being typically based on an aggressive, violent masculinity, women are not usually promoted as a media image – unless the message can show the superiority of the nation over other identifications and allegiances (including family). When it is for the sake of the nation, local nationalist discourse can even build on the remnants of egalitarian ideology: 'a woman is the equal of man, she can fight equally, she can love her nation equally', etc.[25] The superiority of the nation and the impossibility of living together was also a constant image in the international media. That kind of message was, for instance, promoted in the German weekly *Der Spiegel* in summer 1991,[26] at the time when, at least in their official statements, the European states and the USA still supported the integrity of the Yugoslav state.[27]

A photograph showed a young woman holding a machine gun and wearing a uniform of the Croatian militia. She was from a town in the mixed Serbo-Croat area where the hostilities started sporadically in 1991 before degenerating into an open conflict. The woman declared to the reporter that 'she would not hesitate killing her ex-husband if it were necessary'. He is, namely, fighting on the 'other' side. The couple (in that area there was a very high rate of inter-ethnic marriage) 'had a child and used to live happily'. But nevertheless the woman is reported to have said, 'he left me because he could no longer be married to a Croat. If one day we run into each other, I will kill him, otherwise, I know he will kill me'.

It is irrelevant whether the story is true or not: what is important is that this kind of testimony is perceived as true, the woman has a name, she is pretty, blonde and carries an important message: 'We cannot live together any more, we are prepared to kill each other for a higher cause, the Nation'. The pattern is the same as in the other images of women with guns mentioned above which were used in Yugoslavia during the preparatory stages of the war: the individual is prepared to renounce her or his personal autonomy and happiness for the sake of a higher cause and is ready to use violent means to achieve it. Stories like this one, whether true or not, contributed to building distrust and constructing hatred in the population which was then more ready to accept war and violent 'solutions' to existing tensions which originally did not necessarily have an ethnic component. When a neighbour, friend and even wife or husband is ready to kill, what can one expect from a more distant 'Other'? And once the athmosphere of fear and distrust is established, a neighbour or friend can even show readiness to help and make peace, but can no longer be trusted. Hardly any newspaper, local or international, was prepared to bring stories of love, tolerance and solidarity if they were taking place across those borders that the nationalist leaders and their followers were determined to draw for ever, even by means of terrible bloodshed.[28]

Nevertheless, it is a fact that in this war as in other wars women show incomparably less violent behaviour than men and manifest a desire to help and understand the other side (Ivekovic 1993: 192). Women whom I talked to seldom expressed hatred or hostility towards the Other, whether they participated actively in military actions or were among the numerous victims of the war (or both at the same time). Most did not go to fight of their free will, nor did they 'fight for life', but for sheer economic survival.

'When the war started, we had just come back from Slovenia, built a house, nicely settled down and thought we had saved enough for a decent living. We thought that we would not have to go and work somewhere else again. This is all gone now,' says L., a woman in her thirties, from the Tuzla region. She looks back to the outcomes of the recent war and peace for herself and her family: 'We were all in the war, my husband, my two teenage daughters and myself.' Why? Which army? She says she does not really know what the war was about, why she took part in it except that 'We all had to survive' and the army she joined provided for that – while the war lasted. 'We went there where the conditions were the best', she says, 'Now we have to look for work outside of Bosnia again as guestworkers, as before; our daughters who were children when the war started, married in the war. One is already a widow, alone with their child. . . . Her husband was killed only a few months after their marriage.'

Peace activists

The first genuine opposition to the war came from the mothers of soldiers drafted into the Yugoslav Federal Army, who happened to be stationed in Slovenia and were sent at the end of June 1991 to 'protect the borders' of the state. The parents' (mainly mothers') protests against the war took place all over Yugoslavia and soon gave birth to peace movements. Helke Sander (1992) noted that there was a real potential for opposition to the war. Yet in the first spontaneous actions mothers appeared more as protectors of their sons than opponents of war. The movement was immediately manipulated by the nationalists in power for their own purposes. Broad media coverage was given to those mothers who were against their son's participation in the Federal Army, but who encouraged his 'patriotic duty' towards his nation and 'his own people'. On Croatian television one could listen to mothers who were prepared to 'sacrifice their sons for the Nation'. This was also the theme of a number of songs which were supposed to raise the morale of the troops. In Belgrade mothers with patriotic messages to convey found it easy to enter parliament where the TV cameras were ready and waiting.

Public demonstrations of mothers against the war were also used to create distrust and hostilities between national groups. For instance, in the town of Temerin in Vojvodina, where Hungarians and Serbs have been living together for the past few centuries, several dozen women of all nationalities, mothers of Federal Army soldiers sent to fight on Croatian territory, gathered in the autumn of 1991 to express their solidarity with other mothers protesting in front of the army headquarters in Belgrade. This display of transnational solidarity among mothers was soon destroyed by the arrival of Milosevic's ruling party delegates and some Serb refugees from Croatia, shouting slogans which were hostile to Hungarians, 'Hungarians should go to Hungary, Serb mothers have suffered enough from them in the Second World War'. The refugees were presented as 'the victims of Croats, who are friends of Hungarians'. Accused of treason and under threat, the Serb mothers then withdrew and only the Hungarian mothers continued their protest the next day.[29]

CONCLUSION

This chapter has attempted to approach the violent disintegration of Yugoslavia from the women's perspective. As an observer of the catastrophe embracing the country which used to be mine and therefore as an indirect participant, I would like to finish this account with a drop of optimism.

As I have already said, we were all taken by surprise. And yet now, after the state has collapsed in a violent outburst, in this relative 'post-war' period, we continue to search for good reasons for the collapse and discover/analyse all the evil that has germinated over the years in the country that today does not exist any more except with the prefix 'former'. That is also what I have done in this chapter. However, by doing so one tends to minimise or even forget the forces that tried to produce something else but lost because they were weaker. And yet in this long and painful process of learning about democracy these forces are likely to play an important role. The initiators of protests against the war and activists in various peace groups are in the majority women. These peace groups are among those rare political groups which, in the context in which 'pure ethnic entities' have been created on the territory of former Yugoslavia and isolated from one another, still keep in touch and try to communicate. Feminist and autonomous women's groups who are actively opposed to nationalism, sexism and war are numerous,[30] but their activity has so far been located in big urban centres and their political influence is limited (Djuric 1995).

As organisers and co-ordinators of peace groups and anti-war campaigns, women are likely to derive awareness and strength from their resistance to war. Therein lies a hope. Although some have fallen into the nationalist trap, many feminist groups all over former Yugoslavia have kept their networks in spite of the communication blockade. Because they have the moral integrity to declare that 'this is not their war', they are the ones who can best express the feelings of the silent majority of the population. Beyond women's issues they can raise the common issues and propose global choices to counter the global (but always male) choice of destruction. And as Dubravka Zarkov said, 'as long as solidarity exists between women's or other groups across the borders, transnationally, it will be a reminder of other possibilities, even if these are obscured, erased or reinterpreted in nationalist discourses' (Zarkov 1995: 116).

NOTES

1   In my case it was my grandmother, my mother, my aunts and their friends.
2   From a speech Gyorgy Konrad (a famous Hungarian writer and human rights defender, president of PEN International) gave in October 1991 in Frankfurt/ Main, when receiving the peace prize, in the presence of the German President von Weißzäcker. He received one of the highest peace prizes and applause. But Germany acted precisely in the way Konrad warned against: only two months later it decided to recognise Croatia, independently of its other European partners (i.e. it was not prepared to await the results of the Badinter Commission on Yugoslavia).
3   Namely, through the scenes around the threatened Serbian minority in Kosovo: raped Serbian women, the forced migration of Serbs, intimidation and discrimination against the Serbian minority by the Albanian majority in power. The 600-year anniversary of the Kosovo battle in June 1989, a commemoration of one of the foundation myths of the Serbian nation, was a blow in the face of the local Albanian minority (but the majority in Kosovo).
4   Yugoslavia used to be a federal state consisting of six republics: Croatia, Bosnia-Herzegovina, Macedonia, Montenegro, Serbia and Slovenia. Serbia had two autonomous provinces: Vojvodina and Kosovo. The initiatives include: amendments to the constitution of Slovenia in 1989 (a possiblility not foreseen in the federal constitution of 1974); the economic blockade of Slovenian products by Serbia in 1989; the removal of the autonomy of the regions of Vojvodina and Kosovo in 1989 by the Serbian government; the declaration of sovereignty by the state of Slovenia in 1990; the declaration that Kosovo was a republic by the Albanian delegates to the Kosovo assembly; the proclamation of the Croatian state as the state of the Coratian people in 1990.
5   The fact that they were not paid for their work (i.e. that they were not officially active) does not imply that they 'did not work'.
6   This was for instance the case in Croatia where seven women and 134 men were elected in 1993 (*Freitag* 17 1993); six of the women belonged to the party in

power. In Federal Yugoslavia in the 1992 elections women won less than 3 per cent of the seats (Djuric 1995).

7 From an interview with Sonja Liht, *Pacifik* 1991.

8 Drakulic (1993) mentions that in November 1991 doctors in the largest Zagreb hospital were prevented from practising abortions.

9 While admitting that there is gender-specific victimisation in war, some authors warn that it should not be reduced to the dichotomy female victims and male aggressors (Jones 1994): men are victims too, more often singled out for killing, torture and elimination. Although this occurs to women as well, Jones argues it is not on a gender-specific basis. Quoting Amnesty International (1993) the author argues that the atrocities due to sex assault constitute the central and perhaps the sole case where women have been subjected to specific forms of human rights abuse which they face primarily because of their sex. Some field data tend to confirm that women themselves, in their self-perception as victims of violence in war, tend to restrict violence to sexual violence (Nikolic-Ristanovic *et al.* 1995).

10 *Antiratni Bilten SOS-a*, Belgrade: SOS telefon za zen idecu zrtve nasilja 4, 8 March 1993.

11 For more information about the strategies the Milosevic government employed to strip the population of their hard currency savings, including superinflation, see the fascinating analysis by Mladjan Dinkic; *Ekonomija destrukcije*, Belgrade: VIN (this now exists in English, *Economy of Destruction*).

12 Ibid.

13 Men are more likely to have the support of their families to flee abroad and are considered more under threat, especially if they are avoiding being drafted. Women are less likely to be granted asylum because, so far, no gender-specific grounds for granting political asylum have been officially recognised. Women fleeing persecution are generally put into the category of economic and poverty refugees.

14 *Tageszeitung* 9 December 1992.

15 *Borba* 1–2 August 1992.

16 The same demand has been made in other similar situations. Eye-witnessing the convulsions in the Congo in 1961, which was seen in Europe from the angle of the rapes of Belgian nuns, the journalist Edward Behr (1978) entitled his book *Y a-t-il ici quelqu'un qui a été violé et qui parle anglais?* (*Anyone here been raped and speak English?*) New York: Viking. Fact finding about rapes and the raped women themselves are ultimately unimportant: it is the message that can easily be spread around the world (in English) and that can capture attention which is important.

17 At the end of 1992 and beginning of 1993, from the *Vancouver Sun* to the *New York Times*, from *Tageszeitung, Bild, Frankfurter Allgemeine,* to *Le Monde, Libération* etc., the rape story was on the front pages until the first scandals occurred concerning the accuracy of information about the number of rapes, 'estimated' as between 50,000 and 60,000, and the first critical voices were heard after the controversial Zagreb Women's conference on mass rapes in Bosnia-Herzegovina on 7 February 1993. On that occasion one of the prominent participants in that well publicised meeting, the president of the Bundestag, Rita Sismuth, visited the 'Home for raped women' and instead of the expected women found only drunken Croatian soldiers (Erich Rathfelder in *Tageszeitung* 8 February 1993).

18 See interview with Neva Tölle from the Autonomous Women's house in Zagreb (*Freitag* 23 April 1993).
19 S. Drakulic, 'Women hide behind a wall of silence', *Nation* 1 March 1993, quoted by A. Jones (1994).
20 In the German press, which I followed most carefully at that time, I found only a couple of articles which stressed that rapes are committed on all sides in war implying that Serbian women were also among the victims (Helga Hirsch in *Die Zeit* 11 December 1992; Gaby Mizchkowski, *TAZ* 7 December 1992).
21 From an interview with woman activist Marsha Jacobs, quoted by A. Jones (1994: 119).
22 See interview with C. Mackinnon in *Tageszeitung* 5 February 1993. Mass rapes are seen by her as an instrument in the policy of 'genocide by Serbs'. Therefore this is the opportunity to 'legally recognise the nature of the crime', (i.e. to establish the rape of women in war as part of a crime against humanity. This can be done only by proving the link between genocide and rapes in war. So far this has not been done: mass rapes were not explicitly stated to be part of Nazi war crimes for instance. According to the interpretation of other jurists, however, the issue is not to create new legal instruments but to implement those that already exist (H. Fischer in *Die Zeit* 11 December 1992).
23 *Tageszeitung* 25 January 1993.
24 *Bedem ljubavi* in Zagreb or the *Women's Movement for Yugoslavia* are examples.
25 A good example is the Yugoslav comic Kninja, where the main protagonist is a woman named Milica who is presented as an equal fighter.
26 *Der Spiegel* 19 July 1991.
27 See the EU Declaration on Yugoslavia of 13 May 1991 and James Baker's declaration of 21 June 1991 both supporting a 'democratic and united Yugoslavia' (Goati 1996).
28 The same is true of some surveys of refugees where the narratives basically convey the message 'never together again' (see also Jambresic-Kirin and Povrzanovic 1996).
29 P. Kende and M. Morokvasic (1994): *L'Evolution des rapports interethniques entre les Hongrois et leurs voisins dans L'Europe Danubienne*, Paris: Datar.
30 They include, for present Federal Yugoslavia: the Women's Party; Women's Lobby; Women's Parliament; Women and Society; Women in Black; SOS line for women and children victims of violence; women's studies; group for women raped in war; centre for rape victims. In Croatia there are, among others: Zenska Infoteka, Zenski Lobi, centre for women victims of war, women's groups' anti-war campaign.

REFERENCES

Amnesty International (1993) *Bosnia-Herzegovina: Rape and Sexual Abuse by Armed Forces*, report, 21 January, London: Amnesty International.
Bausinger, H. (1996): 'Concluding remarks', in R. Jambresic-Kirin and M. Povrzanovic (eds) *War, Exile, Everyday Life: Cultural Perspectives*, Zagreb: Institute of Ethnology and Folklore Research.
Blagojevic, M. (1991) *Zene izvan kruga – profesija i porodica*, Beograd: Faculty of Philosophy, Institute of Sociology.

Djuric, T. (1995) 'From national economies to nationalist hysteria: consequences for women', in H. Lutz, A. Phoenix and N. Yuval-Davis (eds) *Crossfires: Nationalism, Racism and Gender in Europe*, London: Pluto.

Drakulic, S. (1993) 'Women and the new democracy in the former Yugoslavia', in N. Funk and M. Mueller (eds) *Gender Politics and Postcommunism*, London: Routledge.

Glenny, M. (1990) *The Rebirth of History*, Harmondsworth: Penguin.

Goati, V. (1996) 'Politicke elite, gradjanski rat i raspad SFRJ' (Political elites, civil war and dislocation of Yugoslavia), *Republika* (Beograd) 147 (September).

Greverus, I. M. (1996) 'Rethinking and rewriting the experience of a conference on "War, Exile, Everyday Life"', in R. Jambresic-Kirin and M. Povrzanovic (eds) *War, Exile, Everyday Life: Cultural Perspectives*, Zagreb: Institute of Ethnology and Folklore Research.

Helsinki Watch (1993) *War Crimes in Bosnia-Herzegovina*, vol. 11, New York: Human Rights Watch.

Ivekovic, R. (1993) 'Femmes, nationalisme, guerre', in M. Morokvasic (ed.) *Yougoslavie: Logiques de l'exclusion*, special issue of *Peuples Méditerranéens* 61: 185–200.

Jambresic-Kirin, R. and Povrzanovic, M. (eds) (1996) *War, Exile, Everyday Life: Cultural Perspectives*, Zagreb: Institute of Ethnology and Folklore Research.

Jones, A. (1994) 'Gender and ethnic conflict in ex-Yugoslavia', *Ethnic and Racial Studies* 17(1): 115–34.

Kavcic, B. (1990) 'Women and power structure: the Yugoslav case', *Sociology*, supplement to vol. 23.

Korac, M. (1996) 'Ethnic-national conflicts and the patterns of social, political and sexual violence against women: the case of Yugoslavia', in M. Anglin (ed.) *Identities: Global Studies in Culture and Power*, Toronto: Gordon & Breach.

Krulic, J. (1991) 'Yougoslavie: les transitions perilleuses', in P. Kende and A. Smolar (eds) *La Grande Secousse: Europe de l'est 1989–1990*, Paris: Presses du CNRS.

Lutz, H., Phoenix, A. and Yuval-Davis, N. (eds) (1995) *Crossfires: Nationalism, Racism and Gender in Europe*, London: Pluto.

Mackinnon, C. (1994) 'Turning rape into pornography: postmodern genocide', in A. Stiglmayer (ed.) *Mass Rape: The War against Women in Bosnia-Herzegovina*, Lincoln, NB: University of Nebraska Press.

McNeil, P. and Coulson, M. (1994) *Women's Voices: Refugee Lives*, Woonona: The Book People.

Madzar, L. (1994) *Suton socijalisticke privrede*, Beograd: Institut ekonomskih nauka.

Martinet, G. (1971) *Les Cinq Communismes: russe, yougoslave, chinois, tchèque et cubain*, Paris: Seuil.

Meznaric, S. (1994) 'Gender as an ethno-marker: rape, war and identity politics in the former Yugoslavia', in V. Moghadam (ed.) *Identity Politics and Women*, Boulder, CO: Westview.

Milic, A. (1993) 'Women and nationalism in Yugoslavia', in N. Funk and M. Muller (eds) *Gender Politics and Postcommunism*, London: Routledge.

Morokvasic, M. (1984) 'Being a woman in Yugoslavia: past, present and institutionalized equality', in M. Gadant and A. M. Barrett (eds) *Women of the Mediterranean*, London: Zed.

—— (1992) 'La guerre et les réfugiés dans l'ex-Yougoslavie', *Révue européenne des migrations internationales* 8(2): 5–25.

—— (1996) 'La mobilité des élites scientifiques de l'autre Europe: exode ou circulation', *Revue d'études comparatives est-ouest* 27(3): 31–73.

Mrdjen, S. (1996) 'La mixité en ex-Yougoslavie: integration ou ségrégation des nationalités', *Revue d'études comparatives est-ouest* 27(3): 103–43.

Nahum-Grappe, V. (1996) 'La haine ethnique et ses moyens: les viols systématiques', *Confluences-Méditerranée* 17: 39–55.

Neier, A. (1993) 'Watching rights', *The Nation* 1(March).

Nikolic-Ristanovic, V., Mrvic-Petrovic, N., Konstantinovic-Vilic, S. and Stevanovic, I. (1995) *Zene, nasilje i rat* (*Women, Violence and War*), Beograd: Midim Print.

Papic, Z. (1993) 'Ex-citoyennes dans l'ex-Yougoslavie', in M. Morokvasic (ed.) *Yougoslavie: Logiques de l'exclusion*, special issues of *Peuples Méditerranéens* 61: 205–16.

Pavlowitch, S. (1988) *The Improbable Survivor*, London: Hurst.

Pejic, N. (1993) 'Media and the war', in M. Morokvasic (ed.) *Yougoslavie: Logiques de l'exclusion*, special issue of *Peuples Méditerranéens* 61: 35–46.

Popov, N. (1993) *Srpski populizam od marginalne do dominantne pojave*, special issue of Vreme (Belgrade) May.

Rupnik, J. (1988) *The Other Europe*, London: Weidenfeld & Nicolson.

Sander, H. (1992) Interview in *Tageszeitung* 6 August.

Scierup, C. U. (1991) 'The Post-communist enigma: ethnic mobilisation in Yugoslavia', *New Community* 18(1): 115–31.

Sklevicky, L. (1984) 'Organizirana aktivnost zena Hrvatske u NOB-u, 1941–1945', *Povijesni Prilozi* (Zagreb) 3.

Stiglmayer A: (1993) *Massenvergewaltigung: Der Krieg gegen die Frauen*, Frieburg: Kore-Verlag (trans. M. Faber, 1994, *Mass Rape: The War against Women in Bosnia-Herzegovina*, Lincoln, NB: University of Nebraska Press).

Woodward, S. (1995) *Balkan Tragedy*, Washington DC: Brookings Institution.

Woolf, V. (1938) *Three Guineas*, London: Hogarth (repr. 1992) *A Room of One's Own, Three Guineas*, Oxford: Oxford University Press.

Yuval-Davis, N. and Anthias, F. (eds) (1989) *Woman-Nation-State*, London: Macmillan.

Zarkov, D. (1995) 'Gender, orientalism and the history of ethnic hatred in the former Yugoslavia', in H. Lutz, A. Phoenix and N. Yuval-Davis (eds) *Crossfires: Nationalism, Racism and Gender in Europe*, London: Pluto.

5 When society was simple

Gender and ethnic divisions and the Far and New Right in France

Eleonore Kofman

The title of this chapter refers to the type of society the Far and New Right in France have sought to create, one which seeks a return to a point of origin from which society can be regenerated and its decadence brought to an end, especially through the return to a bygone era. Ideas of decadence and regeneration have usually included two components, that of biological reproduction and the transmission of values (Winock 1990), hence the significance of the family seen as the foundation of the natural and established social order. Families are deemed to function through complementary sexual divisions and so egalitarian ideologies, which seek to break down sexual differences, are considered to produce nefarious effects on this key institution, serving as it does as a metaphor for the nation.

In many respects, these themes are not all that different from those put forward by earlier fascist and national-socialist regimes, as in Austria, France, Germany, Italy (Thalmann 1986), or by other Far Right movements in present-day Europe, for example in Britain (Durham 1991), Belgium (*Chronique Féministe* 47 1993) and Germany (Skrzydlo *et al.* 1992). Yet these different situations demonstrate that there is not a single and consistent attitude to the family and its social relations among Far Right movements. National front movements have had to confront women's changing roles, despite (or rather because of) their desire to turn their back on modernity; feminism is seen as a threat to a natural hierarchy and an ordered society. As Durham (1991: 279) concludes, the British National Front remains an expression not only of racism, but often of an embattled masculinity. Without any doubt these are heavily male organisations, permeated by patriarchal values, but where in some cases a few women have held important posts. Yet women who support or are active in these movements do not necessarily share their same views about women's place in society as housewives and mothers. They may not necessarily agree with rigid sexual divisions, authoritarian sexual morality or be opposed to abortion. On the other hand, those who are older or closer to Catholic teaching may see such traditional attitudes as a valorisation of women's status (Erdenet 1992). As we shall see subsequently, the desire to preserve the nation against immigrants can be a major reason for women to take an active role in Far Right movements (Peyrebonne 1979; Skrzydlo *et al.* 1992).

It should be noted that despite the importance of sexual and gender differences, and their role in fixing racial boundaries through dichotomies of cultural difference, women and gender relations have until recently been little studied (David 1982; Durham 1991; Lesselier 1990a, 1990b; Seidel 1988). Earlier research tended to focus on women, feminist movements and national-socialism (Bock 1983; Koontz 1987; Mason 1976; Thalmann 1986). Kandel (1990) is highly critical of analyses which have presented women as the primary victims of Nazism, or Nazism as simply a pinnacle of patriarchy, and questions whether the feminism that emerged in the 1970s is capable of thinking theoretically about extreme forms of racism, including the extreme cruelty of the conflicts in former Yugoslavia (Kandel 1994; see also Morokvasic, Chapter 4 in this volume). It is worth noting that French feminists tended to focus their attention on Germany and Italy, and only since the early 1990s has there been a growing attention being paid to the Vichy period and its impact on women's lives and implications for sexual divisions (Muel-Dreyfus 1996; Eck 1992).

In relation to contemporary France, research initially focused on the discourse and ideology of New and Far Right movements concerning women and gender divisions. More recent studies have investigated women's own views and participation in a variety of Far Right and related movements. Erdenet's (1992) study of about fifty women of different ages was drawn from four broad categories: traditional Catholics who reject the reforms of recent decades; the National Front and its associated groups; radical nationalists who are more extreme than the National Front and who adopt a totally biological notion of race; and finally groups with specific interests such as anti-abortion or respect and support for motherhood (such as Union féminine pour le respect et l'aide à la maternité).

Not only are gender divisions and relations extremely important in right-wing discourses, ideologies and practices, but also they are an essential element of ideas about how society should function and be reproduced, of how values should be transmitted, and the ways in which the national is to be demarcated from that which lies outside its boundaries. As with Benton's myths of origin (Chapter 2 in this volume), right-wing discourses in particular present society as the product of laws of nature, which mask the socio-historical relations of power and maintain that relations of domination, exploitation and inequality are socially necessary (Guillaumin 1988). Though by no means restricted to the Right, such discourses articulate certain social facts as non-political and non-social, belonging to the realm of the natural and biological order, and thereby impenetrable to critical scrutiny. For women this means their confinement to biological materiality. In arguing for the determination of the social and political by the biological, such naturalisation reinforces men's appropriation of women's bodies (Bisseret-Moreau 1988). Particular attention is paid to demographic policies, especially rates of reproduction and motherhood, and the threat that supposedly insufficient replacement may pose for national decline and the preservation of national identity.

This does not mean that attitudes to sexual differences are straightforward, since sexual differences are used instrumentally by the Far Right in vaunting and at the same time castigating modern developments in women's changing role in society. On the one hand, sexual and gender relations of European populations are seen to be more progressive than the traditional and globally misogynist ones characteristic of immigrant communities in western Europe (Peyrebonne 1979). On the other hand, the more permissive and liberal relations, and the consequent lower birth rates of the indigenous population, threaten the ability of the nation to survive. These have been some of the general preoccupations of New and Far Right movements in France.

In this chapter I shall focus on the role of sexual differences and gender relations in the constitution of an ordered society according to the New and Far Right in France. First, I shall show how crucial sexual differences have been in their ideology, and how they have been a major element in designating racial boundaries. As Guillaumin (1988) has argued, such right-wing discourse posits in an extreme form the relationship between patriarchy, nationalism and religion. Second, I shall consider the way that women themselves see their role in the Far Right in France.

FAR AND NEW RIGHT IN FRANCE

In the French context a distinction is usually made between the Far Right and the New Right (Dupont 1988; Taguieff 1993/4). The Far Right is morally conservative, supporting a return to traditional Catholicism, and is in favour of neo-liberalism within France but economically protectionist in relation to external actors. Its social values are Petanist, that is, those of the Vichy regime with its slogan of *Famille, travail, patrie* (Family, work, country). The New Right, however, is against economic liberalism and rejects Judaeo-Christianity in favour of paganism.

The best known Far Right party in France is the Front National (FN), which since its electoral breakthrough, in a by-election in Dreux in September 1993, has polled well nationally, scoring 10 per cent in the European elections in 1984 and 12.5 per cent in the 1995 legislative elections. In the March 1995 local elections it gained control of three local authorities (Marignane, Orange and Toulon, all in the South). It has also begun to make inroads into trade union organisations. Other smaller and more radical right-wing groups, such as the Parti Nationaliste Français et Européen and the Parti Nationaliste Français, refer overtly to a biological notion of race. For them, to be French means being white (Terreblanche 1989). The FN, on the other hand, euphemistically speaks of race in terms of culture and national identity.

The discourses and practices of the FN in relation to sexual differences, and, more specifically, Le Pen's references and use of sexual images have given rise to political and psychoanalytical analyses (Jouve and Magoudi 1988; Lallemand 1991). The *affaire des foulards* (headscarves) in 1989 also drew attention to second-generation and immigrant Muslim women and their part in the process of integration (Gaspard and Khrosrokhavar 1995; Kaltenbach and Kaltenbach 1991; Kofman 1996; Schnapper 1991).[1] The wearing of headscarves has continued to arouse considerable debate and resulted in new administrative circulars, such as that by the Education Minister, François Bayrou in September 1994 (Hargreaves 1995).

Intellectually, the New Right is politically isolated and has developed a vehemently differentialist conceptualisation of the relationship between groups or 'races'. For them, anti-racism is associated with the preservation of difference, and racism with the support of universalism (Guillaumin 1991; Taguieff 1991). The major New Right association is GRECE (Groupement de Recherche et d'Etudes pour une Civilisation Européenne) which was founded in 1968; those disaffected with GRECE left it to form the Club de l'Horloge in 1974. Members of the Club opposed the vehemently materialist and anti-Judaeo-Christian stance adopted by GRECE. A history of the various intellectual currents is presented by Taguieff (1993/4). For GRECE, the return to Grecian civilisation signified a means of bypassing Judaeo-Christian morality, and its sense of compassion and grace for others. In the pursuit of its counter-hegemonic project, GRECE questioned the foundations of Europeanness which it considered should be a culture untainted by Semitic elements. Alain de Benoist (1977), GRECE's key intellectual, defined right-wing thinking as based on positive attitudes towards diversity and viewed the inequalities resulting from it as beneficial. In contrast, the progressive homogenisation of the world, propounded by two thousand years of egalitarian discourse, is deemed harmful.

De Benoist (1977: 350) considered sexual difference and the female condition to be a major characteristic differentiating Graeco-Roman from monotheistic religions. In the former, the inegalitarian status between the sexes was founded on diversity that led to an enriching complementarity;

in the latter the regressive aspiration for uniqueness reduced one to the other. For him, social behaviour stems from innate biological conditions resulting from natural selection. Genes determine men's tendency towards aggression and their itch to conquer and dominate. Women possess qualities of submission, passivity, sensibility, tenderness and intuition, and have, as the principal biological role, the gift of life. Overturning the natural order is thus threatening; men and women should be complementary and not seek to eliminate virile values. Echoing Spengler, de Benoist stated

> Man makes history, woman is history; the feminine is eternal, maternal, vegetable, history without culture and never changing. . . . The complementarity of two temperaments – masculine individualism and feminine altruism – are equally necessary for human progress. . . . The more woman strives to approach the masculine principle, the more she loses the power of inspiration, which is the appendage of femininity – and the less creative man becomes.
>
> (de Benoist 1978: 9–10)

Liberation from external constraints is painful, for it means that women must submit to self-discipline. If differences are not maintained, men will be transformed into women of masculine sex, which is the worst form of decadence (Dupont 1988: 20). Woman's role is thus to be a faithful wife, fertile mother and a sexual object and lover for her man. The latter, as Dupont notes, differentiates the pagan aspect from the Catholic and traditional Front National.

The New and Far Right have been given prominence, not just in minority journals, but in mass circulation newspapers such as *Figaro Magazine*, which has included Domesday scenarios of a France populated by immigrants in an article entitled 'Serons-nous français dans trente ans'. This issue shows on the cover a picture of a Marianne wearing a *chador* (Hargreaves 1987; Le Bras 1991) and includes critiques of feminism and women's demands for equality. The scenario contributed, on the basis of inflated and incorrect figures and calculations, to the demographic obsessions and fears concerning the decline of the French population and invasion by a foreign element. It was not, however, an isolated publication for the heavily pro-natalist stance has been harnessed increasingly by the Right and the Far Right since the 1970s for nationalist projects (Bisseret-Moreau 1988; Le Bras 1991, 1992). I shall return to the demographic theme when discussing women's roles and rights in society.

The Front National has had numerous outlets to air their views of a simpler, ordered society and has increasingly had the capacity to influence the policies on immigration and immigrants of the traditional Right, which won the French elections in March 1993. While immigration lies at the nexus of the normal and the deviant, the indigenous and cosmopolitan, a traditional socio-sexual order also underpins the Far Right vision of a homogeneous and consensual national society and identity. It is a society in which each person has and knows her or his place; sexual difference emanates from a natural order heavily influenced by socio-biology and arguments derived from the animal world of supposed male aggressiveness and female compliance, complemented by traditional Catholic morality. The FN has been closely involved with anti-abortion commando raids on clinics. A woman's responsibility is to reproduce and nurture the national community and transmit its value. Her place is in the home; man's place is to protect her and the nation, symbolised in feminine terms, from violation. (For further discussion of men's protection of women, see Benton, Chapter 2, and Allen, Chapter 3 in this volume.) *Figaro Madame* argued that women were pushed into work to sustain the frenetic race for consumption. Women should stay at home and some in the FN have proposed a minimum wage for housewives.

For the FN, the cultural identity of the national community is to be defended; both French and immigrants have a right to difference (*droit à la différence*), a discourse adopted from regionalists and feminists in the 1970s. It now forms the core element of the neo-racist arguments concerning the inability of non-European immigrants to assimilate into a French, and by extension, European identity. Culture is conceived of as being rooted in biological qualities that have evolved over time and become stable and fixed. Multiculturalism is thus seen as a threat to the survival of the French (Harouel 1985). Quantitative indicators, such as the *seuil de tolérance* (threshold level) (MacMaster 1991) are also utilised to prove the relative incapacity of immigrants (for which one can read North Africans) to assimilate.

La vérité c'est que les peuples doivent préserver et cultiver leurs différences. . . . L'immigration est condamnable parce qu'elle porte atteinte à l'identité de la culture d'acceuil aussi bien que l'identité des immigrés.

(The truth is that people must maintain and cultivate their differences. . . . Immigration is to be condemned because it threatens both the identity of the host and of immigrants.)

(*Eléments pour la civilisation européenne* 45 1983)

In 1982 Le Pen stated:

nous avons non seulement le droit mais le devoir de défendre notre personnalité nationale et nous aussi notre droit à la différence.

(We not only have the right but the duty to defend our national character and *our* own right to be different.)

Carl Lang, the general secretary of the FN, too spoke of '*le droit de notre peuple de disposer de lui-même*' (the right of our people to self-determination), a sentiment appropriating Third World discourse and epitomised by the title of the book *Europe, Third World, Same Struggle* (de Benoist 1986).

In this schema, gender and racial identities intersect; a constellation of sexual, medical and martial metaphors serve to distinguish those who cannot be assimilated into the nation, and who are to be excluded from social and political rights, and those who can be assimilated. Sexual metaphors, signifying transgression of the body politic and normal behaviour, have always been an underlying thread in discourses of decadence (Winock 1990). Medical metaphors, closely related to the biological, and requiring intervention in the social body, suggest that simple and effective treatment can be practised. It invokes the idea of disease as contagion brought in by outsiders, and calls for the closure of frontiers against contamination. Such reasoning has of course a long history in fascist thinking (Gilman 1992) and has been reactivated with the spread of AIDS. Lastly, the martial metaphor is infused with male sexual imagery and the surgically oriented strategies of the medical metaphors. These metaphors are all the more hard hitting, given their direct references to the daily life of the home, the family and neighbourhood, in which the immigrant may live but not share the values of the indigenous population.

If the French are not safe in public places, neither can they feel secure in their own homes, especially when they share their neighbourhoods with immigrants. The force of this insecurity is conveyed by the threat of invasion of the home in strong peasant images. As Le Pen (1985a) declared:

Demain ces immigrés s'installeront chez vous, mangeront votre soupe et coucheront avec votre femme, votre fille ou votre fils.

(Tomorrow immigrants will come and live in your homes, eat your soup and sleep with your wife, daughter and son.)

Not only do women figure prominently in Le Pen's universe, symbolically and in reality, as they do in most nationalist discourses and strategies (Parker *et al.* 1992; Yuval-Davis and Anthias 1989), but they also link the family with the nation. Women reinforce the idea of inheritance, kin and closed worlds. Le Pen speaks of France as a beautiful and ideal woman, a fiancée to be coveted. Notions of family, roots and heritage are not just part of his programme; they also determine the opposition between national and foreign.

The task of the revived family as the basic social unit is to save the nation from its ills – delinquency, insecurity and unemployment. Just as significantly the family supplies the analogy for the concept of national preference and the rationale for policies of exclusion and discrimination against immigrants, and on the basis of which, education, housing and welfare can be legitimately denied them. Increasingly social benefits for immigrants are tied to their legal status, while family reunification has been curtailed by a series of restrictive measures brought in by Charles Pasqua in 1993.

For the FN, ties of blood, which take precedence over contractual links, can be justified (see also Benton's discussion of the relation between national identity and bodily fluids, Chapter 2 in this volume). It would seem there is nothing more natural than family ties, a theme which was expounded in *L'Heure de Vérité* (17 March 1984), a television programme in which famous figures are interviewed. The family is the basis of society and where it is most natural for the father to exercise authority. Indeed, for Le Pen the future of western civilisation depends upon it. Decadence arises from the general loosening of discipline in the family and the nation. Thus the new order must be practised here. Confusion of sexes is both the sign and cause of decadence. Internally within the family, the threats to the socio-sexual order are modernity and feminism, externally delinquency and immigration.

Le Pen has denounced the 'rights of man' for refusing exclusion. The family is exclusive, and without closed families and nations we would collapse into anarchy. (As Benton shows, such closure is essential for maintaining the racial purity of the nation: Chapter 2 in this volume.) 'Il n'y a pas de vie sociale sans discrimination, sans différentiation.' (There exists no social life without discrimination or without differentiation.) Indeed, the notion of familial and national preference was frequently repeated by supporters and activists in interviews conducted in 1985 (Orfali 1990).

While there is nothing more natural than family preferences, Le Pen alone has dared counter the taboo of incest in his famous saying:

J'aime mieux mes filles que mes nièces, mes nièces que mes cousines, mes cousines que mes voisines, mes voisines que des inconnus et les inconnus que mes enemis.

(I prefer my daughters to my nieces, my nieces to my cousins, my cousins to my neighbours, my neighbours to strangers and strangers to my enemies.)

His book *La France est de retour* was of course dedicated to his three daughters and his Celtic lineage. It is worth noting that these preferred links with family are formed through blood and lineage, not alliance, and that the father–daughter relationship and paternal power are privileged over the marriage relationship (Paul-Lévy 1986).

This working out of affiliation in concentric circles from the core of the family is firstly transposed to Europeans, and then other westerners, especially if they support France. Non-European immigrants, who lie beyond the pale, are the primary target of such discourses. They both threaten the socio-sexual order and fail to conform to it. The principal focus is on the nexus between immigrant men and French women. Immigrant men undermine the virility and primary protective functions of French men and threaten French women. Women, as the guardians of the family, have to be protected against outside invaders and also risk being raped by foreign males. Much play is made on *viol* (rape) and *vol* (theft). These are of course terms frequently used in nationalist discourse in speaking of the nation as a person to be defended by men against an aggressor (see Benton, Chapter 2 in this volume). After attacks on women in Paris in 1985, *National Hebdo* (the FN weekly) spoke of women in permanent danger. After a white French woman was attacked in Avignon in 1989, French women were presented by the FN as martyrs of uncontrolled immigration fallen in front of the occupier (i.e. immigrant). 'It isn't just about rape and assassination but real symbolic appropriation of our land and our people' (Le Pen 1989b).

However, sexual violence appears to be a primarily masculine worry, since women supporters and activists of the Front did not necessarily associate sexual harassment and rape with immigrants (Erdenet 1992) But then immigrant men are to be feared and pitied because of their unbridled sexuality and polygamous behaviour. As inhabitants of temperate zones (in all senses), western men are privileged to experience a later sexuality supposed to be advantageous for the development of their intellectual capacities. For those who originate from hotter climates, precocious sexuality detracts from their intellectual attainment. No one of any age is safe from immigrants, for French women from puberty to old age may be attacked.

French women, on the other hand, are failing to respect traditional sexual divisions and are sometimes led astray by feminists. For Le Pen feminism is essentially a revolutionary project animated by Marxists and with which some people are involuntarily complicit. The problem with feminist struggles is that the traditional authority of men and their virile responsibilities have been weakened, thereby increasing insecurity. Le Pen rejects the accusation that the FN is a macho party and refers to the fact that many women attend public meetings and are members (*National Head* 1985). Women too have responsibilities, and he cites devotion to figures such as Joan of Arc (Warnock 1991) and the fundamental role of women as mothers (Lesselier 1991).

Soraya Djebbour, a member of the Le cercle national des femmes d'Europe (CNFE), set up in May 1985, argues that while feminists see social relations between men and women in terms of power, members of the CNFE, on the other hand, see these relations as complementary. There is a need to preserve harmony, not to create rebellion against men and nature. Martine Lehideux, who launched CNFE and has been a FN member of the European Parliament since 1984, cautions against the Enlightenment attack on families that leaves the individual starkly facing the state. She contends that the CNFE is opposed to this inhuman totalitarian scenario; its vision is one of a child cuddled and raised by the mother, protected by the father and growing up among its own blood kin. A cosy and inclusive world. French women are thus called upon to preserve the integrity and survival of the national community by fulfilling their natural role as mothers and guardians of their children's education.

The decline and ageing of the French population and the multiplication of the immigrant population are key themes, and strongly pushed by the CNFE, for whom Alfred Sauvy, formerly director of INED (the national demographic institute), was the greatest demographer. French demographic thinking is closely associated with pro-natalist policies, rooted in biological and organicist imagery. While demographic concern is also prevalent throughout a wide political spectrum, and not restricted to right-wing circles, the origins of INED and its leading demographers in the Vichy regime (Fondation Carel), and the sympathetic views on population policies and close relationships with the Front National, have been highlighted by several researchers (Bisseret-Moreau 1988, 1989; Le Bras 1991). Until about 1970 INED propounded a discourse of law, order and the 'duty of procreation' which was toned down with the rise of the women's movement. However, subsequent demographic decline immediately aroused cries of decline of the west and an evil to be combated (Bisseret-Moreau 1988: 107). Furthermore, demographers such as F. G. Dumont presided over the Association pour une renaissance démographique set up in 1976 after the passing of legislation on abortion (Bisseret-Moreau 1988: 95). The spurious calculations of the *Figaro* dossier had been supplied by Bourcider de Carbon from INED, who soon after sat on the FN scientific committee. In 1979 Sauvy and the then current director of INED, Calot, participated in a conference organised by Le Club de l'Horloge. Their papers and Sauvy's book *Le Défi démographique* were published under its auspices (Le Bras 1991: 216–17). Sauvy questioned the equality of the sexes and women working.

The FN exhorted women not to take up employment but to stay at home, looking after the families they should be producing. It has suggested that rents should be reduced and family allowances increased to facilitate this. However, some of these exhortations, together with criticisms of abortion, have had to be tempered because of the support the FN receives from women members and electors. Indeed, the CNFE does recognise that women may not find fulfilment exclusively through the home and has suggested ways that they could combine bringing up children with work and outside activities (Foucault 1990: 11). Research on female Far Right activists in France and Germany (Skrzydlo *et al.* 1992) shows that they do not correspond to the image of the non-working housewife and do not necessarily share the views of their party on such traditional roles.

Women, as we have seen, are portrayed by the FN as victims of immigrant violence and therefore in need of French men's protection. On the whole, little specific attention was paid to immigrant women, usually shorthand for Muslim and Arab women, until the headscarf affair of November 1989. The headscarf affair brought together many of the contradictory representations of immigration and the persistence of stereotyped images. North African women are caught between demands for modernity and conforming to traditional representations (Barbara 1992). Muslim women have served as evidence of the cultural gulf between 'misogynist' Islamic attitudes and 'liberated' western values. Yet they are harder to categorise and are considered less threatening than their male counterparts, partly because they draw a certain degree of sympathy for the social control imposed on them within familial surroundings. So, on the one hand, the traditional forms of orientalisation of prolific and tantalising sexuality of harems and belly dancers still linger, although this may be counterbalanced by a different kind of orientalisation, that of the traditional submissive woman portrayed as living in a closed world. On the other hand, girls' success in the educational system gives them a positive image and they are seen as the greatest potential for the integration of Muslims into French society (Kofman 1996). This is exemplified by their greater propensity to register for voting and declare themselves to have no religion (survey published in *Cahiers de l'Occident* 11, 1988, cited by Kaltenbach and Kaltenbach 1991).

In recent years the socio-sexual order has also been undermined by homosexuality and AIDS, a theme which has allowed Le Pen to bring together both his sexual and medical metaphors and remedies for cure. AIDS has inevitably been high on his list of diatribes. Le Pen announced on *L'Heure de Vérité* (6 May 1987) that AIDS could be transmitted through saliva, tears and contact. AIDS combines the sexual and biological contagion for which there is no known remedy. However, it is used to warn us of the danger of mixing and pollution brought into the social body by outsiders, and a development which may lead to the disappearance of the nation (see also Benton, Chapter 2 in this volume). The therapy is to identify the heterogeneous and dangerous presence in one's midst and to segregate or exclude it. *Sidatorium* (the French term for AIDS is SIDA), rhyming with crematorium, has been the remedy suggested by the FN for those with AIDS (Hastings 1991: 203).

As for homosexuality, Le Pen declared that it was not a crime but a biological and social anomaly (*L'Heure du Vérité* February 1984). It is presented as a grave threat to the preservation of the human species and in particular the French, and is associated with decadence and disorder, the corruption of youth and the destruction of the family. For the New Right, homosexuality represents a backward stage in human evolution in which sexual differences have not yet been clearly delineated (de Benoist 1977). In general, the FN was opposed to legislation which made discrimination illegal on grounds of homosexuality (enacted in August 1982), while a large number of its members are in favour of legislation outlawing it (Lesselier 1990b: 12).

WOMEN AND THE FAR RIGHT

What roles do women actually play in the Far Right, and particularly the Front National, which is the most studied part of the Far Right movement? In particular how do many of them, especially the younger members, reconcile traditional values of sexual difference with women's presence in the public sphere at work and in politics? (These questions are explored in another context by Afshar, Chapter 6 in this volume.) Women are in a minority in the Front National, as in all political parties, and for the most part, hold subordinate positions. However, there are notable exceptions, such as Ariane Biot, Le Pen's press secretary in the mid-1980s, Marie-France Stirbois, who substituted for her husband as a Member of Parliament after he died in a car crash in 1988 and had a reputation as a superwoman, and Le Pen's own daughter, Marie-Claire (Lesselier 1991).

In general, women in the Far Right would not see themselves as feminists; where younger activists use terms such as 'equality', it is within the context of complementarity and difference. On the other hand, UFRAM (Feminine Union for the Respect and Support of Motherhood) interpreted real feminism as the defence of a feminine nature. Earlier feminist movements had fought for the right causes: votes for all, rights for married women, equal education for girls and boys, and opening up of the professions. The problem with second wave feminism, and its ties with Marxism, was that it had encouraged the war between the sexes and the destruction of society which would be replaced by an atheist society, dangerous for both the family and the country (Erdenet 1992: 8).

Throughout the various groups, 'women' and 'men' are seen as natural constructions such that each sex is expected to conform to its norms and and not deviate through, for example, male homosexuality or lesbianism.

However, this does not mean that women activists wish to be confined to the home, though the family remains a constant theme. Women may work, but their role is also to reproduce values and educate children, familiar Rousseauian sentiments. The Front National has gone out of its way to present itself as a party that is itself a family and represents the family. We have seen this in Le Pen's discourse and it is one of the reasons activitists gave for adhering to the Party (Orfali 1990). Among younger members of the Front National, the degree to which they desire to balance work and family varies with age, educational level and background. For some female theoreticians of the Far Right, women's work had led to higher rates of divorce and was harmful for children and the family; others saw it as oppressive (Erdenet 1992: 7).

Mixing moderate and radical stances on different issues is not uncommon. Some women in the FN support the mixing of cultures but are opposed to abortion; others are socially liberal but anti-immigrant. Within the Front National those holding moderate positions thought they could alter things from within; they were against lashing out against men. On the other hand, the most traditional and nationalist discourses on women tended to be expressed by older female activists and those in radical nationalist movements for whom homosexuality was a perversion, while women's essential role was to reproduce values and transmit life to the next generation.

CONCLUSION

As we have seen, sexual and gender differences for the New and Far Right in France are central to their conception of an ordered and simple society; they are key elements in the maintenance of an established socio-sexual order in which each person knows and has her or his place. There are female activists in the Front National who are very much in the public sphere, and sometimes portrayed as superwomen, but the family and the clear demarcation of sexual and gender differences are common themes among female members.

Moreover, these very differences serve to demarcate who belongs and who is excluded from the national community, from which stems a far from innocent politics of difference. Diversity is vaunted, but those who do not conform, or are incapable of being included, are to be expelled where they cannot trouble an existing consensus or culture that has taken a long time to construct. Differentialist thinking is intimately intertwined with the premise of incapacity to assimilate and the fixity and naturalisation of cultural and social traits.

The Front National may have only a minority of women activists and fewer female than male voters, but its discourses of insecurity and privileging of the family, at a time when national identity has become problematic and unemployment a serious issue, have an impact beyond its own circles.[2] These ideas are not isolated from other movements and parties with political influence. Their attitudes on the family, abortion and divorce find resonances and support among traditional Catholics. (The influence of Catholicism on political parties is discussed by Waylen, Chapter 8 in this volume.) Anti-abortion raids have continued in the 1990s. Their proposals for the control of immigration and the view of the immigrant as the *bouc émissaire* of all ills in French society found a ready echo in the most recent right-wing government. Changes in the nationality code, restrictions on family reunification and pursuit of those working illegally and without papers have been adopted and have made the lives of many immigrants far more precarious. Fortress Europe and European preference have become the basis of policies towards immigrants and asylum seekers.

NOTES

1 In 1989 three Muslim girls at a secondary school in Créil (Paris Region) wore headscarves, for which they were expelled. Discussions have raged ever since about the wearing of religious symbols and the secular tradition in educational spaces in France.

2 Mossuz-Lavau and Sineau (1988: 16) argued that many women, especially at the top and bottom of the social hierarchy, are turned off by the Front National's fundamental anti-feminism. For example, in the first round of the 1988 presidential elections, 17 per cent of men but only 10 per cent of women voted for Le Pen. Some of the largest disparities between a high male and a low female vote were recorded for the liberal professions and workers. Greatest support came from female shopkeepers and artisans and unemployed women.

REFERENCES

Barbara, A. (1992) 'Représentations de la femme musulmane par les non-musulmanes', *Migrations Société* 20: 11–22.

Benoist de, A. (1977) *Vu de droite*, Paris: Copernic.

—— (1978) 'The feminine condition', *Spearhead* 113: 8–10.

—— (1986) *Europe, tiers monde, même combat*, Paris: Robert Laffont.

Bisseret-Moreau, N. (1988) 'The discourse of demographic "reproduction" as a mode of appropriation of women', in G. Seidel (ed.) *The Nature of the Right*, Amsterdam: John Benjamin.

—— (1989) 'Pensée animiste et démographique: de la décadence de la race au vieillissement de la population', *Sexe et Race* 4: 121–44.

Bock, G. (1983) 'Racism and sexism in Nazi Germany', *Signs* 8(3): 400–21.

David, R. (1982) 'La Nouvelle Droite et les femmes', *Combat par la Diaspora* 8: 33–47.

Dupont, G. (1988) 'FN, GRECE: deux discours sur la femme', *Article 31*, 36: 18–20.

Durham, M. (1991) 'Women and the National Front', in L. Cheles, R. Ferguson and M. Vaughan (eds) *Neo-fascism in Europe*, London: Longman.

Eck, H. (1992) 'Les Françaises sous Vichy: femmes du désastre, citoyennes par le désastre?', in F. Thébaud (ed.) *Histoire des femmes en occident: le XXe siècle*, vol. 5, Paris: Plon.

Erdenet, G. (1992) 'Une autre manière d'être féministe', *M. Mensuel, marxisme, mouvement* 53–4: 21–8.

Foucault, F. (1990) 'Le cercle national des femmes d'Europe: Maréchale, nous voilà', *Les Cahiers du Féminisme* 54: 9–11.

Gaspard, F. and Khosrokhavar, F. (1995) *Le Foulard et la République*, Paris: La Découverte.

Gilman, S. (1992) 'Plague in Germany, 1939/1989: cultural images of race, space and disease', in A. Parker *et al.* (eds.) *Nationalisms and Sexualities*, London: Routledge.

Guillaumin, C. (1988) 'Sexism: a right-wing constant of any discourse – a theoretical note', in G. Seidel (ed.) *The Nature of the Right*, Amsterdam: John Benjamin, reprinted in C. Guillaumin (1995) *Racism, Sexism, Power and Ideology*, London: Routledge.

—— (1991) '"Race" and discourse', in M. Silverman (ed.) *Race, Discourse and Power in France*, Aldershot: Avebury.

Hargreaves, A. (1987) 'Images et identités culturelles: vers une société multi-ethnique', in J. Bridgford (ed.) *France. Image and Identity*, Newcastle: University of Newcastle.

—— (1995) *Immigration, 'Race' and Ethnicity in Contemporary France*, London: Routledge.

Harouel, M. (1985) 'La société pluriculturelle: une illusion suicide', in Le Club de l'Horloge, *L'Identité de la France*, Paris: Albin Michel.

Hastings, M. (1991) 'Les métaphores medicales dans le discours du Front National en France', in H. Schamphelaire and Y. Thanassekos (eds) *L'Extrême Droite en Europe de l'Ouest*, Brussels: VUB Press.

Jouve, P. and Magoudi, A. (1988) *Les Dits and les non-dits de Jean-Marie Le Pen*, Paris: La Découverte.

Kaltenbach, H-H. and Kaltenbach, P. P. (1991) *La France: une chance pour l'Islam*, Paris: Editions du Félin.

Kandel, L. (1990) 'Le mouvement féministe aujourd'hui et le national-socialisme', *Les Temps modernes* 524: 17–53.

—— (1994) 'Faurisson-"Détective": même combat? Les féministes, entre la "fin des utopies" et la naissance du révisionnisme', in L. Crips, M. Cullin, N. Gabriel and F. Toubent (eds) *Nationalismes, féminismes, exclusions*, Frankfurt am Main: Peter Lang.

Kofman, E. (1996) 'In search of the missing female subject: comments on French migration research', in M. Cross and S. Perry (eds) *Population and Social Policy in France*, London: Pinter.

Koontz, C. (1987) *Mothers in the Fatherland: Women, the Family and Nazi Politics*, London: Cape.

Lallemand, M. (1991) 'La métaphore sexuelle dans le discours de Jean Marie Le Pen', *Celsius* 42: 3–9; 43: 3–8.

Le Bras, H. (1991) *Marianne et les lapins*, Paris: Olivier Oban.

—— (1992) 'Le fantôme de la population française', *Esprit* 181: 172–8.

Le Club de l'Horloge (1985) *L'Identité française*, Paris: Albin Michel.

Le Pen, J. M. (1985a) *La France est de retour*, Paris: Editions Carrère/Michel Lator.

—— (1985b) *Pour la France: programme du Front National*, Paris: Editions Albatross.

—— (1989a) *Europe: discours et interventions 1984–89*, Paris: Groupe des Droites Européennes.

—— (1989b) 'Immigration, les femmes entrent en résistance', *National Hebdo*, November.

Lesselier, C. (1988) 'The women's movement and the extreme right in France', in G. Seidel (ed.) *The Nature of the Right*, Amsterdam: John Benjamin.

—— (1990a) 'Dieu, famille, patrie: les "intégristes" catholiques et les femmes', *Les Cahiers d'Article* 31(1): 59–68.

—— (1990b) 'L'extrême droite et l'homosexualité', *Cahiers de féminisme* 54: 12–16.

—— (1991) 'De la vierge Marie à Jeanne d'Arc: images de femmes à l'extrême droite', *L'Homme et la Société* 99/100: 99–114.

MacMaster, N. (1991) 'The "seuil de tolérance": the uses of a "scientific" racist concept', in M. Silverman (ed.) *Race, Discourse and Power in France*, Aldershot: Avebury.

Mason, T. (1976) 'Women in Nazi Germany', *History Workshop* 1: 74–113; 2: 5–32.

Méricourt, O. (1990) 'L'extrême droite en France: Enfants, cuisine, église . . .', *Cahiers du Féminisme* 54: 5–8.

Mossuz-Lavau, J. and Sineau, M. (1988) 'Le vote des femmes: l'autre évenement', *Le Monde* 5 May, p. 16.

Muel-Dreyfus, F. (1996) *Vichy et l'eternel féminin: contribution à une sociologie politique de l'ordre de corps*, Paris: Seuil.

Orfali, B. (1990) 'Le FN ou le parti-famille', *Esprit* 9: 15–21.

Parker, A., Russo, M., Sommer, D. and Yaeger, P. (eds) (1992) *Nationalisms and Sexualities*, Routledge: London.

Paul-Lévy, F. (1986) 'Le Pen: attention danger', *Les Temps modernes* 475: 147–52.

Peyrebonne, M. (1979) 'Immigration – a crime against women', *Spearhead* 129: 14–15.

Schnapper, D. (1991) *La France de l'intégration: sociologie de la nation en 1990*, Paris: Gallimard.

Seidel, G. (1988) 'Right-wing discourse and power, exclusions and resistance', in G. Seidel (ed.) *The Nature of the Right*, Amsterdam: John Benjamin.

Silverman, M. (1992) *Deconstructing the Nation*, London: Routledge.

Skrzydlo A., Thiele, B. and Wohlaib, N. (1992) 'Frauen in der Partei "Die Republikaner": sum Verhaltnis von Frauen und Rechtsextremismus', *Beiträge zur femistische Theorie und Praxis*, 33.

Taguieff, P. A. (1984) 'Alain de Benoist: philosophe', *Les Temps modernes* 451: 1439–78.

—— (1991) 'Les métamorphoses idéologiques du racisme et la crise de l'anti-racisme', in P. A. Taguieff (ed.) *Face au racisme: analyse, hypothèses, perspectives*, vol. 2, Paris: La Découverte.

—— (1993/4) 'From race to culture: the New Right's view of European identity', *Telos* 98–9: 99–126.

Terreblanche, E. (1989) 'Entretien avec Christelle Dugue, Présidente du CNF (Combat Nationaliste Féminin)', *Tribune Nationaliste* 38: 5–9.

Thalmann, R. (ed.) (1986) *Femmes et fascisme*, Paris: Editions Tierce.

Warnock, M. (1991) *Joan of Arc: The Image of Female Heroism*, London: Vntage.

Winock, M. (1990) *Nationalisme, antisémitisme et fascisme en France*, Paris: Seuil.

Yuval-Davis, N, and Anthias, F. (eds) *Woman-Nation-State*, London: MacMillan.

6 Strategies of resistance among the Muslim minority in West Yorkshire

Impact on women

Haleh Afshar

For its adherents Islam can, and often does, provide a strong sense of identity as well as guiding religious principles. But the level and intensity of the immigrant Muslim community's identification with their faith in the west vary considerably over time and place. At times of national, international or even community-level political crisis, faith, as an empowering identity, can gain considerable ascendancy. It can result in Muslims in general and Muslim women in particular adopting mores and practices that are in marked contrast to those of the host society. At such times, the assumed process of integration through time, education and birth of new generations of migrants can appear totally fallacious. It is therefore worth considering why and when Muslim migrant women are more likely to reject the supposedly liberal, western values of the host society for the apparently more restrictive Islamic values of their society of origin (or that of their parents).

To understand this question I have been working since the early 1980s with three generations of Muslim women living in West Yorkshire. The views offered here are the result of long interviews, conducted with the women in groups and individually over the years. But the particular period focused on is the mid-1980s, when a combination of privatisation policies, erosion of social services, heightened racism and race-aware education created a sense of despair among the minority groups in West Yorkshire (see Foster-Carter 1987; Honeyford 1983, 1984a, 1984b; Murphy 1989: 103–42). This feeling of insecurity was in part responsible for a revival of interest in Islam and for Muslims attempting consciously to carve out a social niche for themselves. Encouraged by the international growth of Islamic fundamentalism, Muslim minorities sought refuge in the strength of a universalist empowering Islam to combat the realities of deteriorating socio-economic conditions within their daily lives. Muslim women too found the idea of an all-powerful, united Islamic *umma* (or people), alluring, though their responses varied according to age, economic and political circumstances. Some of those who had become the most ardent supporters of Islam in the mid-1980s came to revise their views in the early 1990s, while others became more fervent. This chapter tries to unravel some of the elements that contributed to the choices made by these women.

ISLAMIC REVIVALISM

Revivalist Islam, though dating back to the early years of the twentieth century, has gained considerable momentum and political importance in its final decades. Like the Far Right in Europe (discussed by Kofman, Chapter 5 in this volume) revivalist Islam harks back to an idealised/idolised past, when the world was set right by the arrival of the Prophet and when a 'golden age' was created. This means that unlike some other utopian ideologies, Islamists do not merely promise a heavenly future to their adherents, but actually claim a real historical past which exemplifies the successful implementation of its policies (see e.g. Afshar 1991; Chhachhi 1991). This idealised past or myth of origin (to use Benton's phrase, Chapter 2 in this volume) is all the more useful since at the time, some fourteen centuries ago, the Prophet of Islam ruled both as a source of enlightenment and as a political ruler. So Muslims can lay claim to a real state at a real time when a powerful righteous ruler governed the *umma* and laid the foundation of the glorious Islamic empire. It is claimed that all that Muslims have to do now is to revert to that past and all will be well. What is needed most of all is strength of purpose, purity, morality and the determined pursuit of Islamic law to the letter.

Some Muslims, such as Dr Kalim Sadighi in London, have even gone so far as to declare that Muslims living in Britain should endorse, not vote for (as is customary in the west), an Islamic parliament to run their affairs. In the event this particular call fell on deaf ears. But given the enormous diversity of creed, even among Muslims in West Yorkshire, political unity has never been successfully forged. What has been effective, however, is the aspiration towards a notional Islamic unity and grandeur. This became particularly important during the 1980s when Thatcherite policies resulted in severe cutbacks in welfare and educational provisions which were of considerable importance to the less well-off in the Muslim community. At the same time the intensification of racism, fuelled by shortages of jobs and the generally lower wages paid to immigrants, exacerbated a sense of dislocation and alienation, particularly among the young. As a result they chose to believe that the Islamic utopia could provide an alternative to the feelings of inferiority and isolation for minority women. The Rushdie affair and the Gulf War added to the sense of crisis (also discussed by Allen,

Chapter 3 in this volume) and fuelled the ardour for Islam and its unifying strength among Muslims in West Yorkshire.

ISLAM AND WOMEN

Where there is a much greater sense of unanimity among Muslims is in the understanding that the standard-bearers and signifiers of a high moralistic profile would, inevitably, be women. Their modesty would denote achieved dignity, not only for themselves, but also for the community of Muslims. Conversely, women's failure to live up to the prescribed standards spells dishonour both for women themselves and for the entire kin and clan. The need to protect women, and extreme sensitivity to women's sexual vulnerability, can become an almost obsessive fear among some women and their menfolk and (as other chapters show in different contexts), can have deleterious consequences for women.

It would, however, be quite wrong to assume that the excessive emphasis on modesty, expressed often in terms of the need for some form of veiling and segregation, is all that Islam offers women (see Ahmed 1992; Mernissi 1991). There is an ever-growing body of literature written by enlightened Muslim women in defence of their creed which they claim, with much justice, has given them considerably more than any other faith has to its women. (see e.g. Hoffman 1985; Rahnavard nd). They note that, some fourteen centuries ago, Islam bestowed a separate personal and economic identity on women; they did not become the chattel of their husband, but retained their name and property and had inalienable rights of inheritance from both their parents and their husband.[1] Marriage was a matter of contractual agreement between consenting partners and women were required, by Qur'anic dictum, to stipulate a *mehre* (marriage price) before the consummation of marriage. Furthermore, whereas women's resources are their own, men are required to spend their wealth on women and a husband must maintain his wife in the style to which she has been accustomed. In addition, mothers are entitled to payment for suckling their babies. Marriage and motherhood are revered and Islam has little respect for celibacy. Thus although practices and interpretations vary, there is much in the body of the Qur'anic dictum, which Muslims must obey absolutely, which benefits women and protects their rights.

It is the combination of these absolute rights and entitlements and the idealised visions of marriage and motherhood which have created a view of Islam which is acceptable both to the devout and to enlightened women of the creed. At times of difficulty, when all else fails, the creed, with its positive approach and protective embrace can offer an alluring alternative to minority women.

ISLAM AS THE CHOSEN IDENTIFIER FOR WOMEN

It is at times of crisis or hardship that Muslim women, particularly those who were born and bred in the UK, have consciously chosen to adopt their creed as their personal identifier. Among the myriad of selves and identities that are open to them – those offered by school, television, friends, neighbours and parents – it is not always easy to understand why some may opt for one that seems to separate them so clearly from the host society. (This provides evidence of the situational nature of identity discussed by Allen, Chapter 3 in this volume).

For many of the young girls and women that I have been working with, Islam represented a haven of support, honour and dignity in the jungle that racism at school had created. There is plenty of evidence to show that if schools and/or teachers are supportive, encouraging and positive towards these girls, then notions such as a separate culture or identity become less important (see Tomlinson 1984). They no longer need to define themselves primarily as Muslims. But when young girls find themselves failing at every turn, failing to achieve the grades, the standards, the expectations of the school and its teachers, then they resort to their faith. For those who do not make the grade because of racism, cultural and other problems, there is always the option to be bad pupils, but be or become good Muslims.

THE HONEYFORD AND RUSHDIE EPISODES

It was very much this utopian image of Islam, as a powerful, unified, morally superior and wholly protective faith, which spearheaded the growth of Islamic revivalism in West Yorkshire. In the city of Bradford, local political developments did much to nurture a return to the faith. The international revival of Islam coincided with the Honeyford episode, when a local headmaster publicly denounced Muslim immigrant children as inferior and as having a 'purdah mentality' (see Honeyford 1983, 1984a; some points made by Honeyford were repeated in a BBC TV *Panorama* programme in 1993). He was promptly rewarded by Prime Minister Margaret Thatcher, who made him her 'Racial Issues Adviser'. His views were very much shared by the Right in British and French politics (Seidel 1985; see also Kofman, Chapter 5 in this volume). The mobilisation of parents in Bradford against Honeyford did, after a long struggle, result in his early retirement. (For detailed discussion see Foster-Carter 1987; Murphy 1989). But the débâcle underlined a new heightened sense of racism within the community of Bradford. In the name of free speech, Honeyford shattered many racist taboos that had been carefully nurtured by black and white citizens alike. Bradford Council's racial equality guidelines, seeking to respect cultural differences, had been in place for less than five years when they were so blatantly flaunted. *Hallal* meat (meat slaughtered according to Islamic rules) had been introduced to schools in 1982, and guidelines for better treatment of minorities in schools in 1983.

A second and equally devastating issue for the Muslim community was the Conservatives' success at the local elections which resulted in a hung council in Bradford. By 1985 the Conservatives held forty-six seats, Labour had forty-one and the Liberal Democrats six. Nevertheless the Lord Mayor was determined to make the city a flagship of privatisation. Using his casting vote, he repeatedly backed measures which eroded what meagre public resources were available to the migrant community. The Muslims in Bradford were getting poorer and getting fewer and fewer benefits from the state; the time was ripe for an eruption, and Salman Rushdie's (1988) novel *The Satanic Verses* provided the fuel. In a country where blasphemy against Christianity is against the law, where films like *The Life of Brian* are barred from some towns, the censorship laws had allowed an author to blaspheme against Islam and its Prophet. In the name of free speech the Muslim community was to consider itself under direct attack. Yet Bradford was the only city in the UK where Muslims responded to Kalim Sadighi and Khomeini's call to organise demonstrations and burn the book.

In my view it was not so much what Rushdie said, but the timing of the book that resulted in the eruption. In Bradford Muslims and Islam were considered under siege and the Muslims saw it as their duty to rise and protest.

MOTHERS AND GRANDMOTHERS

It was very much in the context of heightened tensions locally that I talked to a group of Muslim schoolgirls about their views of themselves, of their faith and of their future. The girls were all in their teens, and all lived with their mothers and grandmothers in close proximity, either in the same house or in the same neighbourhood. I had assumed that in such three-generational households I would find a gradation of integration, with the grandmothers being the most distinct and devout group exercising a 'traditional' and 'conservative' influence and the youngest group generating a dynamic force for change and integration into the host community.

It was therefore with some surprise that I discovered that the opposite appeared to be the case. The women I talked to ranged from well-to-do professional and business backgrounds to homeworkers and mill workers. For the oldest generation, who had chosen to come to the UK in the 1960s, the overall expectation had been, if not integration for themselves, at least a much greater degree of receptiveness to the British way of life for their children. As Mrs B, a grandmother who had followed her businessman husband to the UK in 1965, told me:

> We wanted to come because we thought of Britain very much as a second home. I was worried, of course, but I thought things would be much better after a while.

As considerable as the changes were for Mrs B, she recalls little discrimination:

> When I got here I felt shamed and covered my head when I left the house. But my husband said 'no matter'. He said that things were different here. People were quite nice, they did stare, but they smiled as well.[2]

Mrs B dreamed of her daughter becoming educated, and getting both a good job and a good husband.

> Of course I wanted her to know her own culture, but I felt that she could do both. I did not want her to be too different from her school friends. So she never wore *shalwar kemiz* [long trousers and a loose top] or anything like that at school.

Her daughter S was an achiever and certainly fulfilled many of her mother's expectations. She obtained high grades at school and went to the local college. Her parents did not wish her to leave home, and although they bought her a car, she always had to be home straight after her classes. Still, she met a young man at college. It was at this point that Mrs B's best intentions were most severely tested. Mrs B herself had had an arranged marriage and had been happy and willing to leave everything in the hands of her parents, but she accepted her daughter's views.

> I had tried to teach her the difference between good and bad. I had tried to teach her about our culture. But here things are different. Still I told her to tell him to come and ask permission for my daughter's hand and not mess about with her and shame the family.

Luckily the young man had all the 'appropriate' qualifications: he was a Muslim, from a 'good' family, well educated and with good prospects. When S's daughter C was born, Mrs B decided to take charge of her religious education.

> You have to guide children. . . . You have to do your best to tell them about Islam and tell them to guard their *izzat* [honour] till they get married.

Mrs D, a grandmother who had come over from Pakistan to join her husband in his small business, was equally enthusiastic:

I had to be less strict about the veil and about talking to strangers when I started working in my husband's business. But I made sure that my daughter knew her religion. I taught her to read the Qur'ān and say the *namaz* [daily prayer].

Her daughter too went to college and got good qualifications. But her marriage was more or less arranged; her parents suggested a couple of men, whom she refused. But the third suggestion seemed all right.

He looked OK and had a good job. We met and I thought that he was quite nice, so I said OK and we went ahead.

Her daughter E was a good pupil. She had gone to the Brownies when at primary school and had managed to pass the entrance exams and get a scholarship to a private single-sex school nearby. Her mother had done her best to teach her about Islam but initially E had not been very interested in learning her mother tongue and religious rituals.

Mrs F was a widow. She had come over from Pakistan with her family in the early 1970s and her husband had died soon afterwards. Hers had been a hard life, with no knowledge of English, and few skills that could be transferred to the UK; she had eked out a precarious living doing what she could. In the still caste-conscious Muslim Pakistani community, she did what lowest-caste women did back home – she washed and prepared the dead for burial. But, like all her contemporaries, she had enormous faith in the British education system, and believed that her children were going to succeed through studying. In this respect her daughter had done better than her son. She had gone to the local school, and had always had a paid job on the side to help with the household finances. In some respects not having a father and facing poor marriage prospects within the community had meant that the daughter X could to some extent decide her own future. She married one of the many employers she had over the years. He had had great difficulty getting the consent of his family to what they considered a 'bad marriage'. Their daughter G is the apple of her grandmother's eye; it was Mrs F who largely looked after G while her parents pursued their full-time demanding careers. Mrs F had insisted on giving her granddaughter a thorough religious education.

In our society religion is very important. Girls who understand about religion respect their parents and are good girls.

Mrs B's idea of a well-brought-up Muslim girl was much the same.

She would say her *namaz*, speak Urdu, wear Muslim clothes and be of good character and obedient. She should respect people and speak well.

In practice, however, few of the teenagers I talked to said their five regulatory daily *namaz*.

These three families are typical of the range of those whom I worked with and talked to over the years. As I watched the youngest generation grow, I, like the grandmothers, had hoped that they would put racism and divisiveness behind them and become 'British', like everyone else.

REVIVALISM AND SCHOOL AND PLAYGROUND POLITICS

For most of the women that I talked to education was perceived as the best road to success. Whether they were themselves highly educated or not, the women seemed to have implicit faith in the system. Grandmothers on the whole were not too sensitive to racism, and mothers, who had experienced the traumas of taunts and mockeries themselves, had hoped for improved conditions for their daughters.

At the same time all mothers and grandmothers expected their daughters to remain 'good Muslims'. Exactly what this term meant varied considerably from parent to parent; for some it was merely a matter of good behaviour,[3] for others there was a continuous struggle to teach daughters the Qur'ān, Urdu, and the rudiments of rituals of feasts and fasts. They were also sometimes aware that their demands could create problems for their daughters, as Mrs B pointed out:

> Children go to school and see different things and they see different things at home. They are living a double life. They think that what they see outside their homes is the real thing. But we have to tell them about life. We have to do the teaching and the loving and the caring.

As for the youngest generation, they cherished their mothers and grandmothers and valued the love and care; they tried to be 'good' Muslims. But they also had to survive school where, far from disappearing, racism had become more intense and immediate. The values promoted by grandmothers and mothers frequently conflicted with the values on offer from the media, the school and in the playground; those of the grandmothers were frequently the least acceptable. As G explained:

> Who wants to be 'goody goody two shoes'? If you are quiet and always do what the teachers say, then you get bullied by the kids. They'll think you are doing it to make yourself all right . . . you know what I mean? Not different colour and things.

'Making yourself all right' was indeed the main aim of the teenagers I talked to when they first went to school. Being all right meant being invisible, like the others, not different – a difficult task when you are clearly of a different colour and sometimes have to wear different clothes. Being like the rest becomes less and less easy for those Muslim girls who also try to please their parents and wear modest clothes (see Husband 1982: 182–9).

> Well I do put my scarf over my head to school. But when you come in, you just got to move it. If my dad finds out he'd be mad. But you've got to leave it or else everybody laughs at you.
>
> (U, a 15-year-old of Pakistani origins)

Little or nothing at school reflects these girls' life experiences at home; the implicit content of what they learn in history, literature and geography places them very much at the margins of realities (Puar 1993). The curriculum is firmly anchored in an assumed uniformity of white British Protestant experience which is postulated as a norm and renders everything else 'different'. As Saifullah Khan has noted,

> the child's move to school presents him/her with a disjunction between two meaning systems. The education system presents a new set of relations and references, some of which have already been absorbed by the child through media or local neighbourhood contacts. It is through the school's lack of contact with community aspirations and systems of support and education, and the lack of recognition of the child's existing social and linguistic skills that children of ethnic minorities assess the relative value placed upon their identity and affiliation. . . .
>
> The children of ethnic minority families belong to both systems. . . . But the second generation child and adolescent is 'of' two systems and creating a new one.
>
> (Saifullah Khan 1982: 211)

The teenage Muslim girls make every attempt at conforming and becoming part of the group or being as unobtrusive as possible. E told me:

> I never talk to 'them'. There is a few of 'us' and we just keep together and don't do much at play time. It's best to keep away from 'them'.

For most of their contemporaries they remain 'immigrants' and 'blacks'. Being born and raised in Britain does not make them British in the eyes of the other pupils. Far from being a melting pot or a haven of integration, for most of these girls the experience of schooling borders on the infernal. But, so long as there was any hope of success, be it in terms of academic grades or future prospects, it was a price worth paying. The mothers of the teenagers I talked to had all gone through some years of schooling in Britain. Some had obtained tertiary education too. Almost all had protected their mothers and not allowed them to know about the pains of schooling (Afshar 1989);

now their daughters were doing the same. But in the 1980s there was considerably less hope of success.

For the second generation of migrant women who entered the labour market in the early 1970s, 'qualifications' had been an invaluable asset enabling some to move away from the constraint of the *chardivari* (the four walls), and most to have some kind of paid employment. This in turn had made them better able to deal with marriage and, in a couple of exceptional cases, divorce (Afshar 1994).

Their daughters, however, had less cause for optimism, that is until the Iranian revolution took hold and Islamic revivalism gained momentum. It is very much in this specific context of school, national and international politics that in the mid-1980s Islam began to emerge as a positive, rather than negative, group identifier for these girls. The west, the chains of imperialism and the decline of moral standards all appeared intertwined. Suddenly the high moral ground was occupied by the faith, the family and the *umma*; Islam ceased to be the boring recitations at the mosque that these young girls had sought to avoid. It became a vision of strength, an empowering alternative. The youngsters wanted to be Muslims.

The groups of 'immigrant' girls in the playground no longer wanted to be invisible, they had a message, a righteous view and a sense of self that was valued. Of course it all happened very slowly. I was still asking them about conventional notions of feminism and liberation, when they, slowly, began telling me about femininity, *izzat* and the historic duties of Muslims, which became grander as time went by. In her first year at middle school, G wanted to avoid being 'good'; by the time she was 15 she had decided that she wanted to be devout.

> I didn't know what it really meant to be a Muslim. It's not just about praying and all that. It's about being part of a whole world, a much bigger world than England. You have Muslim girls fighting for the veil in France, in Lebanon, all over. It's a real sign of honour. Instead of being 'cheap', you can be respected.

C too had gradually moved towards the new Islam:

> It was not easy before. Your mum and dad didn't approve of your friends, your friends thought your mum and dad were too strict. If I wanted to mess about with my friends, I couldn't tell my parents. I'd have to invent all kinds of stories about after school art club and all that to get away and then I didn't even enjoy it. I didn't want to smoke. Cinemas were so scary, all dark and you couldn't see where you were. I wouldn't go to the pub. So most of the time we used to go to the shopping centre. But my friends thought I was a bit wet and so they'd ask me less and less.

Then this Muslim girl started talking to me about Islam and all that and brought me newspaper cuttings and all that and then we started going to sort of meetings; you know in the shopping centre, or at McDonald's. You know it's not like they say in the Mosque. You get lots of rights and lots of history and all that. It's nice going around with the Muslim girls. I am glad about it all.

For C, Islam was as much about having friends, belonging to a group and holding your head up as it was about faith and rituals *per se*.

For E, Islam was far more than a social or political allegiance. She had begun reading around the subject and was very keen to find out more. For her, Islam, the veil, the prayers and fasting and all the rules and rituals were a welcomed and necessary part of growing up and becoming her own self. She felt that her creed gave her strength, and a real sense of purpose.

Of course my grandma had told me about it, but I hadn't really understood it all. I still don't, but it's incredible. You know we have all these rights and all this religion and I knew so little; I still know so little. But I am going to read everything and find out all about it. It's incredible!

In practical terms, with the exception of E, who did her best to follow all the religious rituals, the return to Islam for the teenagers I talked to was more about selecting a positive identity and gaining self-respect, than actually following a creed.

ISLAM AS A NEGOTIATION STRATEGY

I returned to talk to my young friends last year. C, E and G were still at school, but I met up with K, L and M, who also grew up in a three-generational household of Muslim women. They too had, to a greater or lesser degree, adopted Islam in the 1980s. They too saw their creed as an empowering, protective shield in the jungle that is school. To the extent that they had chosen the Islamic identity, they had also gained the approval of the community. M explained:

It was really nice, I didn't feel so ashamed of my name, or of my mum and dad. You felt you belonged, not just to the *biradary* [the extended family], but to the whole big world of Muslims. You know, you could do things.

Most of the young girls and young women I talked to did not regularly say their five daily prayers. Few knew their Qur'ān well enough to read or recite correctly and most resented learning even Urdu. None had a working knowledge of Arabic. For them it was not the Islamic daily rituals, so much as the universal sense of Islamic identity that was important. This pragmatic view of Islam, though useful in the playground, at school and in dealing with the host community, was more of a handicap when it came to dealing with their own community. This was particularly problematic for the young women who faced difficult decisions concerning tertiary education, employment, marriage choices and lifestyles. The conflicting agendas of the community, the family and individual women had not been resolved; revivalism had been empowering, but it was also debilitating when it came to life choices. As young adults these young women were at a point when they could choose to abandon the boundaries of their Islamic identity and transfer to the host community's colleges, universities and workplaces and perhaps move away from their families.

Those who wished to retain their Islamic identity had to come to terms not only with Islam, but also with Islamists within the community. It was as adults seeking jobs and moving towards the marriage market that these young women had to exercise enormous tact and use their understanding of Islam to best effect. It was then that the young women decided to organise some Islamic classes. They felt that the Islamists within the community, male and female, chose to interpret the faith in the most restrictive of terms; Islam had become a means of asserting community control, particularly over young women (see Yuval-Davis, Chapter 9 in this volume). There was a sense that revivalism had gone hand in hand with a level of moral policing that was not necessarily valid in the best Islamic terms. So the young women decided to find out for themselves what they were really entitled to, in terms of Islamic law as stated in the Qur'ān. It was a brave decision to demystify the faith and to use it not only as a badge of identity, but also as a means of negotiation and as a pathway towards an 'Islamic' liberation. They spent about six months coming to weekly evening sessions, with several English translations of the Qur'ān and reading the texts, comparing the commentaries and reading in greater depth around some of the issues concerning women and their rights. They were determined to gain a better understanding of their religion and use this knowledge to the best effect.

As we have already seen, some fourteen centuries ago Islam recognised women's legal and economic independence as existing and remaining separate from that of their fathers and/or husbands and sons. Islamic marriage was conceived as a matter of contract between consenting partners (Qur'ān 4:4, 4:24), and one that stipulated a specific price, *mehre*, payable to the bride before the consummation of marriage. The holy book demands that women are maintained in the style to which they have been accustomed (2:238, 4:34) and paid for suckling their babies (2:233). So these young women could use the text of the Qur'ān, which for Muslims is the undisputed word of God, to defend their rights. They could state categorically that they could not be married off without their own consent and that it was they and not their families who were entitled to payment for marriage and subsequently entitled to payment for housework and motherhood.

Faith gains considerably more importance when the girls and women believe that it offers them not only salvation in the next world, but better opportunities in this one. Though diverse in its forms and interpretations, the mores and normative demands of Islam were very much the framework within which life chances were negotiated among these women and their kin (Afshar 1992). Different generations of women used their knowledge and understanding of Islam differently to negotiate the best possible outcomes, particularly where education, matrimony or employment prospects were being considered. Given the importance of the creed, this group of school leavers, facing the future, decided that knowledge of the faith in general and the holy Qur'ān in particular could play a central role in their bargaining with patriarchy and the matriarchs of the family (see Kandiyoti 1988).

The decision to set up a Qur'anic study group was initially welcomed by the community since daughters, like sons, were not always willing to attend the Qur'anic schools run by religious leaders. There young boys and girls are taught to recite the Qur'ān. Although an estimated 90 per cent of Muslim children do at some time or another attend these schools, most do not stay for long or learn much while they are there (Parker-Jenkins 1991).

For its adherents, Islam is not an oppressive belief, confining women to the *purdah* (veil) and the *chardivari* (for detailed discussion see Khawar and Shaheed 1987; Shaheed 1989). It is seen as a dynamic terrain for new discourses, for formulating possible alternatives and negotiating a path forward. It is this dynamic and flexible approach to Islam that has made revivalism so attractive to some. Islam demands that its adherents, women as well as men, be well educated, that mothers and daughters be loved and respected. These, as well as the economic provisions it makes for women, permit a degree of flexibility which is a far cry from the more repressive, authoritarian view of Islam projected by the western media. But this dynamic view is also rather threatening to the old-established ways that migrant communities, in particular the older men, wish to continue 'guarding'.

Nevertheless, the parents were initially pleased that their daughters were going to a religious meeting and the young women enjoyed the gatherings. I was invited to attend the sessions and participate in the discussions. The group's conclusions about their Islamic rights were somewhat different from those traditionally recognised and granted by the community. It was in part a matter of interpretation and emphasis on particular parts of a Qur'anic verse rather than others. For example, in terms of arranged marriages, the young women referred to the Qur'anic stipulation that it must take place with the *consent* of both partners (Qur'ān 4:4, 4:24), something that has not always been observed by their parents.

But once they began questioning some of the prevalent practices and referring their parents to the holy text, once they began using knowledge as a strategy for foiling some of the parental dictates, then of course the group and its meetings became less popular with the older generation.

Given that all Muslims are supposed to believe absolutely that the Qur'ān is the very word of God as recited by the Prophet of Islam, it was not easy to refute or deny absolutely the God-given rights that the young women were demanding. For these young women knowledge could become power; the power to refuse, legitimately and in the name of Islam, the parental dictate. But, like many familial struggles, the gains were more theoretical than real. Sometimes parents admitted that what they asked in the name of Islam was perhaps not strictly speaking a Qur'anic duty, but they still asked for compliance on arranged marriages, on appropriate employment, and appropriate clothing and behaviour. Newly discovered, and apparently God-given rights were at times discarded by the young women for parental love, for empathy with the problems faced by the minority community and for the real sense of solidarity that existed within the families.

MARRIAGE AND THE LABOUR MARKET

To have a strategy, to have knowledge, or even to be right, does not necessarily mean that the struggles become any easier. For young minority Muslim women, particularly those who have chosen to adhere to the faith in a context of revivalism and heightened Islamification, it is none too easy to negotiate terms and conditions when it comes to life chances.

The chances of success were much higher when mothers and daughters formed an alliance. It was when the women of the family united that they managed to loosen the constraints and move beyond the limits imposed and guarded by the men. The woman who for me embodies the best example of successful strategisation of Islam is Mrs R. She had come over with her mother and had stayed at home cooking, cleaning and helping her mother look after the younger children. She had had an arranged marriage and had become a homeworking garment maker. She was determined that her daughter would do better and had, single handed, launched a campaign against her husband.

> Sometimes I used to cry. I had to look after six children. It was very difficult to get out to do a job because in my family it was a forbidden thing for women to do. My daughter T works, which is against our

family's tradition. My husband asked me to ask T to stay at home and he said he would give her the same amount of money which she gets by doing her job. I had to persuade him to allow her to work.... I never learned driving, but I wanted all my daughters to learn driving. Again I had to get their father's permission to let them learn driving. I know I suffered a lot. I spent hours waiting in bus stops in the snow. Eventually he agreed and now T has her own car.

For Mrs R it was neither Islamic theory nor western immorality, or for that matter racism, that had acted as a catalyst to defend her daughter's greater degree of liberty. It was the consciousness of the pain and hardship that her husband's notions of appropriate morality and appropriate locality for women had caused her and her children. The gender divide was not in terms of questioning the morality, but rather in defying the practical degradation that such an imposed morality created in women's lives. It was the practicalities of day-to-day living that had made Mrs R into a fierce defender of her daughter's rights.

All the young women I talked to intended to work in the formal labour market (for detailed analysis see Brah 1993; Brah and Shaw 1992). But, particularly for the Islamists among them, male notions of propriety as well as the general absence of real opportunities, placed serious constraints on the choices open to them. Most did not have mothers like Mrs R. Many families were wary of 'unsuitable' jobs, though the levels of restriction varied from views that stipulated appropriate 'modest' clothing, often condoned by mothers, to fierce opposition to 'working with white men', generally adopted by fathers.

On the whole it was the fathers who were most likely to police the boundaries of the gender divide. I did, however, meet one 'conservative, traditional grandmother', Mrs N, who had come over from Pakistan in the 1960s with her teenage daughters. She was most worried about her granddaughter O.

You have to think of the family, you don't want everyone gossiping about you. I don't mind her working, but I want her to have a decent sort of job, maybe with a Muslim employer, or working at home. But it's not easy when O [her granddaughter] goes and trains as a hairdresser.

Hairdressing has the added disadvantage of being a low-caste employment and an occupation that was likely to ruin her daughter's chances of matrimony.

These girls, they don't think. If they follow our traditions, they'll be considered good girls, but if they copy English girls and English ways, then they will lose face. My daughter is fashion conscious and I keep on telling her that it is not good. How can you find a decent husband if you have a bad attitude or a bad job?

O had joined our study group, but she was stuck; she wished to be not only a good Muslim but also a hairdresser. The Holy Qur'ān could not help her out of this one! Eventually O gained her mother's agreement to become a home-based hairdresser. This way, at least the family honour would not be publicly eroded, even though her marriage chances were considered to be not as good as before.

The tensions of Islamist politics were most intensely experienced by the few young women who had managed to get well-paid jobs and were working with Muslim men. As P, a social worker, explained to me:

> Of course I am a good Muslim, I've been devout all my life. But these Muslim men, they don't want us to open our mouth. They are much harder on us than on the English women. They watch the way we dress, they watch the way we talk, where we go. And they just tell you straight out and that isn't proper. I mean not about the work, but about you. Then they go and talk to your dad and mum and it's hell to pay.

P's case was not an isolated one. In the public domain the devout Muslim men thought of active Muslim young women as a threat to the entire community's honour. They wished 'their' women to maintain the highest standards by being silent and submissive and never contesting their directives. The situation of women working in the private sector for Islamist men was far worse; there the men asserted and maintained their 'policing' rights.

Some of the women decided to use their new-found conscientisation, through the study group, to contest the authority of one such employer. He was approached privately, quietly and tactfully by one of the older women who was willing to act as a negotiator. Mrs Q, who had been born in Pakistan and came over with her parents to study and become a professional in the UK, agreed to act as an intermediary. She provided chapter and verse quoting from the Qur'anic injunctions that Muslims respect each other and respect each other's privacy.

Sadly she failed to convince the employer. Using Islam as a strategy works best in a climate of harmony and informality, among parents and children, within households. At the workplace issues of power, hierarchies and personality become too intense. All that happened was that P lost her job as well as her faith and her zeal. It was fortunate for her that her training and skills enabled her to find alternative employment and she eventually chose to abandon her Islamic identity without totally losing contact with her family and relatives.

For those who succeeded in maintaining their self-definition of Islamism, being a devout, practising and veiled Muslim woman, working in the public domain entailed its own difficulties. Among the women I knew V was by far the best versed in the Qur'ān and Islamic dictum. She decided to wear the veil as soon as she went to university and spent as much time learning about Islam as she did about her degree. She was an outstanding student and obtained excellent grades throughout. But when it came to finding a job, her decision to wear a headscarf and modest clothing led to discrimination at every turn.

They say that they don't want to have someone that looks so different. But maybe they're scared of Islam and what it means; they worry that I might suddenly do something crazy. Who knows? It took me three years to get a proper job and then I had to settle for a relatively low pay and position, working with 'immigrants'. Still what matters most to me is to be a good Muslim, everything else will be all right in the end.

CONCLUSION

What the experiences of growing up in three-generational households in West Yorkshire suggests, more than anything, is that being a Muslim 'immigrant' means very different things to different women. Even at the height of revivalism, the Islam that different women adopted or aspired to was different in every case and rarely did it involve the daily devotional and ritualistic practices.

There is a political Islamic discourse that the male community leaders espouse and generally attempt to enforce. Regarding women's status, this version of Islam is remarkably similar to the teachings of the political Right now and in the past (for a comparison with fascism, see e.g. Afshar 1982). It assumes a permanent sexual vulnerability for women and posits a view that any divergence from the stipulated norms and practices would in-evitably 'dishonour' a woman, making her unmarriageable and leading her family to disgrace (for detailed analysis see Sabah 1984). The assumption is that the family and particularly the male kin are the only protection a woman has. At least in the UK, the state does not figure in this equation; it is firmly located in the domain of 'the other', an institution which the minority are resisting and which threatens rather than assists them. In the British context there is just enough truth in these views to deter women from turning to the state and its apparatus for help against their kin and community.

In this context, the group of women that I worked with found the best solution to be a return to Islam and a serious attempt at redefining the faith in terms beneficial to them. Without a doubt, the political contexts, both nationally and internationally, had much to do with this choice of strategy. The intensified experience of racism in Bradford in the late 1980s and early 1990s, the Gulf War, the burning of *The Satanic Verses*, the decision of Bradford Council, arrived at by the casting vote of the Thatcherite Mayor, to cut back on welfare provisions, all played a part in sustaining the resolve of those who wished to remain Islamic. Though not always strategically successful in terms of familial negotiations, they nevertheless sometimes found this form of return both empowering, in terms of providing self-respect and pride in their faith, and illuminating, in terms of the teaching and learning work of the group. Many discovered much that they did not know about Islam. For others the realities of dealing with Islamist men outweighed the advantages of revivalism. Among this latter group those who had the needed skills, and the support of their mothers, decided to abandon Islam as their primary badge of identity, and some actually lost their faith.

ACKNOWLEDGMENTS

I am most grateful to Nickie Charles and Helen Hintjens for their detailed and extremely helpful comments on the earlier draft of this chapter. All errors and misunderstandings are, however, entirely due to me.

NOTES

1 It should be noted, however, that although under Islamic law women are entitled to inherit, their entitlement is half of that inherited by men.
2 Fenella Jeffers interviewing Black Caribbean women who migrated to Leeds in the same period found that they too had experienced little direct, personal racism (Jeffers 1995).
3 I am grateful to Sheila Allen for pointing out to me that in this respect grandmothers the world over have similar expectations of their descendants. The Muslim grandmothers seem to ask similar things of their daughters as do good Irish Catholic grannies.

BIBLIOGRAPHY

Afshar, H. (1982) 'Khomeini's teachings and their implications for women', in A. Tabari and N. Yeganeh (compilers) *In the Shadow of Islam*, London: Zed.
—— (1989) 'Education: hopes, expectations and achievements of Muslim women in West Yorkshire', *Gender and Education* 1(3): 261–72.
—— (1991) 'Fundamentalism and its female apologists', in R. Prendergast and H.W. Singer (eds) *Development Perspectives for the 1990s*, London: Macmillan.

—— (1992) 'Gender roles and the "moral economy of kin" among Pakistani women in West Yorkshire', *New Community* 15(2): 211–25.

—— (1994) 'Values real and imaginary and their ascription to women: some remarks about growing up with conflicting views of self and society amongst Muslim families in West Yorkshire', in H. Afshar and M. Maynard (eds) *The Dynamics of 'Race' and Gender: Feminist Interventions*, London: Taylor & Francis.

Ahmed, L. (1992) *Women and Gender in Islam*, New Haven, CT: Yale University Press.

Brah, H. (1993) '"Race" and "culture" in the gendering of labour markets: South Asian young Muslim women and the labour market', *New Community* 19(3): 441–58.

Brah, H. and Shaw, S. (1992) *Working Choices, South Asian Young Muslim Women and the Labour Market*, a Report for the Department of Employment, Research Papers 91, London.

Chhachhi, A. (1991) 'Forced identities: the state, communalism, fundamentalism and women in India', in D. Kandiyoti (ed.) *Women, Islam and the State*, London: Macmillan.

Foster-Carter, O. (1987) 'The Honeyford Affair: political and policy implications', in B. Troyna (ed.) *Racial Inequality in Education*, London: Tavistock.

Hoffman, V. J. (1985) 'An Islamic activist: Zeinab al-Ghazali', in F. E. Warnock (ed.) *Women and the Family in the Middle East*, Austin, TX: University of Texas Press.

Honeyford, R. (1983) 'Multiethnic intolerance', *Salisbury Review* summer: 12–13.

—— (1984a) 'Diary of a week at Drummond Middle School', *The Times Educational Supplement* 13 April.

—— (1984b) 'Education and race: an alternative view', *Salisbury Review* Winter: 30–2.

Husband, C. (ed.) (1982) *'Race' in Britain: Continuity and Change*, London: Hutchinson.

Jeffers, F. (1995) 'Different faces filling different spaces: Black Caribbean women and the trade unions in the 1950s and early 1960s', MA dissertation, Centre for Women's Studies, University of York.

Kandiyoti, D. (1988) 'Bargaining with patriarchy', *Gender and Society* 2(3): 274–90.

Khawar, M. and Shaheed, F. (1987) *Women of Pakistan: Two Steps Forward, One Step Back?*, London: Zed.

Mernissi, F. (1991) *Women and Islam: An Historical and Theological Enquiry*, Oxford: Blackwell.

Murphy, D. (1989) *Tales from Two Cities*, Harmondsworth: Penguin.

Parker-Jenkins, M. (1991) 'Muslim matters: the educational needs of the Muslim child', *New Community* 17(4): 569–82.

Puar, J. K. (1993) 'Challenging the white gaze: the deconstruction of relational discourse', MA dissertation, Centre for Women's Studies, University of York.

Rahnavard, Z. (nd) *Toloueh Zaneh Mosalman* [The Dawn of the Muslim Woman], Tehran: Maboubeh.

Rushdie, S. (1988) *The Satanic Verses*, London: Viking.

Sabah, F. (1984) *Women in the Muslim Unconscious*, Oxford: Pergamon.

Saifullah Khan V. (1982) 'The role of culture of dominance in structuring the experience of ethnic minorities', in C. Husband (ed.) *'Race' in Britain: Continuity and Change*, London: Hutchinson.

Seidel, G. (1985) 'Culture, nation and "race" in the British and French New Right', in R. Levitas (ed.) *The Ideology of the New Right*, Oxford: Polity/Blackwell.

Shaheed, F. (1989) 'Purdah and poverty in Pakistan', in H. Afshar and B. Agarwal (eds) *Women, Poverty and Ideology in Asia*, London: Macmillan.

Tomlinson, S. (1984) *Home and School in Multicultural Britain*, London: Batsford.

7 Citizen warriors, workers and mothers

Women and democracy in Israel

Valerie Bryson

Israel has been described as a 'developed, westernized democracy that happens to be located in the Middle East' (Safir 1993: 57). The circumstances of its foundation were, however, unique. In the late 1990s, the continued threat or reality of war means that it remains a highly militarised society, in which soldiers are political actors and the physical defence of the nation is not simply the stuff of legend but a current reality. The status of religion and the political significance of ethnic divisions also make it strikingly different from most other western democracies. Such a combination of similarity and difference casts fresh light on gender roles; it also throws into sharp relief the ways in which women may be separated from one another by nationality, religion and ethnicity and the ways in which the pursuit of feminist goals may at times conflict with the defence of national identity or traditional culture.

In this chapter I draw upon recent work by western feminists who have developed a critique of the concept of *citizenship*, which they say requires serious reformulation if it is to be used to empower women (Jones 1990; Lister 1992, 1993; Phillips 1991; Young 1989). I argue that many of the feminist demands derived from this critique appear to have been met in Israel, and that Jewish women in particular have made some significant gains. This suggests that a determined feminist movement and appropriate public policies and legislation can do much to defend and advance women's interests, even in a hostile environment. Nevertheless, even Jewish women remain second-class citizens in comparison with Jewish men. For Palestinian women, the disadvantages of their gender are not simply added to those of minority status but can interact with them, making it difficult for them to fight for their rights as women without appearing to betray their own culture. The example of Israel both confirms the experience of other states in which the goal of full citizenship for women has met with some success and suggests that the pressures of nationalism and militarism can confirm the marginalisation of even apparently privileged women, while intensifying the subordination of others.

The feminist critique of traditional approaches to citizenship rests upon two underlying and interrelated points. First, in line with the whole of the western political tradition, the concept of citizenship claims universality, but is based upon the particular needs, experiences and contributions of men and ignores those of women. This has important implications for our perception of the obligations and entitlements of citizenship. These have traditionally centred upon men's military role: from this perspective, a full citizen is one who is expected and prepared to risk his life defending his country, and women's usual lack of such responsibility has in the past been used to justify denying them full citizenship rights (see Benton, Chapter 2 in this volume). In most modern societies, this idea of the citizen-warrior has been replaced by that of the citizen-worker. This means that full-time paid employment has become the key to economic security, social welfare and the resources needed for political participation. Meanwhile, the domestic and caring work for which women retain primary responsibility remain invisible; as these are not seen as civic duties they do not normally provide access to civic rewards.

Feminists have therefore also attacked the perception of citizenship as an essentially *public* activity. The abstraction of citizenship from private life ignores the socially essential work performed by women within the home; it also ignores inequalities within the family and the ways in which these condition economic and political behaviour.

All of this has led some feminists to argue for a reconceptualisation of citizenship based on a recognition of the social necessity of caring work and an analysis of the private bases of public activities and inequalities. Such analysis has produced a number of public policy demands which cluster around three main areas (Bryson and Lister 1994). The first of these concerns the caring needs of society and women's domestic work. Reforms advocated here are intended to provide state support for women's traditional caring responsibilities, to enable these to be combined with employment and to facilitate and encourage greater domestic involvement on the part of men. They include parental leave, shorter working weeks and affordable, good-quality child care. The second set of reforms rests upon the belief that personal economic dependency is incompatible with full citizenship. It seeks to provide economic independence for women by improving their employment prospects, securing greater rights for part-time workers and giving women independent access to state welfare benefits. The final area is defined in narrower political terms and includes a demand for electoral reform and the introduction of quotas, in the belief that these will facilitate an increase in the political representation of women.

Although not universally agreed on, such demands represent an influential strand of modern feminist thinking on citizenship. They represent both a response to the immediate and practical needs of many women and a synthesis of analyses by feminist political theorists and those concerned with more immediate public policy issues. They also draw upon comparative data from other western societies, particularly the Scandinavian nations.

This chapter broadens the basis of such comparative material by examining a nation which has in some ways gone further than most in satisfying the conditions that feminists have identified as prerequisites for equal citizenship. It finds much that is familiar and that confirms the experience of women in long-established western democracies in terms of both the gains that have been won and the obstacles that remain. However, the situation of women in Israel is also the product of unique circumstances stemming from the history of the land and its peoples, the founding of the Jewish state in the aftermath of the Holocaust and the continuing military nature of the society. This means that the idea of the citizen-warrior remains a potent one; although most women undertake some military service, their role is largely supportive and not equal to that of men. Taking Israel as a case study therefore shows the specificity as well as the commonalities of gendered inequalities and patterns of resistance.

CITIZENSHIP IN THE JEWISH STATE

Israel was founded in 1948 as a Jewish state. As such, it represented the fulfilment of a dream achieved through military and political struggle by both men and women: the establishment of a homeland for the Jewish people after 2,000 years of exile and persecution. In 1950, the Law of Return granted every Jew in the world the right of entry and citizenship; the 1950s saw a period of mass immigration, with the Jewish population doubling from some 650,000 at Independence; in the mid-1990s it stood at over 4 million (Israel Information Centre 1993).

According to the Declaration of the Establishment of the State of Israel, non-Jews would have equal citizenship rights in the new state:

> The State of Israel . . . will foster the development of the country for the benefit of all its inhabitants . . . it will ensure complete equality of social and political rights to all its inhabitants irrespective of religion, race or sex; it will guarantee freedom of religion, conscience, language, education and culture.
>
> (Israel Information Centre 1993: 56)

However, hundreds of thousands of Palestinian Arabs left the country during the ensuing 1948–9 War of Independence. Although 20 per cent of Israelis are not Jews, Jewishness remains central to full Israeli identity and citizenship. Unlike those in the occupied territories, non-Jewish citizens within the Green Line do have a degree of equality including political rights and there are Arab members of the Knesset.[1] The first language of the Knesset is, however, Hebrew and the marginalisation of non-Jews is symbolised in the very fabric of the Knesset building, with its carvings and rich tapestries depicting key moments in Jewish history. More generally,

> Israeli Arabs have low social status, because in Israel the social status of the citizen is determined not only by education and professional achievements, but by the degree of identification with the central goals of Israel as a Jewish Zionist state.
>
> (Palestinian educator, quoted in Swirski and Safir 1993: 9)

Palestinians do not simply constitute a marginalised ethnic minority, but are seen as an actual or potential threat to national security. As such, Palestinians have of course no equivalent of the Law of Return and they do not normally serve in the armed forces. As will be discussed later, such service is of central importance as a source of national identity and full citizenship; it is also a key route into political power.

While Palestinian men are second-class citizens in relation to the Jewish state, Palestinian women have also traditionally been subordinated within their own community. As gender equality has been equated with the Jewish tradition, defence of Palestinian cultural identity has therefore sometimes involved women in defence of their own subordination (Mar'i and Mar'i 1993; Najjar 1992). Contrary to popular belief, therefore, the fact of living in a western democracy has *not* meant that Palestinian women within the Green Line enjoy a higher status relative to men than women in most other Arab nations (Hassan 1993).

Although the processes are less immediately obvious, Jewish women can also become invisible as citizens. As is well known, they have long played an unusually active role in the armed forces and they still remain eligible for conscription; however, their service has not been on the same terms as men, and the continued importance of the citizen-warrior emphasises masculine military virtues and offers men a route into political power which is denied to women. From this perspective, Jewish women become primarily the mothers and carers of citizens, rather than independent actors. The male experience of active military service is also of vital importance in forging a sense of solidarity, comradeship and national identity which crosses class and generational differences so that 'Israeli Jewish national cohesiveness is . . . a major product of the patriarchal male bond of the military' (Yuval-Davis 1985; see also Benton's discussion of war creating brotherhood, Chapter 2 in this volume).

There is also a broader sense in which the very meaning of Jewishness has been equated with the cultural and religious experiences of Jewish men. The marginalisation of women is dramatically clear in the Diaspora Museum in Tel Aviv. This celebration of Jewish identity documents the continuity of Jewish life and culture throughout the centuries of the diaspora; not only is its portrayal of Jewish life silent on the role and experiences of Jewish women (there is, for example, no mention of their ritual lighting of the Sabbath candles or their work in maintaining religious observances around food) but also it clearly equates Jews with Jewish male persons (as when the visitor is informed that 'all Jews' are circumcised). A visit to the museum is considered an important part of the education of young Jewish citizens: its lessons would seem to include the marginality of women.

EARLY JEWISH FEMINISM, EQUAL RIGHTS AND THE WELFARE STATE

Despite the cultural marginalisation of women, women have enjoyed a high degree of formal legal equality with men since the earliest days of the state of Israel. The Israeli Declaration of Independence promised equal rights regardless of sex as well as 'religion and race'. Three years later, the Women's Equal Rights Law opened with a declaration that

> with regard to any legal act, the same law shall apply to a woman and a man and any provision of law that discriminates against women shall be of no effect.
>
> (Lahav 1978: 195)

These declarations were in part a recognition of the work done by women in the founding of the new state. Such recognition was not automatic, however. Rather, it was the outcome of a long tradition of feminist activity by Jewish women that extends back to the early years of the twentieth century, when many of the early pioneering women, who had expected to be equal partners in the founding of a new society, found instead that they had to fight for this right (Izraeli 1993; Pope 1993a; Swirski 1993). Their claims against exclusion were based on socialist ideas of fulfilment and participation through productive labour. Such ideas found their clearest and most direct expression on the Kibbutz (Safir 1993) and were also reflected in women's involvement in military activity. At a more general level, they also clearly established the right of women to work and ensured that the needs of women were linked to ideas of collective responsibility for social welfare.

The new state of Israel also recognised the importance of women's child-bearing role and of their traditional domestic activities in preparing for and developing the new nation. At the most basic level, this arose from the need to build up the Jewish population in the aftermath of the Holocaust and to ensure the defence of the new nation. It also involved an emphasis on the centrality of the family to Jewish identity and the critical role of women in maintaining cultural traditions within the Jewish community. From this perspective, raising a family was a matter of public responsibility rather than simply one of private satisfaction; as such, it was much more visible than in Britain at the same period, and received much more state support.

This recognition of both the importance of women's work within the home and their right to paid employment has, from the first days of the Israeli state, produced a set of public policies aimed at supporting Jewish women in their dual role. As early as 1954, working women were given the right to three months' paid maternity leave and another year's leave without pay. Collective agreements enabled mothers of young children to work one hour less a day and to care for sick children without loss of pay and, in contrast to many other nations, part-time workers were given the same rights as full-timers in terms of security of tenure, social security and worker benefits. In 1965 the law established that men and women should be paid the same rate for the same work and in 1973 this was amended to include work of equal value. Working mothers were further helped by government-supported provision of good quality daycare for young children; a 1975 tax reform made allowance for their additional housekeeping and child-care expenses. In 1988, many of the rights of working mothers were converted to *parental* rights (Izraeli 1993; Lahav 1978; Raday 1993).

Such policies are necessary preconditions for women's economic independence and have been well in advance of those in Britain. Jewish women in Israel have also benefited from welfare policies in which entitlements, including pensions, are to a greater extent than in Britain based on need and family responsibilities rather than on workplace contributions. This partly reflects the state's acceptance of responsibility for the welfare needs of Jewish immigrants: whole families arriving with no wage-earner are entitled to many benefits on the same basis as established citizens. All Israeli Jewish women receive a birth allowance, all Jewish families get a non-means-tested children's allowance and housing policies favour those with children. War widows receive particularly generous welfare payments (Katz 1993); following vigorous lobbying by feminist groups, legislation in 1994 extended single-parent entitlements to unmarried mothers, and all single, divorced and separated parents are now eligible for additional family benefit.

These policies appear to be in line with the western feminist demands outlined earlier and suggest that the logic of nationalism is not necessarily hostile to the interests of all women. They have, however, not been applied equally to all groups of women, and many of the benefits outlined above are restricted to Jewish or Jewish and Druze families alone, sometimes disguised by the rubric 'families who have relatives in the Israeli army' (Yuval-Davis 1989: 96). Their goal is not simply to recognise and support women's role in building up a healthy work-force, but also to maintain an ethnic balance in favour of Jews. They can therefore be seen as part of a conscious policy of 'demographic racism' (Abdo 1994: 151) in which the respective birth rates of Israeli Jewish and Arab women are central military and political issues for both Jewish and Palestinian nationalists. Such demographic strategies are clear at a popular level: pregnant Jewish woman used to be congratulated with the words 'I see you are going to bring a small soldier into the world!' (Yuval-Davis 1985: 669), while Palestinian slogans proclaimed that 'The Israelis beat us at the borders but we beat them at the bedrooms' (Yuval-Davis 1989: 96) and 'Victory will come not on the battlefield but in the delivery room' (Grossman 1993: 27; see also Abdo 1994; Najjar 1992).

Women have therefore been given or denied rights according to the value which the Israeli state places upon their reproductive capacities, rather than as independent citizens. This explains why only Palestinian women can obtain free contraceptives (Yuval-Davis 1989: 96). The prioritisation of nationalist over feminist principles has also meant that although abortion is now legally obtainable, it is strongly opposed in both communities, with nationalist arguments reinforcing religious objections to a much greater extent than in most western nations.

'SECOND WAVE' FEMINISM FROM THE 1970s

As the above sections show, Israel was well in advance of Britain in supporting women in their domestic role and helping them to combine this with paid employment. Its policies were, however, motivated by nationalist rather than feminist goals, and by the 1970s, even Jewish women were far from achieving substantive equality in politics or employment, while traditional gender roles had never really been challenged and 'personal' issues such as domestic violence and sexual exploitation remained un-examined. When the ideas of 'second wave' feminism were imported into Israel in the early 1970s (largely by new Jewish immigrants from English-speaking countries, particularly the United States) they therefore found fertile ground.

The resulting new Jewish women's movement in Israel was very much a product of American culture and its development in many ways followed a similar course to that of US feminism (Pope 1993b; Swirski 1993). University-based consciousness-raising groups and seminars developed a radical analysis of women's oppression by men, and early campaigns against beauty contests and for abortion rights widened into a range of activities centring on domestic violence, rape and sexual harassment. New scholarly analysis included the development of women's studies and feminist cultural criticism; this now extends into more popular discourse, questioning the patriarchal construction of Jewish identity. Some women are also reinterpreting religious texts and seeking changes in religious practices; most dramatically, the Women at the Wall have been campaigning for the right of Jewish women to conduct public prayers, under strictly limited conditions, at the sacred Wailing Wall in Jerusalem. Women peace campaigners have developed non-hierarchical methods of political organisation and new forms of symbolic protest, such as the silent vigils of the Women in Black (discussed by Yuval-Davis, Chapter 9 in this volume; see also Chazan 1993; Pope 1993b, 1993c). Campaigns for improved health provision for women (such as breast screening) are receiving support from all groups of women, including some in the Ultra Orthodox Jewish community. As elsewhere, child sexual abuse has been the most recent problem to be 'discovered' and is now the subject of widespread feminist concern.

The situation of the Palestinian minority in Israel has led many Palestinian female political activists to prioritise nationalist over feminist issues; it has been difficult for Palestinian women both in Israel and in the Occupied Territories to challenge repressive practices without appearing to betray their own culture (Abdo 1994; Espanioly 1993; Hassan 1993; Mar'i and Mar'i 1993; Najjar 1992). However, some Palestinian women have been addressing a whole range of issues around women's economic, social, cultural and sexual subordination. Their activities have included working for daycare centres, community health projects and income-generating cooperatives. Some have been challenging conventional interpretations of the Qur'ān and some have been tackling the widespread problem of female illiteracy (for a discussion of similar processes in Britain, see Afshar, Chapter 6 in this volume). Others have attacked the traditional concept of 'family honour' which centres upon female purity; from the late 1970s, Arabic-language rape crisis services have been organised by and for Arab women in Jerusalem, and in 1994 the first refuge specifically for Arab women victims of domestic violence in Israel was opened (Grossman 1993; Kessel 1994; Swirski 1993).

Today, there are a significant number of grassroots groups that address the practical needs of women in all sections of Israeli society, whether these be for legal advice, rape counselling, health programmes or helping newly arrived immigrant women to find employment. Most of these are for either Arab or Jewish Israeli women. However, a few do cross the Arab–Jewish divide, and some women are deliberately setting up links and establishing social and personal contacts based on their common role and experience as mothers.

As in the United States, the radical feminist agenda developed in tandem with more conventional demands for improvements in women's career prospects and representation in elite positions. These demands stem from a more liberal and individualistic tradition, and today this strand of feminism is represented by the high-profile Israel Women's Network, which helps women to run for public office and campaigns and lobbies on a wide range of women's issues. Although the leadership has been exclusively Jewish, membership is open to both Jewish and Arab women.

Founded in 1984, the Network is a non-partisan group and has particularly close links with women members of the Knesset, most of whom now have a stated commitment to feminism. The Network not only supports women in their electoral campaigns, but also now has its own office in the Knesset building and is an important source of information and resources for elected members. Recent successes include legislation in 1993 which aims at ensuring a more balanced representation for women and men on the boards of directors of government companies and allows some scope for affirmative action to achieve this. By April 1994, one-third of the private Bills which had been passed by the current Knesset were on women's issues supported by the Network.

THE LIMITS OF EQUALITY: EMPLOYMENT AND FAMILY LIFE TODAY

As in other western nations, changing social attitudes, an increasing need for two incomes to maintain family living standards and a rise in demand for women's labour in service industries have contributed to a steady rise in women's paid employment, and women now constitute over 40 per cent of the Israeli work-force (Israel Women's Network 1993). Again as elsewhere, however, this has not produced the kind of economic independence which many would argue is a prerequisite for full citizenship. Inequalities remain particularly acute for Palestinian women, who have traditionally been excluded from education as well as employment, who face a labour market acutely divided on ethnic lines and who receive less state support for their family responsibilities. Although even here employment rates are increasing, by 1985 the participation rate of Arab women was only 11 per cent, compared with 39 per cent for Jewish women (Rakba 1993).

Employment patterns for all ethnic groups remain sharply gendered, with women overrepresented in caring and service work and in part-time and low-status employment, and men retaining a near-monopoly on top positions in both the private and public sectors (Agassi 1993; Izraeli 1993). Unsurprisingly, therefore, the earnings gap between men and women remains large; indeed, like the percentage of women workers in part-time employment, it has actually been *growing* in recent years: in 1993, the average hourly pay of women was just over two-thirds that of men (Israel Women's Network 1993).

In Israel, as in other industrial nations, women's disadvantaged employment situation owes more to their role in the family than to formal barriers. Alice Shalvi, the chairwoman of the Israel Women's Network, has claimed that women will never be equal with men in politics or employment until they are equal within the home (Shalvi 1994). Egalitarian state policies have, however, done little to change traditional patterns of domestic responsibilities, which remain firmly with women. (Similar problems have also arisen in Chile with the return to democracy: see Waylen, Chapter 8 in this volume). Although many rights to leave have been converted from maternal to parental rights, they are rarely taken by men. Moreover, despite the relatively 'advanced' welfare provisions outlined above, the needs of working mothers are still not adequately met by the state: although 92 per cent of Jewish 3-year-olds attend kindergartens, these are open in the mornings only, and even for older children the school day is short and closures for public holidays are frequent. Although employment and welfare policies make more provision for the needs of working parents than is the case in Britain, Israel does not provide an exception to the universal rule that it is still women who are expected to juggle the demands of family and employment. These responsibilities are further increased by men's military role and by public policies which continue to support the centrality of the family in Jewish life and women's pivotal role within it; for example, great efforts are made to enable soldiers to return home on the Sabbath. In general, it remains true that

> Despite the fact that the majority of young women now work outside the home, most social arrangements are organized on the assumption that women are still full-time homemakers.
>
> (Safir 1993: 64)

The problem of large-scale poverty in female-headed, single parent families as experienced in Britain or the United States does not at present exist in Israel, where only one in twenty households is headed by a single parent. Most such families are the result of divorce or widowhood rather than birth outside marriage (Safir 1993). Nevertheless, because women's unpaid domestic work prevents them from entering the labour market on equal terms with men, most Israeli women have less personal disposable income than men. Studies elsewhere have shown that financial resources are in general *not* shared equally within the family and that many apparently affluent married women lack the financial resources that would enable them to participate fully as active and independent citizens of their society (Pahl 1989). They also have much less disposable *time*. Although this has been ignored in traditional political analysis, feminists have recently identified this as a critical citizenship resource, without which women are seriously disadvantaged (Adam 1989; Lister 1990: 456).

POLITICAL UNDERREPRESENTATION

All of the above means that, as in other nations, women in Israel enter political life with few of the resources necessary for success; they are further disadvantaged by the political role and influence of patriarchal religions and by the centrality of war to Israeli politics.

Nevertheless, formal politics in Israel is in some ways relatively favourable to women, and Jewish women have made their voices heard throughout the twentieth century. In 1920, even before women's suffrage was formally ratified at national level, 4.5 per cent of delegates elected to the Jewish Representative Assembly were women. In 1949, eleven of the one hundred and twenty members of the First Knesset were women (just over 9 per cent) at a time when fewer than 4 per cent of the British House of Commons or the United States Congress were women (Swirski 1993). One of the women elected represented an independent Women's List (Freedman 1993). By 1969, the premiership of Golda Meir seemed to symbolise the advanced role of women in Israeli politics.

It might be expected that the nature of the Israeli electoral system (the party list system operates within a single national constituency) would have produced further advances in recent years. Cross-national studies have suggested to some British feminists that in a political climate which officially approves of the political representation of women, the presence or absence of an electoral system based on proportional representation is the most important single variable in predicting its extent (Norris 1991; Phillips 1989). There is no simple causal connection, but most forms of proportional representation make the overall gender balance visible and can make the imposition of gender quotas both less controversial and easier to achieve than in single-member constituencies. As in Britain, women's organisations in Israel are fighting for better representation and the secular parties are increasingly realising that women candidates can be vote winners. Unlike Britain, the list system means that women candidates can be adopted without requiring individual men to stand down, and some of the main secular parties have adopted gender quotas for their list. Combined with continued feminist activity and an increased awareness of gender issues, this led some to expect an increase in female representation in the 1996 election.

In this election, however, only nine women members were elected, a decrease of three from the previous Knesset, and fewer than in 1949 (Networking for Women 1996). This is partly because of a shift in favour of the Orthodox Jewish political parties which have always strongly opposed the political involvement of women. It also reflects the primacy of military and security matters; in this context, efforts to increase women's representation seemed irrelevant to many and positively dangerous to others. In such a hostile political environment, a level of representation which is only marginally lower than that in Britain or the United States might even be considered a success.

The first section of this chapter identified three key areas in which British feminist writers on citizenship are demanding government action or reform: first, employment and welfare policies that support women in their traditional caring role; second, policies that support women's economic independence; third, an electoral system that facilitates the use of gender-based quotas. In all of these areas, feminists could find some satisfaction in Israel, which seems in many ways much closer to Scandinavia than to Britain. Nevertheless, as we have seen, the result has not been any great reduction in gender inequalities or an increase in political representation. This does not mean that feminists have erred in identifying these factors. Rather, it is a reflection of other decidedly woman-unfriendly factors, specific to Israel. These include issues around Jewish national identity and the sense of demographic competition between Jews and Palestinians discussed above. Above all, the role of religion and the militarised nature of Israeli society create obstacles to women's equal citizenship which are not present in other western nations.

RELIGION AND THE RELIGIOUS COURTS

The status of religion in Israeli society and the extent to which Judaism is integral to official Israeli Jewish identity mean that religious interpretations and practices are not simply matters of personal belief (Goodman-Thau 1993). This is particularly true in the Orthodox Jewish community. Here, although some women are developing their own analyses, the rabbinical establishment has imposed an interpretation of the scriptures which opposes any idea of equality between men and women and which requires a high degree of sexual segregation. Such segregation gives Orthodox women a degree of control over their own lives (for example, by running their own schools) and provides the social links and woman-only spaces that secular women have at times struggled for. However, it denies women any public role in religious, community or political affairs. Women, therefore, may not conduct public prayers, become Orthodox rabbis or adjudicate in the rabbinical courts. Until the 1980s, Orthodox political parties instructed women not to use their vote, and women are still unable to hold office in these parties. Such teachings have influence beyond the estimated one-fifth of Israeli Jews who follow Orthodox teaching and religious observations, and mean that socialisation into traditional gender roles goes even deeper than in many western societies.

The opposition of Orthodox men to the public presence of women is not restricted to those within their own community. It creates difficulties for women seeking to enter public life that go beyond the usual problems faced by women in a male-dominated environment. (Similar issues for Muslim women in Britain are discussed by Afshar, Chapter 6 in this volume.) For Orthodox men, a woman in public life can represent a disruptive sexuality rather than another individual human being. As such, the presence of a woman can appear intolerable and generate extreme hostility: a member of the Orthodox-dominated Jerusalem City Council has heard an Orthodox member say of her own presence that he would rather fornicate with a pig than speak after a woman (Hoffman 1994).

Although Jewish religious parties receive only 10–15 per cent of the votes in national elections, they frequently hold the balance of power. The centrality of religious values has combined with the precarious position of coalition governments to mean that when women's demands appear to conflict with Orthodox Judaism, these demands are likely to be sacrificed. Such a sacrifice occurred in 1949 when the Prime Minister, Ben-Gurion, retained the support of the National Religious Party by agreeing to maintain the role of religious courts over personal law. This has significant consequences for all Israeli citizens, and it has been described as 'a compromise between socialist men and Orthodox men at the expense of women' (Swirski and Safir 1993: 12).

As with Judaism, the teachings of Islam on the role of women have been interpreted in many ways, and many Muslim feminists argue that their religion can offer much to women. For Palestinians in Israel whose culture is under threat, defence of their traditional values has, however, included a defence of women's subordinate role which has been justified on religious grounds (Hassan 1993; Mar'i and Mar'i 1993).

The progress of peace negotiations may mean that such attitudes affect the role of women in the Jewish community too: at the signing of the first peace agreement on 13 September 1993, the official Jewish–Palestinian youth delegation was, in response to Palestinian pressure, exclusively male. It may therefore be relevant to ask with Alice Shalvi of the Israeli Women's Network:

Will Israel now be influenced even further by religious fundamentalism
and outmoded preconceptions as to what constitutes women's 'rightful'
role in society? Will Islamic restrictions be added to those already exerted
by Jewish rabbinical authorities and ultra-orthodox political parties?

(Shalvi 1993: 11)

Western feminists have criticised the ways in which dominant political
discourse has artificially distinguished between the private world of
individuals and their families and the public world of citizenship. This
distinction, they argue, enables men to disregard the private inequalities
which inevitably underpin political practices and outcomes (an issue
discussed by Waylen, Chapter 8 in this volume.) The 1949 decision to retain
the religious courts for personal affairs meant that in Israel, this private–
public distinction was institutionalised in the legal system. All Israeli
citizens are bound by one set of state laws conferring rights in the public
worlds of politics and employment and another set of religious laws
governing their personal life. This means that in matters concerning
marriage and divorce, minority groups are governed by Muslim, Druze or
Christian courts and Jews by the rabbinical courts (secular marriage is not
possible in Israel, and all citizens have to register their religious affiliation).
The decisions of these religious courts have a higher status than ordinary
statutes such as the Women's Equal Rights Law of 1952. This means that
in Muslim families, it is the man who is the legal head of household and
who normally gets custody of the children in the event of divorce. For Jews,
it is only Orthodox Judaism and not Reform or Conservative Judaism that
has this privileged legal status. All Israeli Jewish women are therefore
subject to a legal system and a body of law in which only men are judges
and which is positively opposed to gender equality.

THE ARMED FORCES

The recent history of Israel means that the idea of the citizen-warrior is still
potent; military service is also a key route to political power. The exemption
of most Israeli Arabs from conscription reinforces the marginality of their
citizenship.[2] In contrast, Jewish women have played an active military role
both in founding and defending the state. They were involved in the first
Jewish defence organisation in 1909, they were particularly active in the
1947–9 struggle for independence (when some women led combat units)
and they remain eligible for conscription in the late 1990s (Bloom 1993).

The popular image of the young Israeli woman soldier stepping proudly
side by side with her male compatriots is, however, misleading. Although
Jewish women serve in the army, they do not do so on equal terms with

men: they are drafted for a shorter time than men and they are more likely to be granted exemption, only single women under 24 are liable for reserve duty and they are less likely than men to sign up for a career in the army. They are also ineligible for combat duty; such duty is a prerequisite for higher military office, and this means that women are ineligible for the top positions even in the fields of education or medicine. Unlike many male politicians, they are therefore unable to take a sideways step from military to political leadership.

The marginalisation of women in the military strengthens the idea that women cannot understand issues to do with defence and foreign policy and therefore weakens their claim to an equal stake in political life. It also reinforces their traditional role within the family. At a practical level, family life cannot be organised on the assumption that a man will be available to take his children to school or do the shopping, as Jewish men are likely to be called upon for reserve duty for at least a month every year. Perhaps more importantly, Jewish women are less able to complain about their own situation when men's responsibilities at times involve the risk of death. Compared with problems of national defence, feminist issues can appear of secondary importance and Israel's war footing 'imposes something close to self-censorship on women' (Waintrater 1993).

For some Israeli feminists, equality within the army is a central issue. Others, however, see militarism itself as a problem and argue that the values of a militarised, hierarchical society are antithetical to those of feminism and gender equality. Partly for this reason, women have in recent years played a prominent role in a whole range of grassroots peace movements and initiatives. Some of these have involved co-operation with Palestinian women and an awareness of women's peace activities in other nations, such as the British protests at Greenham Common (Chazan 1993; Pope 1993b, 1993c). Israeli women have, however, remained almost entirely absent from the peace negotiations.

WOMEN AND CITIZENSHIP: SOME LESSONS FROM ISRAEL

Jewish women in Israel have benefited from policies which some feminists in Britain see as a precondition for equitable citizenship. These gains owe much to women's own organisational efforts throughout the century, and also to a socialist tradition which acknowledges women's right to employment, understands the social importance of women's work within the family and accepts the need for collectivist solutions and state action to support women and improve their situation. However, as preceding sections have shown, apparently 'woman-friendly' policies in Israel are also a product of interlocking nationalistic, military and demographic pressures and are not aimed at all groups of women. These pressures have made the use of Jewish women's labour in employment and the armed force an economic and military necessity. They have also made clear the public importance of women's reproductive, domestic and caring roles; for Jewish women, these are seen as a matter for state support and encouragement rather than private, individual choice.

At the same time, the politics of nationalism and militarism have led to a celebration of traditionally male qualities and 'heroic virtues'. This has the effect of marginalising even Jewish women, whose prime role becomes that of producing and nurturing citizens (that is, warriors, full-time workers and politicians) rather than playing an active and independent role in their own right. This, combined with the influence of patriarchal religion, largely accounts for the failure of women to achieve the kind of breakthrough in political representation which has been achieved in the Scandinavian countries, which have similar social policies and political institutions.

Israeli-specific factors can also help explain why the earnings gap between men and women is higher than in other nations with similar policies. The importance of 'woman-friendly' social policies is nevertheless confirmed, as the earnings gap is much lower than in the United States, where such policies are lacking.

Israeli-specific factors cannot, however, fully account for all the inter-connected inequalities in employment and the home, for many of these are found in all western democracies. In particular, although men's lack of day-to-day family responsibilities is clearly exacerbated in Israel by their military service, it is not simply caused by it. In Israel as elsewhere, if male citizens continue to opt out of their caring responsibilities, women will continue to be disadvantaged in more public forms of citizenship participation. This kind of inequality is particularly difficult to eradicate and, to the extent that they are privileged by existing arrangements, men are likely to resist real change. Nevertheless, Israeli policies on parental leave and protection for part-time workers do provide the necessary starting point for such change, as does the strength and determination of the women's movement. Moreover, as some women realise a degree of economic independence and achieve a feminist input into decision-making, their domestic 'bargaining power' has been improved; this in turn may facilitate their participation in the public sphere.

A question mark remains, however, about the possible meaning of citizenship in a society that is as profoundly divided as Israel. Most obviously, the situation of the Palestinian minority is at best ambivalent and, even for the economically and socially privileged, falls far short of full membership of the mainstream community. Israeli Jews are also divided and stratified by overlapping ethnic, religious, cultural and class differences.

In this context, an improvement in the situation of a privileged minority of women might seem a rather dubious victory that ignores both the very real oppression suffered by many men and the specific oppression experienced by women in other groups.

Western academic feminism has in recent years become increasingly aware of issues around 'difference'. The development of post-structuralist theory has combined with accusations of racism and elitism to produce a self-conscious disengagement from earlier talk of 'sisterhood' and a reluctance to generalise about women's experience that extends to a questioning of the validity of the very term 'woman'. From this perspective, some sections of the Israeli women's movement can appear too ready to equate the interests of 'women' with 'women like us' (in this case, middle-class, Ashkenazie Jewish women) (Swirski 1993). In practice, however, many feminist organisations in the west are also vulnerable to charges of elitism and marginalisation. It may therefore be that the dramatic nature of the divisions in Israel can, by enabling western feminists to see some aspects of their own society 'writ large', provide a salutary reminder of these dangers. Feminist analysis has clearly raised issues that provide a fundamental challenge to earlier conceptions of citizenship. Although it is also increasingly recognising other sources of difference in theory, it is important that such understandings are translated into political practice if new women-friendly conceptions of citizenship are to be more genuinely inclusive than the old.

ACKNOWLEDGMENTS

Much of the material for this chapter was gathered on a Women's Studies Tour to Israel in April 1994, funded by the Academic Study Group: Israel and the Middle East. My thanks are due to all those involved in the organisation of this intensive learning experience, to the women we met and to the other members of the tour. This is a revised and expanded version of a paper "Women and Citizenship: some lessons from Israel" published in *Political Studies*, September 1996 (Blackwell).

NOTES

1 The Green Line, which was established in 1967 by the United Nations, divides Israel from the occupied West Bank territories.
2 The 'loyal' Druze and Beduin minority communities are an exception. It is, however, only men in these communities who may serve in the army. Women are excluded partly because military service would be contrary to their traditional role and partly because they lack the required level of education (Yuval-Davis 1985).

144 *Valerie Bryson*

REFERENCES

Abdo, N. (1994) 'Nationalism and feminism: Palestinian women and the Intefada – no going back?', in V. M. Moghadam (ed.) *Gender and National Identity: Women and Politics in Muslim Societies*, London: Zed.

Adam, B. (1989) 'Feminist social theory needs time', *Sociological Review* 37(3): 458–73.

Agassi, J. B. (1993) 'How much power do Israeli women have?', in B. Swirski and M. R. Safir (eds) *Calling the Equality Bluff: Women in Israel*, New York and London: Teachers College Press.

Bloom, A. R. (1993) 'Women in the defence forces', in B. Swirski and M. R. Safir (eds) *Calling the Equality Bluff: Women in Israel*, New York and London: Teachers College Press.

Bryson, V. and Lister, R. (1994) *Women, Citizenship and Social Policy*, Bradford: University of Bradford Applied Social Studies/Joseph Rowntree Foundation.

Chazan, N. (1993) 'Israeli women and peace activism', in B. Swirski and M. R. Safir (eds) *Calling the Equality Bluff: Women in Israel*, New York and London: Teachers College Press.

Espanioly, N. (1993) 'Palestinian women in Israel respond to the Intefada', in B. Swirski and M. R. Safir (eds) *Calling the Equality Bluff: Women in Israel*, New York and London: Teachers College Press.

Freedman, M. (1993) 'Breaking new ground in the Knesset', in B. Swirski and M. R. Safir (eds) *Calling the Equality Bluff: Women in Israel*, New York and London: Teachers College Press.

Goodman-Thau, E. (1993) 'Challenging the roots of religious patriarchy and shaping identity and community', in B. Swirski and M. R. Safir (eds) *Calling the Equality Bluff: Women in Israel*, New York and London: Teachers College Press.

Grossman, D. (1993) *Sleeping on a Wife: Conversations with Palestinians in Israel*, London: Picador.

Hassan, M. (1993) 'Growing up female and Palestinian in Israel', in B. Swirski and M. R. Safir (eds) *Calling the Equality Bluff: Women in Israel*, New York and London: Teachers College Press.

Hoffman, A. (1994) Talk given to the Women's Studies Tour by Jerusalem Council Member Anat Hoffman.

Israel Information Centre (1993) *Facts about Israel*, Jerusalem.

Israel Women's Network (1993) *For Justice and Equality*, Israel Women's Network information pamphlet, Jerusalem.

Izraeli, D. (1993) 'Women and work: from collective to career', in B. Swirski and M. R. Safir (eds) *Calling the Equality Bluff: Women in Israel*, New York and London: Teachers College Press.

Jones, K. (1990) 'Citizenship in a gender-friendly polity', *Signs* 15(4): 781–812.

Katz, R. (1993) 'Jewish and Druze war widows', in B. Swirski and M. R. Safir (eds) *Calling the Equality Bluff: Women in Israel*, New York and London: Teachers College Press.

Kessel, J. (1994) 'Sanctuary where women can escape their doom', *Guardian* 5 September.

Lahav, P. (1978) 'Raising the status of women through law: the case of Israel', *Signs* 3(1): 193–209.

Lister, R. (1990) 'Women, economic dependency and citizenship', *Journal of Social Policy* 19(4): 445–67.

—— (1992) 'Citizenship engendered', *Critical Social Policy* 32: 445–67.

—— (1993) 'Tracing the contours of women's citizenship', *Policy and Politics* 21(1): 3–16.

Mar'i, M. M. and Mar'i, S. K. (1993) 'The role of women as change agents in Arab society in Israel', in B. Swirski and M. R. Safir (eds) *Calling the Equality Bluff: Women in Israel*, New York and London: Teachers College Press.

Najjar, O. A. (1992) 'Between nationalism and feminism: the Palestinian answer', in J. Bystydzienski (ed.) *Women Transforming Politics: Worldwide Strategies for Empowerment*, Bloomington, IN: Indiana University Press.

Networking for Women (1996) *Networking for Women, A Quarterly Publication of the Israel Women's Network* 9(3).

Norris, P. (1991) *Politics and Sexual Equality: The Comparative Position of Women in Western Democracies*, Edinburgh: Polygon.

Pahl, J. (1989) *Money and Marriage*, London: Macmillan.

Phillips, A. (1989) *Engendering Democracy*, Cambridge: Polity.

—— (1991) 'Citizenship and feminist theory', in G. Andrews (ed.) *Citizenship*, London: Lawrence & Wishart.

Pope, J. (1993a) 'A conflict of interests: a case study of Na'amat', in B. Swirski and M. R. Safir (eds) *Calling the Equality Bluff: Women in Israel*, New York and London: Teachers College Press.

—— (1993b) 'The place of women in Israeli society', in K. Kyle and J. Peters (eds) *Whither Israel? The Domestic Challenges*, London and New York: I. B. Taurus.

—— (1993c) 'The emergence of a joint Israeli–Palestinian Women's Peace Movement during the Intefada', in H. Afshar (ed.) *Women in the Middle East*, London: Macmillan.

Raday, F. (1993) 'Women, work and the law', in B. Swirski and M. R. Safir (eds) *Calling the Equality Bluff: Women in Israel*, New York and London: Teachers College Press.

Rakba, S. A. (1993) 'Arab women in the Israeli labour market', in B. Swirski and M. R. Safir (eds) *Calling the Equality Bluff: Women in Israel*, New York and London: Teachers College Press.

Safir, M. R. (1993) 'Religion, tradition and public policy give the family first priority', in B. Swirski and M. R. Safir (eds) *Calling the Equality Bluff: Women in Israel*, New York and London: Teachers College Press.

Shalvi, A. (1993) 'From where I sit . . . the chairwoman's view', *Networking for Women: A Quarterly Publication of the Israel Women's Network* 6(4): 11.

—— (1994) Talk given to Women's Studies Tour, Jerusalem.

Swirski, B. (1993) 'Israeli feminism old and new', in B. Swirski and M. R. Safir (eds) *Calling the Equality Bluff: Women in Israel*, New York and London: Teachers College Press.

Swirski, B. and Safir, M. (1993) 'Living in a Jewish state: National, ethnic and religious implications', in B. Swirski and M. R. Safir (eds) *Calling the Equality Bluff: Women in Israel*, New York and London: Teachers College Press.

Waintrater, R. (1993) 'Living in a state of seige', in B. Swirski and M. R. Safir (eds) *Calling the Equality Bluff: Women in Israel*, New York and London: Teachers College Press.

Young, I. M. (1989) 'Polity and gender difference: a critique of the ideal of universal citizenship', *Ethics* 99(2): 250–74.

Yuval-Davis, N. (1985) 'Front and rear: the sexual division of labour in the Israeli Army', *Feminist Studies* 11(3): 650–75.

—— (1989) 'National reproduction and the demographic race in Israel', in N. Yuval-Davis and F. Anthias (eds) *Woman-Nation-State*, London: Macmillan.

8 Women's activism, authoritarianism and democratisation in Chile

Georgina Waylen

This chapter explores the changing and complex dynamics of women's political activism in the context of the transition from authoritarianism and the subsequent consolidation of competitive electoral politics in Chile.[1] The military coup of 11 September 1973 brought an end to the three-year parliamentary attempt to create a 'peaceful road to socialism' by the Popular Unity coalition led by Salvador Allende. The military Junta headed by General Pinochet then unleashed a period of unprecedented repression as 'subversives' were targeted as part of the savage war against communism promulgated by the doctrine of 'national security'. This was combined with the implementation of New Right economic policies, akin to structural adjustment, overseen by the US-trained economists, the 'Chicago Boys'. While these policies were credited with producing high rates of economic growth by the mid-1980s, they were also responsible for two deep recessions and high levels of poverty, suffering and unemployment among much of the Chilean population (Raczynski and Serrano 1985). Despite attempts to institutionalise the regime and depoliticise society, the mass protests of 1983 spurred the Junta to allow some liberalisation which culminated in Pinochet losing a plebiscite in 1988 when the populace were asked to vote 'yes' or 'no' to Pinochet continuing in power. His defeat led to presidential and congressional elections in 1989 and the inauguration, in 1990, of the Concertación government, a centrist coalition of Christian Democrats and 'renovated socialists' with the Christian Democrat Patricio Aylwin as president.[2] The Concertación subsequently was re-elected for another term with Eduardo Frei, another Christian Democrat, as its new president. This transition to democracy has seen the reconstitution of a strong and traditional party system and the subsequent demobilisation of popular movements including many women's movements. While the high rates of economic growth have been maintained, the transition has been narrowly defined to focus on the political to the exclusion of the social and economic: both civilian governments have maintained the liberal economic policies of the previous military government and have a narrow economic focus on social questions such as poverty alleviation.

One consequence of the combination of authoritarianism and economic recession in the late 1970s and 1980s in Chile, as in other parts of Latin America, was the (re-)emergence of women's movements which operated largely outside of the conventional political arena (Alvarez 1990a; Jaquette 1994). Indeed, the repression of the male-dominated conventional political arena through the banning and restriction of political parties, congress and trade unions created the 'political space' which allowed women's activities to achieve a high profile outside of it. The locus of political activity had to shift from an institutional basis, that is, organisation on the basis of the workplace or political party, to a community basis where women often found it easier to participate. The identification of women as apolitical and therefore women's activities as not being political, allowed many women certain initial room for manoeuvre unavailable to men before their activities were seen as subversive. At the same time the impact of the debt crisis and the resulting structural adjustment packages, which cut welfare spending, increased poverty and unemployment and reduced real wages, pushed women into adopting collective survival strategies.

However, it is impossible to talk of *a* homogeneous women's movement in the Chilean context as the diversity of women's movements is very visible. During the authoritarian period several major types of oppositional women's movements stand out, although the sometimes shifting boundaries and links between them make clear delineations difficult. The human rights groups and the urban popular organisations form two of these, and feminist groups yet another. These heterogeneous women's movements played an important role in bringing about the initial opening at a time when the political initiative lay outside the conventional arena, and led to the inauguration of the transition to civilian rule (Waylen 1994). During the consolidation of democratic politics it is clear that some women's organisations, often made up of elite and professional women, campaigning around gender-based issues have had an (however limited) influence on the state, political parties and policy agendas. Others, often in popular movements, active around social and economic issues have become more marginal to the processes of consolidation. It is clear that some women, some movements and some strategies are better placed to influence competitive electoral politics than others. The Chilean case demonstrates that, while alliances can exist, it is important not to assume the existence of shared collective identities among women (an issue discussed by Yuval-Davis, Chapter 9 in this volume). Furthermore, in the examination of women's movements, any analysis of 'identity' cannot prioritise experience and agency without considering structures and the wider context within which movements operate. It is possible to understand these various outcomes only through an analysis of the different movements in the context of the wider processes of transition and consolidation and the interaction between them. This chapter begins with a discussion of the women's movements active during the authoritarian period in Chile, and goes on to analyse their place in the unfolding processes of political change.

WOMEN'S MOVEMENTS

Both the Chilean human rights groups and urban popular organisations had women as the majority of their members and pressed primarily social and economic demands. They also involved the politicisation of women's social roles, that is, as mothers and household providers, as women entered the public sphere on the basis of these roles. This entry occurred in conjunction with the military's attempts to abolish the public sphere which led to the politicisation of the private sphere. In a different context, Schirmer has argued that, through involvement in these activities, women have gained a gendered consciousness of political motherhood which cannot be classified in a rigid dichotomy between practical and strategic gender interests (Schirmer 1993: 60).[3] Feminist groups involved women organising together as women to press gender-based demands, often seen as conforming to strategic gender interests (Molyneux 1985). However, as we shall see, the emergence of popular feminism is evidence that too rigid a dichotomy between different women's movements seen as organising either around practical or strategic gender interests is unhelpful.

Human rights organisations

Human rights groups emerged in several Latin American countries, often growing out of the experience that many relatives had in trying to ascertain the whereabouts of missing members of their families. The best-known human rights groups are the Madres of Plaza de Mayo formed in Argentina in April 1977 (Fisher 1989). Similar groups, namely the Agrupación de Familiares de Detenidos-Desaparacidos (the association of the families of the detained and disappeared), emerged in Chile in late 1974 and 1975, when relatives, primarily women, kept meeting each other while they were making the rounds of the prisons, police stations and government offices trying to discover the whereabouts of their disappeared relatives (Chuckryk 1989). It soon became clear that the accepted machinery of the public sphere – the police, law courts and habeas corpus – would fail them and different action was necessary in order to try and effect the return of their missing relatives with the help of church organisations, particularly the Vicaría. By 1986 there were five different Agrupaciones – relatives of the disappeared, relegated (those in internal exile), executed, exiled, and political prisoners.

It has been argued that the Agrupaciones had a more narrowly 'political' background than the Madres in Argentina because they grew out of a more politicised society and some of the members had a left-wing background (Schirmer 1989: 17). Valenzuela (1990) argued that the Chilean human rights groups were so tied to the political parties of the Left that this prevented the emergence of a gender identity. However, the Agrupaciones resembled the Madres in some of their practice and language. The organisations were comprised mainly of women, who argued that they were not primarily politically motivated nor were they feminists. One member claimed, evoking notions of acceptable motherhood rather than radical activism, 'We are mothers not women. . . . we are looking for our children. Our fight is for our families not to be forgotten and to reclaim justice from the state' (Schirmer 1989: 21). Demonstrations were held by the groups outside the Moneda Palace every Friday afternoon during military rule. The participants carried photographs of their missing relatives. This essentially personal emphasis was used in other ways, a moving book of testimonies from the families of fifty-seven missing women and children was published in 1986 which included their life histories, details of their disappearance, photographs and poems by them (Agrupación 1986). These activities were very clearly oppositional and therefore were defined as being political and subversive. However, the Agrupaciones, like the Madres, could use the military's very traditional notions of women's proper role, that they should be at home, caring for their children, as the pivot of their protest. They were prevented from fulfilling this task, they argued, by the disappearance of their children and therefore they had to search for them.

Feminist academics have interpreted these protests in a variety of different ways. Are these activities regressive in that they involve women entering the public sphere on the basis of their traditional roles (i.e. motherhood) rather than challenging or subverting them? Or is this sort of protest transformative in that it challenges the dominant discourses about motherhood and womanhood, as passive and private, through the use of public space in protests (Waylen 1992)? In the face of charges of essentialism, those influenced by notions of difference, political and revolutionary motherhood argue that this sort of activity is transformative and the foundation for both a new form of politics based on an 'ethic of care' and the development of gendered political identities (Bouvard 1994; Elshtain 1992: 120). Analysis has also focused on the innovative form as well as content of the protests through their use of symbolic and meta-phorical devices highlighting the importance of staging and performance in political action (Franco 1994).

Urban popular organisations

The second major type of organisation to emerge during the period of dictatorship were the urban popular organisations. These movements grew up primarily in the *poblaciones*, the poor and working-class districts, and concentrated on the 'politics of everyday life'. The focus of many of the activities of these organisations was social and economic, particularly around consumption issues, and organised on a neighbourhood basis (Valdes and Weinstein 1989). Schild (1991: 138) estimates that over 90 per cent of those participating in these organisations in Santiago, the capital city, were women.

A variety of different types of organisations was formed. Many implemented collective survival strategies, often in the face of repression, recession and cuts in welfare services, either through income generation or the provision of services, frequently operating under the auspices of the church and non-governmental organisations (NGOs) and often staffed by middle-class feminist professionals (Valdes and Weinstein 1993). Others attempted to pressurise the state, either at a national or local level, to provide services which were lacking in those neighbourhoods (Arteaga 1988). The popular organisations which implemented collective survival strategies were termed popular economic organisations (OEPs). By 1982, in the face of a deep recession and cuts in welfare services, 500 OEPs had sprung up in the *poblaciones* of Santiago and this number had grown to 1,125 in 1985. These OEPs have been divided into four different sorts and women predominated in the two most numerous types, while 43 per cent of the total number were women only (Hardy 1985). Organisations centred around the consumption of food made up 48 per cent of the total. The *ollas comunes* (communal soup pots) dealt with the most immediate needs, through women collectively providing a large number of families with meals, often with the help of the church (Fisher 1993). Other organisations of this type included buying committees, where women joined together to buy basic necessities in bulk and therefore more cheaply.

The second major type of popular organisation concerned with collective survival strategies were those concerned with income generation. *Organizaciones laboral-productivas*, those producing goods and services for exchange in the market, made up around one-third of the total in 1985 (Hardy 1985). Of these, 62 per cent were women only and 65 per cent of the total workers employed were women. More than 50 per cent of this type of OEP took the form of artisanal or craft workshops. The product of some of these workshops which became best-known abroad was the *arpillera* (tapestries, which were made by women, depicting scenes from everyday life and often bearing oppositional messages). Many were produced by women whose relatives had disappeared, and were sold abroad under the auspices of the Catholic church (Agosin 1990). The government had its own non-oppositional ones made through CEMA-Chile which were then sold to tourists through government-controlled outlets. About 10 per cent of these OEPs took the form of communal bakeries. Other related activities included running crèches which enabled other women to engage in income generating activity (Fisher 1993).

These activities were predominantly carried out by poor and working-class women acting in terms of their roles as mothers, household providers and managers, so class and gender identities were interacting. Many analysts have argued that it is a mistake to see these activities as simply economic. For a variety of reasons, they have to be seen as political. First, although there is evidence that many of the women involved did not initially see their activities as political as this was something which men did in the institutional public sphere (Caldeira 1990), but as simply part of doing their 'duty' and fulfilling their family responsibilities, changes occurred both in the ways in which they saw their activities and in the ways they were seen from outside. The military defined most collective activities in the *poblaciones* as subversive, particularly at the height of the mass protests in the mid-1980s. Women began to see their collective activities as 'political' because they were seen as such by the regime. Many of those women involved saw the kitchens as an important visible protest because through their existence they were demonstrating the extent of hunger and unemployment (Fisher 1993). Second, these activities involved women acting collectively and in the public arena. One result of this experience of organising was greater self-awareness and the emergence of a more collective and political consciousness (Walker 1985). With it came a sense of empowerment and a different understanding of certain gender issues (Schild 1992). Alvarez (1990b) describes a similar process in two neighbourhoods of São Paulo where women initially met at church-sponsored mothers' clubs which formed part of the network of the Christian base communities. The consequences of meeting and organising together were that gradually the women extended the range of their discussions and activities. As a result of this, the women's group felt they could no longer remain a church-sponsored group if their interests ranged over topics such as sexuality and reproductive rights and they also became active in other organisations such as the daycare campaign (Alvarez 1990b). Schild (1991) argues that *pobladoras* often came into contact with professionals, often feminists, who influenced their attitudes and actions forming a 'symbolic network'. As we shall see, these experiences have helped the development of a popular feminism, and added weight to the arguments that it is imposing a false dichotomy to see women's involvement in urban popular movements as being solely in pursuit of practical gender interests.

Feminist organisations

The period of military rule also saw the re-emergence of self-consciously feminist organisations in Chile. Earlier in the century Chile had pre-dominantly middle-class suffrage movements which disappeared after women gained the vote. The country then entered what the Chilean feminist Julieta Kirkwood called a period of 'feminist silence' as the majority of women active in politics were involved in conventional party politics and not organising as women (Kirkwood 1990). In the 1970s and 1980s feminist groups began to form, engaging in a variety of activities around issues of women's inequality and subordination (Sternbach *et al.* 1992). Initially many women who became active in feminist organisations had been involved in the Left but had become disillusioned because of the lack of attention given to gender issues and now began to develop analyses which went beyond the parameters of class and imperialism favoured by the Left. Feminists such as Julieta Kirkwood began to make the connections between authoritarianism and patriarchy, linking authoritarianism in the home with that in wider society (Kirkwood 1990).

The feminist movement which emerged was not homogeneous but made up instead of diverse groups with changing relationships to one another (Gaviola *et al.* 1994). The Círculo de Estudios de la Mujer (CEM) founded in 1977 under the indirect auspices of the Catholic church through the Academia de Humanismo Cristiano (AHC) was one of the first and most significant. After the group lost the support of the AHC, CEM divided into two organisations, Centro de Estudios de la Mujer (CEM) which con-centrated on the analysis of women's subordination through research and seminars, and La Morada which concentrated more on activism, running workshops and courses. Some groups have been characterised as 'rights-based'; others such as La Morada as having 'radical feminist' tendencies, in part because of its reluctance to engage with mainstream politics; while yet more such as CODEM have been more identified with the left. The 1970s and 1980s saw an evolving and often tense relationship between the so-called *feministas* (women identified primarily as feminists) and *políticas* (women active in political parties and identified primarily as party activists, often on the left). As we shall see, umbrella organisations, such as MEMCH 83, named after an earlier suffrage organisation and Mujeres por la Vida (formed in 1983) were also created to co-ordinate the various activities of these diverse groups into more of a national movement. A number of feminist demonstrations, for example, around International Women's Day, formed some of the first visible protests to occur under military rule. However, many of the feminist organisations have been seen as primarily made up of educated affluent professional women, who despite the influence of the left, campaigned narrowly around gender issues. The relationship between class and gender within feminist organisations has therefore been a contested one.

Popular feminism

This period also saw the emergence of 'popular feminism'. This grew out of the experience of working-class and poor women organising and campaigning self-consciously as women in community organisations of the types described above, who through their experiences of organising around issues of consumption and collective survival began to focus on issues more often identified with feminism such as reproductive rights, sexuality and domestic violence and set up women's centres in working-class areas. Popular women's organisations emerged, such as the Domitilas (named after the Bolivian activist) and MOMUPO (Movimiento de Mujeres Pobladoras), which while founded in 1982 refused the title 'feminist' until 1985. From these elements has evolved a notion of 'popular feminism' (Gaviola *et al.* 1994)

However, popular feminism is seen by its advocates as being different in its concerns from middle-class feminism (Molina 1989: 142). This latter movement is felt by some to be an import from the United States, and also to have ignored the issues of greatest concern to women of the popular classes, primarily economic survival (Schild 1991). Many women espousing popular feminism argue that they want to work together with men and to try and help and preserve the family, something which they do not see middle-class feminism as doing. Middle-class feminism is therefore seen as predominantly concerned with gender issues to the exclusion of class issues (Schild 1992). Middle-class women, it is argued, can solve many of their problems through the deployment of economic resources such as paying for household workers to fulfil their domestic responsibilities, and their domestic servants are women from the popular classes, reducing the chance of common interests existing between poor and middle-class women. Indeed, many women feel that they have been used by middle-class feminist organisations in the past, for example as 'cannon fodder' in demonstrations. However, they do believe that there can be some links with middle-class feminist movements; alliances are possible but they have to be constructed carefully and certainly do not exist automatically (Fisher 1993). This concept of popular feminism is perhaps closer to Mohanty's (1991) notion of Third World feminism and its relationship to other struggles against domination than the often more rights-orientated middle-class-based feminist movements.

It is now possible to see how these different women's movements both interacted together and with the reconstituting political system during the period of transition and democratisation. The most helpful way of doing this is by examining the changing role and actions of the different women's movements during the transition from authoritarianism and consolidation of competitive electoral politics during the first two civilian governments.

THE BREAKDOWN OF AUTHORITARIANISM AND PERIOD OF SOCIAL MOBILISATION 1983–6

The year 1983 saw the emergence of a mass opposition movement in Chile, moving away from the pattern of sporadic and isolated protests which had been occurring since the military *coup* of 1973, and marked the beginning of the widespread reconstitution of civil society. The mass mobilisations were seen by many as providing the key both to overthrowing Pinochet and his authoritarian regime, and to the creation of a new type of more open and democratic politics. Also running alongside the mass mobilisations was the re-emergence of the political parties whose activities became increasingly central in the opposition movement (Garretón 1989; Petras and Leiva 1988).

During this period of mass opposition to the dictatorship, diverse women's movements had a high visibility. The human rights organisations, the Agrupaciones, highlighted disappearances and other abuses perpetrated by the military government; popular movements, active around social and economic issues, grew rapidly in response to the severe economic crisis faced by Chile; and feminist movements, including 'popular feminist' groups, campaigning around gender inequality (re-)emerged onto the public scene (Arteaga 1988; Kirkwood 1990; Valenzuela 1991). Feminists played a visible role in the opposition, participating in the mass mobilisations, days of protest and organising demonstrations for International Women's Day.

Once political parties began to reconstitute, all social movements (including feminist ones) were under pressure to decide on a strategy: whether it was to be autonomy from or integration into the unfolding political process (Valenzuela 1990). Some feminists decided on integration as the best way of pursuing a feminist agenda and moved into the political parties. They tended to be middle-class professional women, and they were active in the more moderate parties of the Centre and renovated Left. The Christian Democrats were pressed by a group of professional women working in conjunction with the women's department of the party, who produced a set of proposals for inclusion in the party's *proyecto alternativo* in 1984. Women's sections were set up in some of these political parties; in

1986 the Federacion de Mujeres Socialistas (FMS) was established in one faction of the Socialist Party to help increase the influence of feminism in national politics.

The political opposition formed into two groups in 1983, the moderate Alianza Democratica (AD), which increasingly favoured a strategy of *negociacion* (negotiation), and the left-wing Movimiento Democratico Popular (MDP) which advocated *ruptura* – the violent overthrow of the military dictatorship. Women's organisations tried to remain united in the face of a divided political opposition through broad umbrella movements such as Mujeres por la Vida, which attracted over 10,000 women to its first meeting in 1983. It campaigned using the slogan 'Democracia en el Pais y en la Casa' (democracy in the country and in the home), underlining the feminist demand that democracy would have to be rethought if it really was to include women. Despite the efforts to prevent it, party factionalism did have an impact on women's organisations: as the umbrella organisation MEMCH 83 became more associated with the radical strategy of mobilisation associated with the MDP, for example, many of the feminist and more centrist women's groups left it (Molina 1989).

Mujeres por la Vida also played a role in the Asemblea de la Civilidad, a broad and moderate opposition front opposing the dictatorship formed in 1986. A women's petition was included in the Demanda de Chile, a document submitted to the military government in 1986 and (the feminist and socialist) Maria Antioneta Saa sat in the assembly as the women's representative. However, in a trend which was to recur, it was the middle-class women's organisations which became more integrated into national politics and some popular women's organisations felt Mujeres por la Vida did not represent them in the assembly (Angelo 1990).

THE TRANSITION BEGINS AND POLITICAL PARTIES REGAIN HEGEMONY 1987–9

In this period, two events set the tone for the transition to competitive electoral politics and had important implications for the nature of the civilian government which could take power in Chile. First, as the military regime began to allow a limited political opening, the political parties gained control over the unfolding process to the detriment of the social movements. Second, the Centre and Centre-Left parties decided that a change of government would not be achieved solely through the process of social mobilisation and moved towards a strategy of reaching agreement with the military government, that is, a negotiated transition through pacts made within the political elite. The Centre and Centre-Left parties became the dominant force and negotiation the dominant strategy within the transition.

The Left and other organisations, such as human rights groups and popular organisations, not adhering to the strategy of *negociacion* but *ruptura*, became increasingly marginalised in this middle-class transition of negotiated pacts. In 1988 a plebiscite was held in which people voted yes or no to Pinochet continuing as president. As a result of his defeat, competitive elections were held in 1989.

Women's organisations were also affected by these dynamics. The questions of what role they should play in relation to wider political developments became even more pressing. These developments, in combination with the experience of the Asamblea, reinforced the belief of some feminists that more than ever it was necessary to enter the political process, while others decided to remain outside (Molina 1990). Much of the feminist movement reorientated itself and debated the ways in which women should 'do politics' (*hacer politica*), the alliances they should make and the aims they should have. Some organisations such as La Morada remained sceptical about the benefits that a formally democratic government would bring women in terms of any real shift in the balance of power between the sexes (Molina 1989). Meanwhile others argued that the experience of the Pliego and the Assembly demonstrated several things: the shortcomings and deficiencies of women's politics; the difficulty of articulating women's demands in formal politics; and the lack of receptivity of political parties and social organisations to women's demands. The conclusion drawn by many was that while the pressing task was to enter the political process, there was a need to preserve autonomy at the same time.

Some feminists made increased efforts to enter politics during this period and appeared to make significant headway within the political parties of the Centre and Centre-Left. The emergence of a feminist agenda was most noticeable in the Christian Democrats (PDC), the newly formed Humanist Party, the Partido por la Democracia (PPD), the new umbrella party of the renovated Left, and the Socialists (PS). It was these parties which formed the Concertación, the Centre-Left coalition, which contested the 1989 elections and was in many ways a continuation of the moderate alliance tentatively established after 1983. Women had the greatest visibility and presence within renovated socialism: the FMS continued its work within the socialist party and, after its formation, in the PPD, putting forward proposals for inclusion in the opposition's programme. However, Molina (1989) has argued that the proposals of the Christian Democrat women were some of the most fully elaborated of all the opposition, but some of these (e.g. around reproductive rights and divorce) conflicted with the basic moral and religious ideas which inspire Christian Democracy.

Old tensions which had existed between the *feministas* (feminists) and the *politicas* (female activists within political parties) were reduced as many *politicas* became more sympathetic to the aims of feminists. Indeed Serrano (1990) has argued that during this period, tensions were transformed into a debate about the styles and options which were established as alternatives. Many women activists began to value an autonomous women's axis whose existence could help them in their activities in political parties (Angelo 1990). However, while several parties were prepared to make general statements about women's equality they were not prepared seriously to restructure power to allow women greater access to decision-making processes within them, often segregating them in separate organisations. The FMS had little actual power to change the actions of party organisations. The PPD adopted a quota system for women, but ignored it on occasions, such as in its political council and in the selection of candidates (Saa 1990).

The perception of women's continued lack of influence in the run-up to the 1988 plebiscite and the selection of very few women candidates (around 5 per cent of the total) for subsequent elections provided the major impetus for the creation of the autonomous Concertación de Mujeres por la Democracia in 1988. It was formed by women from a wide range of parties in the Concertación (the coalition contesting the elections) together with independent feminists (including academics, and activists, many of whom were middle-class professionals). The Concertación de Mujeres can be seen as growing both out of a tradition of attempts to create a united women's movement to influence the political agenda and out of the attempts of feminists to influence the Centre and Centre-Left political parties. However, as had been the case with some of the earlier attempts to create a united movement, some women active in the popular organisations again felt that the Concertación de Mujeres did not represent their interests (Angelo 1990).

The Concertación de Mujeres had a threefold aim: first, to raise women's issues on the national political scene, second, to work in presidential and parliamentary campaigns on behalf of the Concertación, and third, to formulate a programme on women for future democratic government. These proposals were presented to the Concertación as demands and most of them were incorporated into its electoral programme (Montecino and Rosetti 1990). The visibility of women's movements during all phases of the transition in combination with the activities of feminists within Centre-Left parties had meant that those political parties felt that they could not ignore the demands of the Concertación de Mujeres. The Concertación was now committed to 'fully enforce women's rights considering the new role of women in society, overcoming any form of discrimination', while 'enforcing the measures required to adequately protect the family'. These goals were to be achieved through first, legal changes: improving women's legal position; second, social participation: the incorporation of women into the political system and labour market; and third, the creation of national machinery at state level which would propose policy and oversee its implementation by other ministries.

These proposals came out of the strategy of direct engagement of parts of the Chilean feminist movement with the political process and it is highly unlikely that, without this pressure, the Concertación would have adopted these ideas. According to Maria Elena Valenzuela (1992) (an academic, feminist activist and later part of SERNAM) members of the Concertación de Mujeres assumed that the newly elected government (and by implication the state) was a gender-neutral tool which could be used in gender-based ways, that is, that engaging with the state would be a relatively straight-forward process to bring about an expansion of rights and democratic procedures through which women would also be incorporated as full citizens. There was also an assumption that relationships with women's organisations outside the state would be relatively unproblematic. Neither of these two assumptions has been borne out in practice.

THE CONSOLIDATION OF COMPETITIVE ELECTORAL POLITICS 1990–6

The resurrection of a conventional party political system and the return to a rather restricted form of electoral politics have resulted in a continuation of trends, such as the marginalisation of certain sectors like the traditional left, that were becoming apparent in the run-up to the transfer of power. The Concertación has maintained the neo-liberal economic model of the previous regime, but combined this with efforts to repay the 'social debt' through increased spending on welfare such as health and education and new policy initiatives to help alleviate the legacy of poverty inherited from the military government. Despite the constraints which result from the nature of the pacted transition, such as an electoral system which favours the Right together with Pinochet's continuing role as chief of the armed forces, some changes have occurred, even if they have not lived up to the hopes of some women activists. It is possible to make an assessment by looking first at women in formal politics, then at state policy before examining women's movements active outside conventional politics.

Formal politics

Fewer women had seats in parliament in 1990 than immediately prior to the military *coup*. Only seven (three of whom had been prominent members of the Concertación de Mujeres) women deputies (of a total of a hundred and twenty) took office in 1990, forming just under 6 per cent of the total (as against 9.3 per cent in 1973), together with three of the forty-seven senators (one of whom was appointed by the military). In Aylwin's government the only woman at cabinet level was responsible for SERNAM and only three of the twenty-seven vice-ministers were women. Despite the existence of a campaign 'Mas mujeres al parlamento', fewer women were mobilised around the elections in 1993 than had been in 1989, except to ensure the election of the feminist and socialist Maria Antonieta Saa to represent the district where she had been mayor. However, the second parliament does have nine women deputies (8 per cent of the total) and some women who had been expected to win safe seats narrowly lost. Frei has two women at cabinet level. In addition to the director of SERNAM, the Minister of Justice (previously head of SERNAM) is also a woman. More women stood as candidates at the local level; 12 per cent of councillors elected in 1992 were women.

Despite these low figures, the majority of political parties continue to pay lip-service to the need for greater participation by women in formal politics, including some efforts by the Concertación to increase the number of women deputies.[4] However, despite the large number of women party activists at the grassroots level, which ranges from about 40 per cent of the total for the parties of the Concertación to between 50 and 60 per cent of the right-wing parties, there are few women present in central executive and governing bodies.[5] Two parties, the PPD and the Socialists, have a system of positive action, in the form of quotas of 20 and 25 per cent respectively to increase the number of women in party bodies, and the Christian Democrats are coming under pressure to adopt a similar formula. While the numbers of women have now reached these figures at many levels, many women within the PS and PPD agree that they do not form a 'critical mass' and in fact act as a ceiling so that, once reached, the numbers are not surpassed (Saa 1996). Disquiet has also been expressed about the function-ing of women's organisations within political parties. On the instigation of women activists, the Socialist Party created a vice-presidency for women in 1992 to make gender-related concerns more central to the party, as it was felt that the FMS, the women's organisation, had become ghettoised and was doing little to advance the position of women within the PS (Pollarolo 1996). Despite the longstanding activism of many feminists in political parties, particularly in the Centre and Centre-Left, party structures are still resistant to the increased participation of women at all levels.

State policy

The major way in which the Concertación has tried to implement its programme on women has been through the creation (by law rather than presidential decree) of the Servicio Nacional de la Mujer (SERNAM) modelled on similar bodies in Spain and Brazil and headed, after pressure from women's groups, by a woman at cabinet level. After right-wing opposition, its functions, including its ability to execute programmes, and size were reduced (Macaulay 1995). Many of its staff are activists and academics rather than civil servants and some were involved in drawing up the Concertación de Mujeres, original proposals. While without prior experience in the day-to-day running of the administration many staff are members of Chile's political class with close ties to Concertación politicians. Inside SERNAM divisions with the Concertación have also been replicated for example between the Christian Democrats and Socialists over issues such as divorce. Its budget is small and in the early years in particular much of it came from overseas (Waylen 1995).

SERNAM has concentrated on a number of areas, some with more effectiveness than others. It has established a network of regional offices which include information centres for women's rights (CIDEMs). Because it cannot execute programmes SERNAM has set up pilot projects for others to continue. It has concentrated on programmes geared towards poverty alleviation and training for the labour market, for example for poor women heads of household and women temporary workers and their children (Matear 1993). It has had perhaps its greatest success in some of its campaigns to raise public awareness, for example over the rights of illegitimate children and its domestic violence programme. It has agitated for legal changes and produced an equal opportunities plan together with a large quantity of research. The area of intersectoral co-ordination with other parts of the state has been one of the most problematic. Relationships with other ministries have often depended on personal contacts and civil servants have often been resistant to the consideration of gender issues. SERNAM has also worked in conjunction with other new state bodies, such as FOSIS, the anti-poverty programme, PRODEMU, the women's organisation set up to rival CEMA-Chile which remained under the control of Pinochet's wife, and some of the municipalities, to implement policies directed at women (Valenzuela 1996).

The greatest room for manoeuvre has existed around those issues considered the least controversial such as training for the labour market. While SERNAM has steered clear of highly contested subjects such as reproductive rights, its activities have still been vehemently criticised by the right and the Catholic church for trying to destroy the family. This was particularly evident in the debate surrounding the position of the Chilean delegation to the UN women's conference in Beijing in 1995.

SERNAM's relationship to women's movements outside the state has also been problematic. It has been seen as weakening women's movements as it has become the major interlocutor through which resources are channelled and has absorbed feminists into the state. Many international institutions and NGOs which had given funds directly to women's groups while the Pinochet regime was in power redirected them through the state once an elected government took power. This disbursement of resources has given SERNAM a potentially clientelistic relationship with groups outside. It has close ties with many of the feminist research NGOs such as CEM and the Instituto de la Mujer, providing them with contracts and support through the commissioning of research. Other feminist groups, such as feministas autonomas, have been wary of SERNAM, regarding it as nothing more than an arm of the state to be kept at a safe distance.

Women's movements

Those operating ouside these mainstream political processes have become increasingly incidental during the consolidation of electoral politics. There is consensus that women's movements have declined in levels of activity, there are fewer organisations in existence and some have changed the activities they engage in. Accompanying these trends has been a greater institutionalisation and professionalisation of the remaining organisations.

The marginalisation of the human rights organisations has become particularly marked. The Aylwin and Frei governments have observed the amnesty proclaimed by the Pinochet regime in 1978 and, apart from a few high-level cases, not taken significant action against members of the military implicated in human rights abuses (Loveman 1991). The emphasis of the government has been on 'the whole truth, and justice as far as possible' and on the need for reconciliation. Crimes have been investigated primarily to ascertain what happened through the work of the Rettig Commission and the families of victims have been compensated. By 1995 the Concertación government was trying to close the issue permanently through a plan which would shut the unresolved cases. But amid opposition (including from the Socialists), which claimed that it amounted to a *'punto final'* similar to that implemented in Argentina, this plan was thwarted by the right-wing parties.

Human rights protesters such as the Agrupaciones and the Madres, operating a politics of ethics, often find the transition from a military to a civilian government very difficult in terms of their strategy. However, in the face of the government's attempts to close the issue of human rights abuses, the Agrupaciones have maintained their activities, demanding justice not prudence, but in an increasingly unfavourable climate. The Catholic church closed the Vicaría one year after the civilian government took power on the grounds that its existence was no longer necessary but the AFDD still receives support from FASIC, a Christian organisation active around human rights issues. Its weekly meetings are still regularly attended by sixty to seventy people. While the dilemmas over tactics in the context of electoral politics split the Madres in Argentina, the AFDD has adopted strategies similar to the breakaway Linea Fundadora, by engaging with the political system: dealing with political parties, testifying to the senate and accepting compensation; as well as demonstrating outside the presidential palace on 11 September, the anniversary of the coup, and even hunger striking (Sierra 1996). Despite these activities, there is little chance of their demands being met by a government determined to put the issue of human rights abuses to rest and a populace (except for those on the Left) largely in sympathy with this aim.

The popular organisations have experienced a similar exclusion from the process of transition. In a process which began after the presidential election of 1989, activity levels both in terms of the numbers participating within groups and the number of groups in existence have declined. This trend has been accompanied by a restriction in the types of activities that the Catholic church will support at the same time as international NGOs have begun to channel their resources through the state, leaving many organisations without the support that they had in the past. Many have disappeared. It has been estimated that prior to the Concertación taking office there were forty-four *talleres productivas* (workshops) in existence in the central zone of Santiago, but by the end of 1993 the number had fallen to eight (Rios 1994). The survivors have been encouraged to diversify their activities. In keeping with the government's view that primarily economic solutions are the answer to poverty, OEPs have been encouraged to become *microempresas* (small businesses). Some *ollas comunes* have become *microempresas* with contracts from government agencies to supply school meals in their area. The *Casas de Mujeres* (women's centres) have become more institutional-ised, while the *talleres de reflexion* (discussion and 'consciousness-raising' workshops) display most continuity with the past in terms of their activities. In addition, while the communists and UDI (pro-Pinochet party) have become more active in poor areas, the political parties do not appear to have changed their paternalistic attitudes to the popular organisations. Surveys among women's groups in poor neighbourhoods have shown widespread disillusionment about the spaces and possibilities to participate and the often commented on demobilisation of social movements extends to popular women's organisations (Valenzuela 1992).

The feminist movement has suffered a similar decline in activity and visibility since the Concertación came to power. Some have argued that the existence of SERNAM has resulted in the beheading of the movement as feminists have migrated into the state, while many of the most visible feminist organisations are the feminist NGOs such as CEM, CEDEM and Insituto de la Mujer which carry out research (particularly for SERNAM) and training (often for leaders of popular women's organisations and women politicians). Their agenda is often influenced by the funders, for example during the dictatorship, resources were available for projects investigating popular women's organisations whereas subsequently the emphasis has shifted towards gendered analyses of public policy and the role of the state (Weinstein 1996). Certain issues have provided a focal point for organising in forms which have included both feminist NGOs and representatives of popular women's organisations. There has been increased activity around reproductive rights including the formation of a forum and reproductive rights network in 1992 (Frohmann and Valdes 1993). The 1995 Beijing conference provided a similar stimulus, particularly in the wake of right-wing criticism, leading for example to the formation of the Grupo de Iniciativa which included a variety of different groups, in a process which raised the visibility of women's organisations.[6]

CONCLUSIONS

The levels of diverse forms of women's activism were high under the military regime and played a significant role in the transition to competitive electoral politics. Subsequently women's activism in a whole range of organisations has declined along with many other social movements, as part of a phenomenon which has even been termed a 'remasculinisation' by some commentators (Craske 1998). It is only possible to understand what has happened to women's activism in the context of the particular nature of the Chilean transition. The elite and negotiated nature of the transition, leading as it has to the resurrection of a strong party system, has provided the constraining structures within which women's activism has taken place. Different women's movements have participated in different ways in these processes and in turn been affected very differently by them. Competitive electoral politics has provided some limited opportunities for some women – mainly middle-class activists involved in parties of the Centre and Centre-Left. Others have been left outside. The acceptance of the demands of the human rights organisations cannot be part of this type of transition; and while some popular movements have changed the nature of their activities, and even become *microempresas* to fit this new reality, others have disappeared. But the transition and consolidation have brought some fluidity. Gender issues have a higher profile in public discourse and the establishment of SERNAM has led to some changes. It is clear that SERNAM's most marked achievements have been in those areas considered less controversial but it has also had substantial success in raising awareness of some gender-based issues such as domestic violence. It has experienced far more resistance both inside and outside the state than some had anticipated. While engagement with the state can be problematic, it is also clear that remaining outside the ambit of the state and political parties is not the solution. Many activists argue that both autonomy and integration are the answer. SERNAM for example has far more legitimacy within the state and political processes if there is a vibrant and heterogeneous women's movement active outside it. While it is a mistake to assume a shared collective identity, alliances on certain issues, for example around reproductive rights and Beijing, are possible in the new terrain of competitive electoral politics, and they can influence the formal arena.

ACKNOWLEDGMENTS

Some of the research for this chapter was funded by a British Academy small research grant in the Humanities and some by ESRC grant reference no ROOO221334.

NOTES

1 This chapter takes a broad definition of the 'political' which is necessary in any analysis of women's political activity. For a longer discussion of the issues involved see Waylen (1996: ch. 1).
2 While in exile, members of some left-wing parties modified their views of socialism and, often influenced by the ideas of Gramsci and Eurocommunism, they moved away from an emphasis on class struggle. This process was intensified by the collapse of communism in eastern Europe in the late 1980s. Hence the term 'renovated socialism'.
3 Maxine Molyneux (1985) first put forward the notion of practical and strategic gender interests. Practical gender interests arise from actual situations, are formulated by women in those situations and vary from situation to situation. They are often expressed in social and economic terms. In contrast, strategic gender interests are those interests which can be derived deductively from an analysis of women's subordination and from the formulation of a more satisfactory set of arrangements. They are often called feminist or women's 'real' interests. However, a rigid analytical dichotomy between practical and strategic gender interests is overly simplistic as there is often considerable overlap between the two.
4 See the report produced by SERNAM of an Encuentro Internacional: Politicas de Igualidades de Opportunidades, October 1993, in which representatives of parties from the Right, Left and Centre say that their party is going to improve the situation for women.
5 Much of the information here comes from Riet Delsing, who undertook an analysis of the positive action measures in the political parties for SERNAM in 1995.
6 See the report by Grupo Iniciativa, Documento Preliminar 'Hacia la IV Conferencia Mundial de la Mujer y el foro No Gubernamental', Santiago, 1995.

REFERENCES

Agosin, M. (1990) *Scraps of Life*, London: Zed.

Agrupación De Familiares de Detenidos-Desaparacidos (1986) *Donde Estan: Mujeres Chilenas Detenidas-Desaparacidos*, Santiago.

Alvarez, S. (1990a) *Engendering Democracy in Brazil: Women's Movements in Transition Politics*, Princeton, NJ: Princeton University Press.

—— (1990b) 'Women's participation in the Brazilian "People's Church": a critical appraisal', *Feminist Studies* 16(2): 381–408.

Angelo, G. (1990) *Nuevos Espacios y Nuevas Practicas de Mujeres en una Situación de Crisis: Hacia el Surgiemiento y Consolidación de un Movimiento de Mujeres – El Caso de Chile*, Santiago: Cuadernos de la Morada.

Arteaga, A. M. (1988) 'Politización de lo Privado y Subversión del Cotidiano', in CEM, *Mundo de Mujer: Continuidad y Cambio*, Santiago: Centro de Estudios de la Mujer.

Bouvard, M. (1994) *Revolutionizing Motherhood: the Mothers of the Plaza de Mayo*, Wilmington, DE: Scholarly Resources.

Caldeira, T. (1990) 'Women, daily life and politics', in E. Jelin (ed.) *Women and Social Change in Latin America*, London: Zed.

Chuckryk, P. (1989) 'Subversive mothers: the women's opposition to the military regime in Chile', in S. Charlton, J. Everett and K. Staudt (eds) *Women, State and Development*, New York. SUNY Press.

Craske, N. (1998) 'Remasculinization, politics and the state in Latin America', in V. Randall and G. Waylen (eds) *Gender, Politics and the State*, London: Routledge.

Elshtain, J. (1992) 'The power and powerlessness of women', in G. Bock and S. James (eds) *Beyond Equality and Difference: Citizenship, Feminist Politics and Female Subjectivity*, London. Routledge.

Fisher, J. (1989) *Mothers of the Disappeared*, London: Zed.

—— (1993) *Out of the Shadows: Women, Resistance and Politics in South America*, London: Latin American Bureau.

Franco, J. (1994) 'Crossed wires: gender theory north and south', paper presented to Conference on Latin American Cross Currents in Gender Theory, Portsmouth, July.

Frohmann, A. and Valdes, T. (1993). '"Democracy in the country and in the home": the women's movement in Chile', *FLACSO Serie Estudios Sociales* December.

Garretón, M. A. (1989) 'Popular mobilization and the military regime in Chile: the complexities of the invisible transition', in S. Eckstein (ed.) *Power and Popular Protest*, Berkeley, CA: University of California Press.

Gaviola, E., Largo, E. and Palestro, S. (1994) *Una Historia Necessaria Mujeres in Chile: 1973–1990*, Santiago.

Hardy, C. (1985) *Estratagias Organizadas de Subsistencia: los Sectores Populares frente a sus Necessidades en Chile*, Documento de Trabajo 41, Santiago: PET.

Jaquette, J. (ed.) (1994) *The Women's Movement in Latin America: Participation and Democracy*, 2nd edn, Boulder, CO: Westview Press.

Kirkwood, J. (1990) *Ser Política en Chile: Los Nudos de la Sabiduría Feminista*, Santiago: Editorial Cuarto Propio.

Loveman, B. (1991) Misión Cumplida?, *Journal of Inter-American Studies and World Affairs* 33(3) 35–74.

Macaulay, F. (1995) 'Gender relations and the democratization of local politics in

166   *Georgina Waylen*

the transition to democracy of Brazil and Chile', paper presented to the PSA Annual Conference, York.

Matear, A. (1993) 'SERNAM: women and the Process of democratic transition in Chile 1990–93', paper presented to Society of Latin American Studies Conference, Manchester.

Mohanty, T. C. (1991) 'Introduction – cartographies of struggle: Third World women and and the politics of feminism', in C. Mohanty, A. Russo and L. Torres (eds) *Third World Women and the Politics of Feminism*, Bloomington, IN: Indiana University Press.

Molina, N. (1989) 'Propuestas Políticas y Orientaciones de Cambio en la Situación de la Mujer', in M. A. Garretón (ed.) *Propuestas Políticas y Demandas Sociales*, vol. 3, Santiago: FLACSO.

—— (1990) 'El Estado y las Mujeres: una Relación Difícil', in ISIS *Transiciones: Mujeres en los Procesos Democraticos*, Santiago: ISIS Internacional.

Molyneux, M. (1985) 'Mobilization without emancipation? Women's interests, the state and revolution in Nicaragua', *Feminist Studies* 11(2): 227–54.

Montecino, S. and Rosetti, J. (1990) *Tramas para un Nuevo Destino: Propuestas de la Concertacíon de Mujeres por la Democracia*, Santiago.

Petras, J. and Leiva, F. I. (1988) 'Chile: the authoritarian transition to electoral politics – a critique', *Latin American Perpsectives* 15(3): 97–114.

Pollarolo, F. (1996) Interview with PS deputada and vice-president for women, Santiago, 19 January.

Raczynski, D. and Serrano, C. (1985) *Vivir La Pobreza: Testiminios de Mujeres*, Santiago: CIEPLAN.

Rios, M. (1994) 'Socializacion, Politica y Accion Colectiva: Organizaciones de Pobladoras en Chile 1973–93', unpublished MA thesis, FLACSO, Mexico.

Saa, M. A. (1990) Interview with María Antonieta Saa, *Crítica Social* May.

—— (1996) Interview with PPD deputada, Santiago, 19 January.

Schild, V. (1991) 'The hidden politics of neighbourhood organizations: women and local level participation in the *Poblaciones* of Chile', *North/South* 30: 137–58.

—— (1992) 'Struggling for citizenship in Chile: a "Resurrection" of civil society?', unpublished paper for Latin American Studies Association Congress.

Schirmer, J. (1989) '"Those who die for life cannot be called dead": women and human rights protest', *Feminist Review* 32: 3–29.

—— (1993) 'The seeking of truth and the gendering of consciousness: the comadres of El Salvador and the CONAVIGUA widows of Guatemala', in S. Radcliffe and S. Westwood (eds) *Viva: Women and Popular Protest in Latin America*, London: Routledge.

Serrano, C. (1990) 'Chile Entre la Autonomía y la Integración', in ISIS, *Transiciones: Mujeres en los Procesos Democraticos*, Santiago: ISIS International.

Sierra, S. (1996) Interview with Presidenta AFDD, Santiago, 20 January.

Sternbach, N. S., Navarro, M. A., Chuchryk, P. and Alvarez, S. (1992) 'Feminisms in Latin America: from Bogotá to San Bernardo', *Signs* 17(2): 393–434.

Valdes, T. and Weinstein, M. (1989) *Organizaciones de Pobladoras y Construción Democrática en Chile: Notas para un Debate*, Documento De Trabajo, Santiago: FLACSO.

—— (1993) *Mujeres que Suenan Las Organizaciones de Pobladoras en Chile: 1973–1989*, Santiago: Libros Flacso.

Valenzuela, M. (1990) 'Mujeres y Política: Logros y Tensiones en el Proceso de Redemocratización', *Proposiciones*, 18: 210–32.

—— (1991) 'The evolving roles of women under military rule', in P. Drake and I. Jaksic (eds) *The Struggle for Democracy in Chile 1982–1990*, Lincoln, NB: University of Nebraska Press.

—— (1992) 'Women and democratization in Chile', paper presented to Conference on Women and the Transition to Democracy in Latin America and Eastern Europe, Berkeley, CA.

—— (1996) Interview with Jefa de Deparmento de Planificacion y Estudios, SERNAM, Santiago, 17 January.

Walker, H. L. (1985) 'Transformation of practices in grassroots organizations: a case study in Chile', unpublished Ph.D. thesis, University of Toronto.

Waylen, G. (1992) 'Rethinking women's political participation and protest: Chile 1970–90', *Political Studies* 40(2): 299–314.

—— (1994) 'Women and democratization: conceptualizing gender relations in transition politics', *World Politics* 46(3): 327–54.

—— (1995) 'Women's movements, the state and democratization in Chile', *IDS Bulletin* 26(3): 86–93.

—— (1996) *Gender in Third World Politics*, Buckingham: Open University Press.

Weinstein, M. (1996) Interview, Researcher for FLACSO, Santiago, 19 January.

9 Beyond differences

Women, empowerment and coalition politics

Nira Yuval-Davis

The problematisation of the notion of sisterhood, which we have been witnessing in the last few years in feminist theory and politics, has been promoted to a large extent by the writings and activities of black feminists on the one hand and postmodern feminists on the other hand (e.g. Anthias and Yuval-Davis 1983; hooks 1981; Weed 1989).

However, some of the ways this heterogeneity has been constructed in left politics in general, and feminist politics in particular, are problematic. This chapter will examine some of the theoretical and political issues involved, concentrating on the notions of identity, ethnicity and identity politics and their specific implications for feminist politics. Its main argument is that ethnicity cannot be collapsed into identity and/or culture and therefore women's ethnicity often is and should be different from that of men. The chapter also argues that feminist politics should incorporate the notion of women's positionings and ethnic differences into its agenda and that therefore any feminist politics should be viewed as coalition politics, preferably of the 'transversal' kind.

THE NOTION OF 'IDENTITY'

The study of identity formation in general and of ethnic identity in particular has preoccupied many social scientists and philosophers (for a detailed discussion of this, see Allen, Chapter 3 in this volume). A central dilemma in the field of identity formation is the duality of the individual and society and the equation of 'society' with the small group of 'the family' or even more specifically with 'the father' (as has been the case with Freudian theory regarding the 'super-ego'). Ethnic identities have often been studied in terms of the person's identification with or distancing from fixed external reified 'ethnicities' (e.g. Epstein 1978; Lewin 1952). On the other hand, post-structural analyses which attempted to go beyond this duality of separate reified realities have often led to the denial of the individual's existence by speaking only of 'human agencies' – subjective manifestations of the general symbolic order. A basic question has been the extent to which one can talk about an 'essential self', a 'unitary self' or even a 'minimal self' (see e.g. Hirsch 1982; Shoemaker and Swinburn 1984). Whatever the answer to this question, identity constitutes the conscious 'self' – the answer, or rather answers, to the question 'Who am I?' Whether or not the multiple and changing answers to this question constitute different identities (or Parsonian roles), sub-identities or different facets of a unitary construct, they represent the ways individuals experience themselves at specific times. While some of the answers to the question 'Who am I?' may be transitory or situational (e.g., being of a certain age, occupation, having certain relationships, etc.), others are perceived to be permanent and 'natural' (sex and familial/ethnic/national origin). All identity dimensions can, in specific social contexts, have higher or lower saliency, but often the primordial components of one's identity provoke the most powerful emotions for the individual, through processes of identification which in extreme cases can blur individual and collective boundaries.

However, even these primordial identities are often far from being fixed and unproblematic, because, in spite of their 'naturalistic' character, the collectivities with which they identify are neither fixed nor unproblematic. With the rise of postmodernist theories, identities have become a focus of renewed interest. The exile, the person with fragmented identity, who belongs everywhere and nowhere, has become the symbol of the postmodern epoch. Within the discourse of postmodernism identities have a 'formative, not merely an expressive place in the construction of social and political life' (Hall 1987: 42).

In order to be able to evaluate Hall's statement, we need to examine both the nature of the relationships between identities of individual subjects and more collective social constructs, as well as the nature of these collective constructs themselves. For the purpose of this chapter, I shall concentrate on ethnic collectivities in their widest sense, although they are by no means the only collectivities in relation to which individual subjects construct their identities.

ETHNICITY, CULTURE AND IDENTITY

There is no space here to enter into a full elaboration of a theoretical framework on ethnicity and the ways it is linked with race and racism (see Anthias and Yuval-Davis 1992). Ethnicity relates to the politics of collectivity boundaries, dividing the world into 'us' and 'them' usually around myths of common origin and/or destiny and engaging in constant processes of struggle and negotiation (see also Benton, Chapter 2 in this volume).

These are aimed, from specific positionings within the collectivities, at promoting the collectivity or perpetuating its advantages, via access to state and civil society powers. Ethnicity, according to this definition is, therefore, primarily a political process which constructs the collectivity and 'its interest', not only as a result of the general positioning of the collectivity in relation to others in the society, but also as a result of the specific relations of those engaged in 'ethnic politics' with others within that collectivity. Gender, class, political and other differences play central roles in the construction of specific ethnic politics. Indeed, different ethnic projects of the same collectivity can be engaged in intense competitive struggles for hegemonic positions. Some of these projects can involve different constructions of the actual boundaries of the collectivity. Ethnicity is not specific to oppressed and minority groupings. On the contrary, one of the measures of the success of hegemonic ethnicities is the extent to which they succeed in naturalising their social constructions.

Ethnic projects mobilise all available relevant resources for their promotion. Some of these resources are political, others are economic and yet others are cultural – relating to customs, language, religion, etc. Class, gender, political and personal differences mean that people positioned differently within the collectivity could, while pursuing specific ethnic projects, sometimes use the same cultural resources for promoting opposite political goals. One example is the use of various Qur'ān *surras* to justify pro- and anti-abortion politics, as was the case in Egypt; another is the use of rock music to mobilise people by both the extreme Right and their opponents on the Left in Britain. In other times, different cultural resources have been used to legitimise competing ethnic projects of the collectivity. For instance, Bundists used Yiddish as 'the' Jewish language in an ethnic-national project whose boundaries were East European Jewry, and Zionists (re)invented modern Hebrew (which had until then been in use basically for religious purposes) in order to include Jews all over the world in their project. The same people can also be constructed, within the discourses of different ethnic-racial political projects in Britain, as 'Paki', 'Black Asians' or 'Muslim fundamentalists'.

Given the above, it is clear why ethnicity cannot be reduced to culture, and why 'culture' cannot be seen as a fixed, essentialist category. As Gill Bottomley claims when discussing relationships between ethnicity and culture:

> Categories and ways of knowing ... are constructed within relations of power and maintained, reproduced and resisted in specific and sometimes contradictory ways.
>
> (Bottomley 1991: 305)

Different ethnic projects can also play different roles in the construction of individual identities. I heard a presentation by a Bosnian woman refugee who described how Islam, from being a virtually insignificant 'if quaint' element in her background had become, through the recent war, her primary identity. Similar observations are made by Allen and Morokvasic when discussing former Yugoslavia (Chapters 3 and 4 in this volume). Different historical situations can enforce individual as well as collective identities, and thus promote certain ethnic projects more than others (Chhachhi 1992). Moreover, in certain historical circumstances, ethnic projects can result in the construction of new collectivity boundaries which would include people who previously would not have defined themselves as being part of the same collectivities, and sometimes would have even been hostile. Thus, people from Sikh, Hindu and Muslim origins, from India, Pakistan and Bangladesh, who were fighting each other on the Indian sub-continent, were all subsumed under the category 'Asian' in Britain. As Avtar Brah (1991: 58) points out, 'Difference is constructed differently within various discourses. These different meanings signal differing political strategies and outcomes.'

Moreover, because specific ethnic projects tend to suit certain members of the collectivity more than others who are positioned differently in terms of class, gender, stage in the life cycle and so on, there can be no automatic assumption, as has been so prevalent within 'identity politics' (Bourne 1987) that specific individuals, just because they are members of certain collectivities, can automatically be considered as 'representing their community'. Only those elected in democratic ways can even partially be considered so. Otherwise, the best and most committed community activists should be considered as advocates rather than as representatives of their 'community' (Cain and Yuval-Davis 1990). And in terms of equal opportunities policies, the fact that certain individuals become employed in a category of work that previously excluded members of their grouping, although positive in itself, can by no means automatically guarantee an improvement in the overall situation of those who belong to that group. The widening class divisions among African Americans are a case in point.

The collapsing of ethnicity into culture, on the one hand, and identity, on the other hand, can also create what Kobena Mercer (1988) calls 'the burden of representation', which can handicap members of groupings subject to positive actions and equal opportunities policies. In the collection Mercer edited on this subject, Judith William remarked:

> The more power any group has to create and wield representations, the less it is required to be representative . . . the visible demand to 'speak for the black community' is always there behind the multi-culturalism of public funding.
>
> (Mercer 1988: 12)

Moreover, specific individuals are usually, especially in contemporary urban settings, members of more than one collectivity. The boundaries of these collectivities sometimes partially overlap and often cross-cut each other. 'Identity politics' which called people to organise (and empower themselves) according to their particular identities, came up against this reality. In the 'equal opportunities' policies of the former Greater London Council (GLC) and other local authorities' 'popular planning' groups, for instance, fights broke out concerning whether a certain black woman worker should become part of the 'race unit' or the 'women's unit'. On the other hand, in a context of budgetary restrictions, the same black woman would probably be asked to represent the interests of all minority 'communities' in the area, conflicts and differences of interests among them notwithstanding.

As Kobena Mercer (1988) points out, these assumptions are part and parcel of the ideology of multiculturalism which, with some changes, 'anti-racists' and 'popular planners' have adopted as well (Anthias and Yuval-Davis 1992; Rattanzi 1992; Sahgal and Yuval-Davis 1992; Yuval-Davis 1996).

'Multiculturalism' (and later on 'anti-racism') have been a major ideological response in the west to the obvious failure of previous liberal approaches which assumed that racism was caused by the 'strangeness' of the immigrants, and that with the acculturation and eventual assimilation of the immigrants – or their children – racism would disappear. The 'melting-pot', however, did not melt, and ethnic and racial divisions have been reproduced from generation to generation (Glazer and Moynihan 1965, 1975; Wallman 1979; Watson 1977; see also Afshar, Chapter 6 in this volume).

Multiculturalist policies construct cultures as static, ahistoric and in their 'essence' mutually exclusive from other cultures, especially that of the 'host society'. Moreover, 'culture' in the multiculturalist discourse is often collapsed into religion, with religious holidays becoming the signifiers of cultural difference within 'multicultural' school curricula.

Moreover, multiculturalism constructs society as composed of basically internally homogenous units – a hegemonic majority, and small unmeltable minorities with their own essentially different communities and cultures which have to be understood, accepted, and basically left alone (since their differences are compatible with the hegemonic culture), in order for society to have harmonious relations. Multiculturalism, like 'identity politics', adheres to the ideology of 'the community' (see Allen, Chapter 3 in this volume).

THE IDEOLOGY OF 'THE COMMUNITY'

The ideology of 'the community' is a populist ideology which assumes 'the people' and 'the grassroots' to be the origin of all that is good and 'authentic' in society. It is intimately linked with the ideology of empowerment as the political goal of radical left activities.

'Empowerment' has been a central item, at least since the late 1960s, on the political agenda of all grassroots resistance movements, whether they have called for black power, raising women's consciousness or for a more general 'return' to 'the community' (see e.g. Cain and Yuval-Davis 1990; Gorz 1982; Wainwright 1987). One of the major issues that the anti-racist and feminist movements have been struggling with has been the effects of that self-negation which powerlessness carries with it. These effects and, hence, the solutions called for, often have psychologial implications. For example, Franz Fanon (1986) called on the 'Black man' to 'regain his manhood'; and the feminist movement has called on women to reclaim their 'womanhood' (or 'humanhood' – depending on their specific ideology). These calls are a result of the view that the internalisation by the powerless of the hegemonic value system according to which they are invisible, valueless and/or 'dangerous', is a major obstacle to their ability to resist discrimination and overcome disadvantage. Of particular influence in this trend of thought has been the work of Paulo Freire (1972) which intimately links knowledge and power.

Jill M. Bystydzienski claims:

> Empowerment is taken to mean a process by which oppressed persons gain some control over their lives by taking part with others in development of activities and structures that allow people increased involvement in matters which affect them directly. In its course people become enabled to govern themselves effectively. This process involves the use of power, but not 'power over' others or power as dominance as is traditionally the case; rather, power is seen as 'power to' or power as competence which is generated and shared by the disenfranchised as they begin to shape the content and structure of their daily existence and so participate in a movement for social change.
>
> (Bystydzienski 1992: 3)

This particular construction of the notion of empowerment, however, firmly situates the individual inside a more or less egalitarian and homogenous grouping which is 'the community', the members of which share in the process of empowerment and collectively manage to fight their oppression and become the controllers of their own destiny. This process is presented as non-problematic and the possibility that conflicts of interest might emerge within 'the community', in which the 'power to' of some would also become their 'power over' others, is never discussed.

The ideology of 'the community' has become popular in wide circles of the Left since, in the western world in general and in Britain in particular, representations based on political parties and trade union memberships have recently come to be seen as less and less satisfactory, reflecting imbalances of power and access which exist within civil society itself as well as in the state. Women and ethnic minorities have been the prime focuses of attempts to create new selection mechanisms which will be more 'just' in their representative and distributive power. The notion of autonomous 'community organisations' as the basis of an alternative mechanism of representation to the more traditional ones has been promoted for that purpose (Gorz 1982).

As has been elaborated elsewhere (Anthias and Yuval-Davis 1992: ch. 6; Young 1990; Yuval-Davis 1991), certain analytical (as well as political) problems arise with these formulations. The notion of 'the community' assumes an organic wholeness. The community is perceived as a 'natural' social unit. It is somehow 'out there' and one either belongs to it or not. Any notion of internal difference within the 'community' is, therefore, subsumed within this organic construction. It can be either a functional difference which contributes to the smooth and efficient working of 'the community', or it is an anomaly, a pathological deviation. Moreover, the supposed naturalness of the 'community' assumes a given collectivity with given boundaries – it allows for internal growth and probably differentiation, but not for ideological and material reconstructions of the boundaries themselves (Bhabha 1990). It does not allow for collectivities to be seen as social constructs whose boundaries, structures and norms are the result of constant processes of struggles and negotiations, or more general social developments. Indeed, as Homi Bhabha (in GLC 1984) and Paul Gilroy (1987) have shown, the fascination of left-wing intellectuals with the 'working-class community' has resulted in their adoption of a model of 'Englishness' which is unquestionably racist, culturally discriminatory and invariably sexist. The perspective of the community as fixed can create exclusionary boundaries which keep as 'other' all those perceived as different – in other words, such notions of community can become extremely conservative, racist and chauvinist (e.g. tenants' associations on some British housing estates which mobilise the neighbourhood to exclude Afro-Caribbeans and Asians; and, on a much more horrific scale, some of the fighting in Lebanon, Bosnia and other 'ethnic cleansings').

Moreover, the ideology of 'the community' assumes an unproblematic transition from individual to collective power, as well as a pre-given and unproblematic definition of the boundaries of 'the people'. The automatic assumption that no inherent conflicts of interest can arise among the members of 'the community', has been a cornerstone of 'equal opportunity' policies (Cain and Yuval-Davis 1990; Phillips 1991). Promoters of such policies, both in formal institutions and in the voluntary sector, have assumed that the interests of all the oppressed and disadvantaged – be it women, ethnic and racial minorities, disabled people, and so on – are not only always 'progressive', but also automatically shared and reconcilable. The ideological construction of these policies did not allow for possible conflicts of interests among those they are aimed at. White backlash and working-class racism were, therefore, never taken seriously, except as 'false consciousness' or a personal pathology of despair. Nor were in-fighting and the growing clashes between 'women's units' and 'race units', between 'Afro-Caribbeans' and 'Asians' and so on taken seriously.

I am far from believing, and especially far from hoping, that solidarity among different people, as individuals and as groupings, in struggles against racism, sexism and other forms of discrimination and disadvantage, is impossible. I shall expand on this later. However, I do not believe that such struggles can be taken forward successfully by simplistic notions of empowerment of the oppressed. Fundamentalist leaderships, who use religion in their ethnic political projects, have benefited greatly from the adoption of identity politics and the ideology of 'the community' by multiculturalist policy-makers as well as by the 'Left' (Sahgal and Yuval-Davis 1992).

FUNDAMENTALISM, IDENTITY POLITICS AND WOMEN

Religious and ethnic fundamentalist movements are probably the most important social movements of the late 1980s and 1990s (Contention 1995; Sahgal and Yuval-Davis 1992). Fundamentalist movements all over the world are basically political movements which have a religious or other cultural imperative and which seek in various ways and in widely differing circumstances to harness modern state and media powers to the service of their gospel. This gospel is presented as the only valid form of the 'essential' or 'right' religion, culture or tradition. Specific fundamentalist movements can rely heavily on sacred religious texts, but may also be more experiential and linked to specific charismatic leadership and other means of the 'reinvention of tradition'. Fundamentalism can align itself with different political trends in different countries and manifest itself in different forms. It can present itself as a form of orthodoxy, seeking to maintain so-called 'traditional values', or as a revivalist radical phenomena, rooting out impure and corrupt forms of religion and politics. (Some of these issues have been explored, theoretically and empirically, by Benton, Allen, Kofman and Afshar, Chapters 2, 3, 5 and 6 in this volume.)

Another important difference within fundamentalist politics is between movements of dominant majorities within states, which look for universal domination in society (such as the evangelical New Right in the United

States and Khomeini's Iran) and fundamentalist movements of minorities, who aim to use state and media powers and resources to promote and impose their gospel primarily within their specific constituencies, which are usually defined in ethnic terms.

The recent rise of fundamentalism is linked to the crisis of modernity – of social orders based on the belief in the principles of Enlightenment, rationalism and progress. Both capitalism and communism have proved unable to meet people's material, emotional and spiritual needs. As Afshar illustrates (Chapter 6 in this volume), a general sense of despair and disorientation has opened people up to religion as a source of solace. It provides a compass and an anchor which gives people a sense of stability and meaning, as well as a coherent identity.

In the Third World, and among Third World minorities in the west, the rise of fundamentalism is also intimately linked with the failure of nationalist and socialist movements to bring about successful liberation from oppression, exploitation and poverty. Religion and other traditionalist ideologies have also been utilised by militants as 'indigenous' ideologies with which to mobilise the 'masses' and to confront racism, imperialism and the interventions of superpowers.

Fundamentalist claims have been received very ambiguously by both multiculturalists and the Left in the west. Within the multiculturalist logic, fundamentalist leaders' presumptions about being the keepers of the 'true' religious and/or cultural tradition and way of life are unanswerable. External dissent is labelled as racist and internal dissent as deviance (if not sheer pathology, as in the case of 'self-hating Jews'). In the politics of identity and representation these leaders are perceived as the most 'authentic' 'others' to be included in the multiculturalist project. At the same time, they are also perceived as a threat, and their 'difference' can easily be used as a basis for racist discourse and exclusionary policies (such as tightening immigration controls in Britain and France). Unlike previous proponents of multiculturalism, fundamentalist activists refuse to respect the 'limits of multiculturalism' which would confine 'ethnic cultures' to the private domain or to some limited cultural community spheres.

Fundamentalist politics has also proved to be very confusing for the Left, and impossible to grapple with within the paradigm of identity politics and community empowerment. While the ideologies promoted by religious fundamentalist activists are often anathema to all that people on the Left generally believe in, such as women's equality, individual freedom and so on, the Left is committed to 'respecting different cultures and ensuring different identities'. The ideology of autonomous self-determination and empowerment, which underpins identity politics and multiculturalism, condemns 'intervention in the internal affairs of the community' as

Eurocentric and racist, part of a tradition of cultural imperialism which must be rejected.

Women have been primary victims of fundamentalist politics (Sahgal and Yuval-Davis 1992). Nevertheless, many women have also joined fundamentalist movements and gained a certain sense of empowerment from them in spite of this (Afshar 1989; Yuval-Davis 1992). Subjective feelings of empowerment and autonomy, however, cannot be the sole criterion for evaluating the politics of a certain action. In a conference in Ireland on Gender and Colonialism (Dublin, spring 1992) Gayatri Chakravorty Spivak defined 'effective gendering' as 'constructing constriction as choice', which is an accurate description of the situation of these women. Feelings and knowledge are constructed as a result of specific power relations and are not outside them (Haraway 1988). As Richard Johnson points out:

> Frameworks are embodied in practical strategies, tacit beliefs, detailed stories . . . I may feel empowered or disempowered, heroic, a victim, or stoical, depending on the framework.
>
> (Johnson 1991: 17)

'Choosing the framework' is, therefore, not just a question of applying 'positive thinking' – as some of the more simplistic feminist and 'Human Growth' workshops on 'women and empowerment' would tend to imply. As Foucault importantly has shown us

> Power doesn't only weigh on us as a force that says no . . . it induces pleasure, forms of knowledge, produces discourse.
>
> (Foucault 1980: 119)

This is why it is so important to examine questions of women and empowerment in relation to the ways women affect and are affected by ethnic and national processes.

WOMEN, CITIZENSHIP, AND 'THE COMMUNITY'

The specific ways women affect and are affected by ethnic and national processes have been elaborated elsewhere (Walby 1992; Yuval-Davis 1980, 1993; Yuval-Davis and Anthias 1989). They include the roles of women as biological and cultural national reproducers; as cultural embodiments of collectivities and their boundaries; as carriers of collective 'honour' and as participants in national and ethnic struggles. All these ways are vitally important to any analysis not only of the specific position of women, but also for any adequate perspective about the ways state and society operate in general.

The construction by the state of relationships in the private domain (i.e. marriage and the family) is what has determined women's status as citizens within the public domain (Pateman 1989; Vogel 1989). In some non-European countries, the right of women even to work and travel in the public domain is dependent on formal permission of her 'responsible' male relative (Kandiyoti 1991), and until 1948 women marrying 'aliens' lost their British citizenship altogether.

There have been attempts to explain some of the recent changes in eastern and central Europe in terms of the reconstruction of civil society – a social sphere which is seen as independent of the state. Many western feminist analyses have shown this 'independence' to be largely illusory, as it is the state which constructs, and often maintains surveillance over, the private domain especially of the lower classes (e.g. Showstack Sassoon 1987; Wilson 1977). However, in Third World societies there is sometimes only a partial penetration of the state into civil society, especially in its rural and other peripheral sections, and gender and other social relations continue to be determined by the cultural and religious customs of the national collectivity. This may also happen in the 'private domains' of ethnic and national minorities in other states.

However, it is not only in the 'private domain' that gender relations vary between different groupings. Often the citizenship rights and duties of women from different ethnic and racial groupings are also distinct. They may have different legal positions and entitlements; sometimes they may be under the jurisdiction of different religious courts or under different residential regulations, including rights of re-entry after leaving the country; they may or may not be allowed to confer citizenship rights on their children, or, in the case of women migrant workers who have had to leave their children behind, they may or may not receive child and other welfare benefits as part of their social rights. Bryson's discussion of women in Israel provides an illustration of these differences (Chapter 7 in this volume).

With all these differences, the one characteristic which structures women's citizenship is its dualistic nature. On the one hand, women are always included, at least to some extent, in the construction of the general body of members of national and ethnic collectivities and/or citizens of the state; on the other hand, there is always, at least to a certain extent, a separate body of regulations (legal and/or customary) which relate to them specifically as women.

Marshall (1950, 1975, 1981) defines citizenship as 'full membership in the community' which includes civil, political and social dimensions of citizenship. The problematic notion of 'the community' discussed above notwithstanding, the ambivalent nature of women's citizenship creates an inherent ambivalence within women's politics *vis-à-vis* their own collectivities, on the one hand, and women from other collectivities, on the other hand. The famous quotation by Virginia Woolf (1938) that 'As a woman I have no country' emphasises the realisation of many women that they are positioned in a different place from men in relation to their collectivity and that the hegemonic cultural and political projects pursued in the name of their collectivities can be against their interests as women. On the other hand, especially among subordinated and minority women, there is a realisation that to fight for their liberation as women is senseless as long as their collectivity as a whole is subordinated and oppressed.

Feminist politics are affected by this ambivalence. Many black and minority women have pointed out the racist Eurocentric and middle-class biases which have been at the heart of most feminist agendas, at least until the last few years. As bell hooks claimed:

> The vision of sisterhood evoked by women liberationists was based on the idea of common oppression – a false and corrupt platform disguising and mystifying the true nature of women's varied and complex social reality.
>
> (hooks 1990: 29)

There are many examples of this varied and complex social reality of women, which problematise any simplistic assumptions about 'the feminist agenda'. Debates relating to these issues can be found in all areas of feminist politics – whether it relates to reproductive rights and the priority given to outlawed abortions versus forced sterilisations, the attitudes that feminists should have towards 'the family' as an oppressive or protective social insitution or whether women should come out against all forms of violence or campaign for participation in the military (Anthias and Yuval-Davis 1983; Hill Collins 1990; Kimble and Unterhalter 1982; Spelman 1988; Yuval-Davis 1996, ch: 6).

If we add to membership in particular ethnic, national and racial collectivities other dimensions of identity and difference among women, such as class, sexuality, stage in the life cycle, and so on, it would be very easy to reach the postmodernist deconstructionist view and a realisation that 'everyone is different'. The question, then, is whether any collective political action in general, and feminist collective action in particular, is possible once such a deconstructionist analytical point of view is conceded as valid (see the critique of Anthias and Yuval-Davis 1983, by Barrett and McIntosh 1985). Are effective politics and adequate theoretical analysis inherently contradictory? My basic answer to this question is the same as that of Spivak when she claimed:

Deconstruction does not say anything against the usefulness of mobilizing unities. All it says is that because it is useful it ought not to be monumentalized as the way things really are.

(Spivak 1991: 65)

Or, to put it in Stuart Hall's succinct way – 'all identity is constructed across difference' (Hall 1987: 44).

WOMEN AND 'COALITION POLITICS' – LINKING THEORY AND PRACTICE

Adopting such a political perspective of boundary construction of 'units' or 'unities' can keep us aware of continuous historical changes and keep our perceptions of the boundaries between collectivities sufficiently flexible and open so that exclusionary politics are not permitted. At the same time such a perspective does not imply political paralysis. Concretely this means that all feminist (and other forms of democratic) politics should be viewed as a form of coalition politics in which the differences among women are recognised and given a voice, while the boundaries of the coalition are not defined in terms of 'who' we are but in terms of what we want to achieve. As Caryn McTighe Musil says:

The challenge of the nineties is to hold on simultaneously to these two contradictory truths: as women, we are the same and we are different. The bridges, power, alliances and social change possible will be determined by how well we define ourselves through a matrix that encompasses our gendered particularities while not losing sight of our unity.

(cited in Albrecht and Brewer 1990: vi)

The question is, of course, how to go about this task concretely. I shall now look critically at several approaches which have attempted to tackle it – two which, although creative and thoughtful in many ways, have, I believe, some major flaws relating to some of the issues discussed earlier, and two which, although very different from each other, might point the way forward in effectively tackling the problem.

The first approach has been described in the article by Gail Pheterson (1990) in the *Bridges of Power* collection. It describes an experiment in the Netherlands in which three mixed women's groups (more or less in half and half proportions) were constructed – one of black and white women, one of Jews and Gentiles and one of lesbian and heterosexual women. The groups operated very much within the usual pattern of the feminist consciousness-raising tradition. Pheterson found that in every group, past experiences with oppression and domination distorted the participants' perceptions of the present and blocked their identification with people in common political situations who did not share their history.

(Pheterson 1990: 3)

She talks about the need to recognise and interrupt how we internalise both oppression and domination in order to create successful alliances. Her position constructs ethnicity as including a power dimension – of oppression and domination and not just as made of 'cultural stuff'. She also shows that women can experience internalised oppression and domination simultaneously as a result of different experiences; people and identities are not just unidimensional. However, her approach implies that there is such a thing as an 'objective truth' that can be discovered. I would say that rather than using a discourse of 'distortion', one should use a discourse of ideological positioning. I shall come back to this point later.

The discourse of 'distortion' creates its own distortions. Pheterson discusses, for instance, the reluctance of some women (black women born in the colonies rather than in the Netherlands; Jewish women who have only one Jewish parent) to identify with their groups and sees it as a distortion and 'blocked identification'. Such a perspective assumes essentialist homogeneity within each category (such as 'Blacks', 'Jews', etc.) and refuses to accept that these women are genuinely located in different positionings from other members of their groups. Moreover, it assumes that the centrality and significance of these categories would be the same to different women and disregards differences of class, age and other social dimensions within the group as inherently irrelevant.

Such an approach is typical of the 'identity politics' which were discussed above and which have been very central to western feminism. The whole idea of consciousness-raising techniques assumes, as a basis for political action, a reality that has to be discovered and then changed, rather than a reality which is being created and re-created when practised and discussed (Yuval-Davis 1984). Moreover, this reality is assumed to be shared by all members of the social category within which the consciousness-raising movement operates, all of whom are perceived to constitute a basically homogenous social grouping sharing the same interests. Individual identity has become equated with collective identity, whereas differences, rather than being acknowledged, have been interpreted by those holding hegemonic power within the movement as mainly reflections of different stages of raised consciousness. Although to a large extent this has been acknowledged by the women's movement(s) in recent years, the solution has often been to develop essentialist notions of difference, such as, for example, between black and white women, or middle-class and working-class women. Within each of these idealised groups, the assumptions about 'discovered' homogenous reality, and the other problems of 'identity politics' and the politics of 'the community' discussed above, usually continue to operate. Moreover, as Linda Gordon points out, such essentialist notions of difference are necessarily exclusive:

> We are in danger of losing any ability to offer any interpretation that reaches beyond the particular groups ... it does not capture the experience of all ... women.
>
> (Gordon 1991: 103)

Even more importantly, as Bonnie Thornton Dill points out:

> As an organizing principle, difference obliterates relation. ... Difference often implies separation, but these relationships frequently involve proximity, involvement.
>
> (Thornton Dill 1988: 106)

An attempt at a more sophisticated type of identity politics was theorised by Rosalind Brunt (1989) who writes in the influential collection *New Times*. Brunt argues that:

> Unless the question of identity is at the heart of any transformatory project, then not only will the political agenda be inadequately 'rethought' but more to the point, our politics aren't going to make much headway beyond the Left's own circles.
>
> (Brunt 1989: 150)

For Brunt, reflecting upon one's own identity (the return to the 'subjective') does not imply withdrawal from politics, but rather the opposite – locating grids of power and resistance (in the Foucauldian way), which are horizontal and not just vertical, while keeping political frameworks of action heterogeneous and floating. She rejects the logic of 'broad democratic alliances' and 'rainbow coalitions' because, she argues, political action should be based on 'unity in diversity' which should be founded not on common denominators but on

> a whole variety of heterogeneous, possibly antagonistic, maybe magnificently diverse, identities and circumstances ... the politics of identity recognizes that there will be many struggles, and perhaps a few celebrations, and writes into all of them a welcome to contradiction and complexity.
>
> (Brunt 1989: 158)

As a positive example of this type of political struggle Brunt points to the support activities which surrounded the miners' strike in 1984–5. This is, however, an unfortunate example, because, with all its positive features, the strike ended up in a crushing defeat, not only of the miners and trade union movement, but of the anti-Thatcherite movement as a whole.

Defeats and real politics aside, Brunt's model of politics can be seen as very seductive – it incorporates theoretical insights of highly sophisticated social analysis, is flexible, dynamic and totally inclusive. However, it is in this last point that the danger lies. What ultimately lies behind Brunt's approach is a naive populist assumption that in spite of contradictions and conflicts, in the last instance all popular struggles are inherently progress-ive. She shares with other multiculturalists a belief in the inherent reconcilability and limited boundaries of interest and political difference among those who are disadvantaged and discriminated against. Such a belief (as discussed above) has created a space for fundamentalist leader-ships to rise.

The third example I want to discuss is of feminist politics which has progressed beyond such assumptions. It is that of Women Against Funda-mentalism (WAF), which was organised in London in the wake of the Rushdie affair to struggle exactly against such fundamentalist leaderships of all religions as well as against expressions of racism which masquerade themselves as anti-fundamentalism.

WAF includes women from a variety of religious and ethnic origins (Christians, Jews, Muslims, Sikhs, Hindus and others). Many of the members also belong to other campaigning organisations, often with a more specific ethnic affiliation – such as the Southall Black Sisters (SBS), the Jewish Socialist Group and the Irish Abortion Support Group. However, except for SBS, which had an organisational and ideological initiatory role in establishing WAF, women come there as individuals rather than as representatives of any group or ethnic category. There is no attempt to 'assimilate' the women who come from these different backgrounds. Differences in ethnicity and points of view, and the resulting different agendas, are recognised and respected. But what is celebrated is the common political stance of WAF members as advocating 'the third way' against fundamentalism and racism.

Patricia Hill Collins in her book *Black Feminist Thought* (1990) discusses the importance of recognising the different positionings from which different groupings view reality. Her analysis – which follows to a great extent the feminist epistemological perspective elaborated by Donna Haraway (1988) – echoes exactly the agenda which has been guiding the members of WAF.

Each group speaks from its own standpoint and shares its own partial, situated knowledge. But because each group perceives its own truth as partial, its knowledge is **unfinished** [to differentiate from invalid (NY-D)]. . . . Partiality and not universality is the condition of being heard; individuals and groups forwarding knowledge claims without owning their position are deemed less credible than those who do. . . . Dialogue is critical to the success of this epistemological approach.

(Hill Collins 1990: 236)

In this Hill Collins sidesteps the trap that Marxists and many sociologists of knowledge have been caught in, of relativism, on the one hand, and locating specific social groupings as the epistemological 'bearers of the truth', on the other hand. Dialogue, rather than fixity of location, becomes the basis of empowered knowledge. The campaigns of WAF on, for instance, state religious education or on women's reproductive rights, have been informed by the different experiences of the women of different positionings and backgrounds in the group.

The last example I want to discuss is also based on dialogue. A dialogue which has been developed by Italian feminists (from the movement Women In Black – especially the women from the Bologna and Torino Women's Centres) working with feminists who are members of conflicting national groups, like the Serbs and the Croats, but especially Palestinian and Israeli Jewish women. On the face of it, such a dialogue does not seem very different from the more common 'identity politics' type of dialogue such as was described by Pheterson (1990). However, several important differences exist.

The boundaries of the groupings are not determined by an essentialist notion of difference, but by a concrete and material political reality. Also, the women involved in the different groups are not perceived simplistically as representatives of their groupings. While their different positionings and backgrounds are recognised and respected – including the differential power relations inherent in their corresponding affiliations as members of the Occupier and the Occupied collectivities – all the women who were sought and invited to participate in the dialogue are committed to 'refuse to participate unconsciously in the reproduction of the existing power relations' and are 'committed to finding a fair solution to the conflict' (Italian letter of invitation, December 1990).

The basic perspective of the dialogue is very similar to that of Hill Collins. The terminology is somewhat different. The Italian women use as key words 'rooting' and 'shifting'. The idea is that each participant brings with her the rooting in her own membership and identity, but at the same time tries to shift in order to put herself in a situation of exchange with women who have different membership and identity. They call it 'transversalism' – to differentiate from 'universalism', which, by assuming a homogenous point of departure, ends up being exclusive instead of inclusive.

Two things are vital in developing the transversal perspective. First, that the process of shifting should not involve self-decentring, that is, losing one's own rooting and set of values. There is no need for it, as Elsa Barkley Brown claims, since

> All people can learn to center in another experience, validate it and judge it by its own standards without need of comparison or need to adopt that framework as their own ... one has no need to 'decenter' anyone in order to center someone else; one has only to constantly pivot the centre.
> (Barkley Brown 1989: 922)

It is vital in any form of coalition and solidarity politics to keep one's own perspective on things while empathising with and respecting others. In multiculturalist types of solidarity politics there can be a risk of uncritical solidarity. This was very prevalent, for instance, in the politics of some sections of the Left around the Iranian revolution or the Rushdie affair. They saw it as 'imperialist' and 'racist' to intervene in 'internal community matters'. Women are often the victims of such a perspective which allows the so-called representatives and leaders of 'the community' to determine policies concerning women.

Second, and following from the first point, the process of shifting should not homogenise the 'other'. As there are diverse positions and points of view among people who are similarly rooted, so there are among members of the other group. The transversal coming together should not be with members of the other group 'en bloc', but with those who, in their different rooting, share compatible values and goals to one's own.

A word of caution, however, is required here. Transversal politics are not always possible, as conflicting interests of people who are situated in specific positionings are not always reconcilable. However, when solidarity is possible, it is important that it is based on transversalist principles so as not to fall into the pitfalls of 'identity politics' of the feminist, nationalist or anti-racist kinds.

CONCLUSION

Empowerment of the oppressed, whether one fights for it for one's own – individual or group – sake, or that of others, cannot by itself be the goal for feminist and other anti-oppression politics. Memoirs by former members, especially Elaine Brown, have brought to light the 'disciplinary' practices of brutality and violence which became part of the daily reality of the American Black Panthers (Walker 1993), and the murder of the teenager, which Winnie Mandela had allegedly been party to, has been just one dreadful demonstration of the old truism that 'power corrupts'. This also applies to the power of previously disempowered people, and to power which is only relative and confined to specific contingencies.

The ideology of 'empowerment' has sought to escape this dilemma by confining 'positive' power to 'power of' rather than 'power over'. However, in doing that, empowerment has been constructed as a process which breaks the boundaries between the individual and the communal. As Bookman and Morgen point out, the notion of empowerment connotes 'a spectrum of political activity ranging from acts of individual resistance to mass political mobilizations that challenge the basic power relations in our society' (Bookman and Morgan 1988: 4).

This chapter has pointed out that such constructions assume a specific 'identity politics' which homogenises and naturalises social categories and groupings, denying shifting boundaries and internal power differences and conflicts of interest. Also, in such an approach cultures and traditions are transformed from heterogeneous, sometimes conflicting reservoirs of re- sources into unified, ahistorical and unchanging essence.

As an alternative to this kind of 'identity politics', this chapter suggests that the idea of 'transversal politics' provides the way forward. In 'trans- versal politics' perceived unity and homogeneity are replaced by dialogues which give recognition to the specific positionings of those who participate in them as well as to the 'unfinished knowledge' that each such situated positioning can offer. Transversal politics, nevertheless, does not assume that the dialogue is boundariless, and that each conflict of interest is reconcilable. However, the boundaries of such a dialogue are determined by the message, rather than the messenger. The struggle against oppression and discrimination might (and mostly does) have a specific categorical focus but is never confined to just that category.

If empowerment of women is to transcend some of the pitfalls discussed in this chapter, it is perhaps wise to adhere to Bottomley's warning:

> The dualistic approach of a unitary Us vs a unitary Them continues to mystify the interpenetration and intermeshing of the powerful constructs as race, class and gender and to weaken attempts at reflexivity. . . . Both the subjective and the objective dimensions of experience need to be addressed as well as the thorny issue of the extent to which observers remain within the discourses they seek to criticise.
>
> (Bottomley 1991: 309)

The transversal pathway might be full of thorns, but at least it leads in the right direction.

ACKNOWLEDGMENTS

An earlier version of this chapter was published under the title 'Women, ethnicity and empowerment', in K. Bhavnani and A. Phoenix (eds) (1994) *Shifting Identities, Shifting Racisms*, a special issue of *Feminism and Psychology* 4(1), published and reprinted by permission of Sage Publications.

REFERENCES

Ackelsberg, M. (1991) *Free Women of Spain*, Bloomington, IN: Indiana University Press.

Afshar, H. (1989) 'Three generations of Muslim women in Bradford', paper presented at the Conference of Socialist Economists, London.

Albrecht, L. and Brewer, R. M. (eds) (1990) *Bridges of Power: Women's Multicultural Alliances*, Philadelphia, PA: New Society.

Anthias, F. and Yuval-Davis, N. (1983) 'Contextualizing feminism: gender, ethnic and class divisions', *Feminist Review* 15: 62–75.

Anthias, F. and Yuval-Davis, N. in association with Cain, H. (1992) *Racialized Boundaries: Race, Nation, Gender, Colour and Class and the Anti-Racist Struggle*, London: Routledge.

Antrobus, P. (1989) 'The empowerment of women', in R. S. Gallin, M. Aronoff and A. Feguson (eds) *The Women and International Development Annual*, vol. 1, Boulder, CO: Westview Press.

Barkley Brown, E. (1989) 'African-American women's quilting: a framework for conceptualizing and teaching African-American women's history', *Signs* 14(4): 921–9.

Barrett, M. and McIntosh, M. (1985) 'Ethnocentrism in socialist feminism', *Feminist Review* 20: 23–47.

Bhabha, H. K. (ed.) (1990) *Nation and Narration*, London: Routledge.

Bookman, A. and Morgen, S. (eds) (1988) *Women and the Politics of Empowerment*, Philadelphia, PA: Temple University Press.

Bottomley, G. (1991) 'Culture, ethnicity and the politics/poetics of representation', *Diaspora* 1(3): 303–20.

Bourne, J. (1987) *Homelands of the Mind: Jewish Feminism and Identity Politics*, Race and Class pamphlet 11, London: Institute of Race Relations.

Brah, A. (1991) 'Difference, diversity, differentiation', in S. Allen, F. Anthias and N. Yuval-Davis (eds) *Gender, Race and Class*, special issue of *International Review of Sociology* 2: 53–72.

Brunt, R. (1989) 'The politics of identity', in S. Hall and M. Jacques (eds) *New Times*, London: Lawrence and Wishart.

Bystydzienski, J. M. (ed.) (1992) *Women Transforming Politics: Worldwide Strategies for Empowerment*, Bloomington, IN: Indiana University Press.

Cain, H. and Yuval-Davis, N. (1990) '"The Equal Opportunities Community" and the anti-racist struggle', *Critical Social Policy*, autumn: 5–26.

Chhachhi, A. (1992) 'Forced identities: the state, communalism, fundamentalism and women in India', in D. Kandiyoti (ed.) *Women, the State and Islam*, London: Macmillan.

Contention (1995) special issue on 'Comparing Fundamentalisms', *Contention* 3(2).

Epstein, A. L. (1978) *Ethos and Identity*, London: Tavistock.

Fanon, F. (1986 [1952]) *Black Skin, White Masks*, London: Pluto.

Foucault, M. (1980) 'Truth and power', in C. Gordon (ed.) *Power/Knowledge: Selected Interviews and Other Writings 1972–1977*, Brighton: Harvester.

Freire, P. (1972) *The Pedagogy of the Oppressed*, Harmondsworth: Penguin.

Gilroy, P. (1987) *There Ain't No Black in the Union Jack*, London: Hutchinson.

Glazer, N. and Moynihan, P. (1965) *Beyond the Melting Pot*, Cambridge, MA: MIT Press.

—— (1975) *Ethnicity, Theory and Experience*, Cambridge, MA: Harvard University Press.

GLC (Greater London Council) (1984) *Challenging Racism in London*, report of the conference held on 12 March 1983, London.

Gordon, L. (1991) 'On difference', *Genders* 10 (spring): 91–111.

Gorz, A. (1982) *Farewell to the Working Class*, London: Pluto.

Hall, S. (1987) 'Minimal selves', in *Identity: The Real Me*, London: ICA Document 6, 44–6.

Haraway, D. (1988) 'Situated knowledge: the science question in feminism and the privilege of partial perspective', *Feminist Studies* 14(3): 575–99.

Hartsock, N. (1981) 'Political change: two perspectives on power', in C. Bunch *et al.* (eds) *Building Feminist Theory: Essays from the Quest*, New York: Longman.

Hill Collins, P. (1990) *Black Feminist Thought: Knowledge, Consciousness and the Politics of Empowerment*, Boston, MA: Unwin Hyman.

Hirsch, E. (1982) *The Concept of Identity*, Oxford: Oxford University Press.

hooks, b. (1981) *Ain't I a Woman? Black Women and Feminism*, Boston, MA: South End Press.

—— (1990) 'Sisterhood, political solidarity between women', in S. Gunew (ed.) *Feminist Knowledge: Critique and Construct*, London: Routledge.

Johnson, R. (1991) 'Frameworks of culture and power: complexity and politics in cultural studies', *Critical Studies* 3(1): 000–00.

Kandiyoti, D. (ed.) (1991) *Women, the State and Islam*, London: Macmillan.

Kimble, J. and Unterhalter, E. (1982) '"We opened the road for you, you must go forward", ANC Women's Struggles, 1912–1982', *Feminist Review* 12: 11–36.

Lewin, K. (1952) *Field Theory in Social Sciences*, London: Tavistock.

Macy, J. R. (1983) *Despair and Personal Power in the Nuclear Age*, Philadelphia, PA: New Society.

Marshall, T. H. (1950) *Citizenship and Social Class*, Cambridge: Cambridge University Press.

—— (1975 [1965]) *Social Policy in the Twentieth Century*, London: Hutchinson.

—— (1981) *The Right to Welfare and Other Essays*, London: Heinemann Educational.

Mercer, K. (ed.) (1988) *Black Film/British Cinema*, ICA documents, London: British Film Institute.

Pateman, C. (1989) *The Sexual Contract*, Cambridge: Polity.

Pheterson, G. (1990) 'Alliances between women: overcoming internalized oppression and internalized domination', in L. Albrecht and R. M. Brewer (eds) *Bridges of Power: Women's Multicultural Alliances*, Philadelphia, PA: New Society.

Phillips, A. (1991) *Engendering Democracy*, Cambridge: Polity.

Rattanzi, A. (1992) 'Changing the subject? Racism, culture and education', in J. Donald and A. Rattanzi (eds) *'Race', Culture and Difference*, London: Sage.

Sahgal, G. and Yuval-Davis, N. (eds) (1992) *Refusing Holy Orders: Women and* , *Fundamentalism in Britain*, London: Virago.

Shoemaker, S. and Swinburn, R. (1984) *Personal Identity*, Oxford: Blackwell.

Showstack Sassoon, A. (ed.) (1987) *Women and the State*, London: Hutchinson.

Spelman, E. (1988) *The Inessential Woman*, London: Women's Press.

Spivak, G. C. (1991) 'Reflections on cultural studies in the post-colonial conjuncture', *Critical Studies* 3(1): 63–78.

Thornton Dill, B. (1988) 'The dialectics of Black womanhood', in S. Harding (ed.) *Feminism and Methodology*, Bloomington, IN: Indiana University Press.

Vogel, U. (1989) 'Is citizenship gender specific?', paper presented at the Political Science Association Annual Conference, April.

Wainright, H. (1987) *Labour: A Tale of Two Parties*, London: Hogarth.

Walby, S. (1992) 'Woman and nation', *International Journal of Comparative Sociology* 32(1–2): 379–95.

Walker, M. (1993) 'Sisters take the wraps off the brothers', *Guardian* 6 May.

Wallman, S. (1979) *Ethnicity at Work*, London: Macmillan.

Watson, J. (1977) *Between Two Cultures*, Oxford: Blackwell.

Weed, E. (1989) *Coming to Terms: Feminism, Theory, Politics*, New York: Routledge.

Wilson, E. (1977) *Women and the Welfare State*, London: Tavistock.

Woolf, V. (1938) *Three Guineas*, London: Hogarth (repr. 1992) *A Room of One's Own; Three Guineas*, Oxford: Oxford University Press.

Young, I. M. (1990) *Justice and the Politics of Difference*, Princeton, NJ: Princeton University Press.

Yuval-Davis, N. (1980) 'The bearers of the collective: women and religious legislation in Israel', *Feminist Review* 4: 15–27.

—— (1983) 'Zionism, anti-semitism, and the struggle against racism', *Spare Rib* September: 18–22.

—— (1991) 'The citizenship debate: women, the state and ethnic processes' *Feminist Review* 39: 58–68.

—— (1992) 'Jewish fundamentalism and women's empowerment', in G. Sahgal and N. Yuval-Davis (eds) *Refusing Holy Orders: Women and Fundamentalism in Britain*, London: Virago.

—— (1993) 'Gender and nation', *Ethnic and Racial Studies* 16(4): 621–32.

—— (1996) *Gender and Nation*, London: Sage.

Yuval-Davis, N. and Anthias, F. (eds) (1989) *Woman-Nation-State*, London: Macmillan.

Index

Note: Information about women in connection with another topic, eg citizenship, will be found under the other heading, eg citizenship. The index entry for women contains only those headings for which no other entry is possible. Women belonging to a specific group will be under the direct heading, eg Muslim women.